how we ended racism

Also by Justin Michael Williams

Stay Woke:
A Meditation Guide for the Rest of Us

Also by Shelly Tygielski

Sit Down to Rise Up:
How Radical Self-Care Can Change the World

how we ended racism

Realizing a New Possibility in One Generation

Justin Michael Williams | Shelly Tygielski

Sounds True
Boulder, CO

Published 2023

Cover design by Frances Baca
Jacket design by Jennifer Miles
Book design by Meredith Jarrett

Printed in the United States of America

BK06362

Library of Congress Cataloging-in-Publication Data

Names: Williams, Justin Michael, author. | Tygielski, Shelly, author.
Title: How we ended racism : realizing a new possibility in one generation / Justin Michael Williams and Shelly Tygielski.
Description: Boulder, Co : Sounds True, 2023. | Includes bibliographical references.
Identifiers: LCCN 2023006371 (print) | LCCN 2023006372 (ebook) | ISBN 9781683648864 (paperback) | ISBN 9781683648871 (ebook)
Subjects: LCSH: Racism--United States. | Racism. | Anti-racism--United States. | Anti-racism.
Classification: LCC E185.86 .W4875 2023 (print) | LCC E185.86 (ebook) | DDC 305.800973--dc23/eng/20230221
LC record available at https://lccn.loc.gov/2023006371
LC ebook record available at https://lccn.loc.gov/2023006372

FSC
www.fsc.org
MIX
Paper | Supporting responsible forestry
FSC® C103098

10 9 8 7 6 5 4 3 2 1

For the children of tomorrow.

Contents

Foreword

I met Shelly a few years ago, virtually, as we were amid the global COVID-19 pandemic. Introduced by a mutual friend as Martin and I were continuing to expand the work of The Drum Major Institute, I remember that even through the screen, I could feel her vibrant energy; in the months and years that followed, she became more than just an ally but also a friend. Through Shelly, I got to meet Justin while in Los Angeles at a Drum Major Coalition event and immediately felt a similar energy. These two souls, together, exemplify what is possible for all of humanity to achieve—an existence beyond the color of skin, beyond religion, beyond generational divides, beyond gender and sexuality. In true sisterhood/brotherhood, Shelly and Justin have modeled, taught, and now codified for us what a world that is safe, just, and equitable can look and feel like. The fabric that they have woven through these chapters invokes these immortal words, spoken by my father-in-law, Dr. Martin Luther King, Jr., that "we are caught in an inescapable network of mutuality, tied in a single garment of destiny. Whatever affects one directly, affects all indirectly." Echoing through the annals of history, these words resonate the resounding call for change that still reverberates in our hearts today.

It is my profound honor to contribute the foreword to this important work, which serves as a guide for the fulfillment of a timeless dream that our family has been relentlessly working toward: the end of racism. To envision a world without racism is not to deny the deep wounds inflicted by centuries of prejudice, discrimination, and systemic oppression. It is instead an affirmation of our capacity to rise above these burdens, to transcend the shackles of ignorance and hate, and to build a future founded on love, understanding, and unity. This book outlines the responsibility each of us has as individuals in the network of mutuality, and it provides the reader with the tools to start and/or continue on that journey.

As I read through the pages you are about to embark on, I realized that the continuation of this work arrives at this noble quest for the vision of the Beloved Communities—a society where love, understanding, and justice prevail over hatred, prejudice, and discrimination. A Beloved Community is not merely a utopian dream, but a tangible reality within our grasp, awaiting our collective determination and commitment. The content of this book provides a roadmap that can help each of us bring that vision into clearer focus.

I often invoke in my work how the eradication of racism is inextricably linked to the eradication of what Dr. King referred to as the Triple Evils: poverty, violence, and racism. These interwoven forces, fueled by systemic oppression, have plagued our world for generations, perpetuating cycles of pain, suffering, and inequality. I know that in difficult times, people can tend to skew toward skepticism. Saying that *we can end racism* is not a small statement. Crossing that finish line will require all of us to do the work, but first it will require all of us to believe that it is even possible. I assure you, however, that the eradication of racism is not an insurmountable task. It is a battle we can win, a flame of hope that burns within the depths of our souls. It was the job of our ancestors to keep this flame burning, and it is our job to stoke that flame into a wildfire that consumes the Triple Evils.

This book is a toolbox filled with tools that we may use, some more frequently than others. There may be tools we decide to lend to others, now and again. There may be tools we aren't ready to pick up yet. What Shelly and Justin reaffirm for us, regardless of which tools we decide to engage, is that the hard work must begin on the inside first. We cannot expect the world to change if we aren't willing to first work on change ourselves. The key to unlocking this transformative change lies in the power within each and every one of us. Within our souls resides the ability to recognize our shared humanity, to embrace diversity, and to celebrate the richness that arises from our differences. It is this power, when harnessed collectively, that can ignite a seismic shift in our society—one that propels us toward a future where racism is but a distant memory.

Ending racism requires us to walk on a path of truth, understanding, and collective action. As you turn the pages of this book, my wish for each of you is that its words ignite a fire within you—an unyielding belief that racism can be dismantled and a resolute commitment to making it so. May the tapestry we are each weaving blanket us with the hope, faith, and strength to cross the finish line once and for all and achieve The Dream.

Arndrea Waters King
President, The Drum Major Institute

Introduction

Who WE Are

We are liberal and conservative.

We are black, white, and brown.

We are Republican and Democrat,
Independent, oppressed, and free.

Standing on the shoulders of all who came
before us, we are the torch bearers,

relaying the torch to a destination that
has never been reached before.

We are a message from the future, ancestors
and descendants at the same time.

We are everything in between.

We are now.

It is time.

We rise together.

It's time to end racism. Does racism need to end systemically? Yes. Governmentally? Yes. Socially? Yes. Institutionally? Yes. Relationally? Yes. Internally? Yes. Is racism more than just a "Black" and "white" issue? Yes. Does it need to end in places all around the world? Yes. Do we, as the authors of this book, know how to accomplish all of that alone? No. **But together, we all can.** "We" means all of us. Together we can create the conditions that need to arise for us to arrive at the finish line, once and for all.

In July 2020, amid the global COVID-19 pandemic and the growing protests surrounding the murder of George Floyd and the increased momentum of movements for social change, we, Justin and Shelly, sat together in a state of despair and outrage and like many, asked "What more can we do that will really make an impact?" So, we—a Black queer millennial man and a white straight Jewish Gen X mother—put our very diverse heads together and decided to try something: we created a curriculum that we thought could help end racism.

We know what you're thinking: "Is ending racism even possible?" Don't worry, we once thought the same thing, too. And we definitely had our doubts. At first we thought it was delusional or at best naïve to be asking such a question. But we decided to challenge ourselves and instead of approaching "Is ending racism even *possible*?" from a place of doubt and cynicism, we forced ourselves to shift our mindset to a perspective that we imagined the most inspiring leaders throughout history must've come from—a place of possibility. That's when everything changed. Making that shift wasn't easy, but it created an opening where there was once only a closed door. What we learned gave rise to this book.

But before we codified the teachings into a book, we tested it with people from across what seemed like every divide and from all over the world, by hosting virtual and in-person workshops. After running several programs, we put our work through a rigorous two-year fellowship at the Garrison Institute, a center on the East Coast of the United States that applies the transformative power of contemplative practice to today's pressing social and environmental concerns, with one goal: to help build a more compassionate, resilient future. At the same time, we hired professional independent academic researchers to host focus groups and conduct surveys with our participants along with studies happening before, during, and six months after the program to examine whether what we were teaching could actually create the conditions we hoped would lead to the type of transformation we were hoping for—the kind needed to end racism. What we found astonished us.

The researchers found that after participants learned this material and applied it to their lives, they felt less reactive and more compassionate, more comfortable being bold when they needed to speak up, more comfortable being authentic and building connections with people who seemed different from them, and more comfortable spreading knowledge about ending racism from a place of confidence. Participants reported being more open-minded and thus better able to find common ground with people who they once considered on the other side of a divide, and researchers found that participants felt more comfortable having difficult conversations about touchy subjects such as race than they had ever been before (and felt that they had learned to have those conversations in ways that actually helped build connection instead of causing more division and harm).

But the thing we're most proud of is that most folks in our program *took action* in their families, workplaces, communities, and schools in ways they never thought possible before taking the program. Internally, participants reported feelings of self-growth, improved self-awareness, improved mental health, improved relationships with the people around them (including those outside of the program), more compassion for others who made mistakes, and most importantly—a renewed sense of hope. We were astonished as we watched our participants become a family and connect across divides while healing their differences. Then, once we wrote the first draft of this book, we sent it to people who are typically considered to be in a battle against one another, such as a PhD chief diversity officer at a social justice organization and a writer for a prominent conservative news outlet. Tears rolled down our faces when we heard their responses: Both said they believed in and were transformed by this work. We were blown away to hear that parties who typically can't even sit in a room together could agree on the work in this book.

Shifting to a perspective of possibility transforms everything. What we discovered on our journey opened our hearts. It changed the way we think about everything, and we hope the same happens for you.

In this book, we will share what we believe to be the primary conditions needed to end racism. **This book is here to teach you the inner work, internal and external perspective shifts, conversations,**

practical tools, and action steps you need so that when racism arrives in your presence, ***you end it.*** We will expand on *how* to do that throughout our journey together. Whether you're starting from zero and have never done a moment of work around racism in your life, or you're on the opposite end of the spectrum and have spent your entire life working for change, or you're somewhere in between—our studies have shown this work can work for you. You don't need a PhD to do it, you don't need to have spent your life in politics—you just need to have an open heart and willingness to start from wherever you are now.

Think of the idea of ending racism as a metaphor for our immune system. In order to have a healthy immune system, we can't just fight sickness—we must also be proactive in cultivating wellness and good health. We invest in our health to build what the mindful researcher Dr. Amishi Jha calls "precovery" and "presilience,"[1] so that when something goes awry in the body or we encounter something toxic, our immune system is strong enough to fight it off. Thus, by cultivating health (not just fighting sickness), *we are changing the conditions and context in which sickness tries to occur*.

Look at ending racism the same way—we are not "fighting racism," ***we are changing the conditions and context in which racism occurs***. This requires us to **evolve our culture**. *We—each of us—create that culture.* And no, we don't need to give up all of our values, beliefs, and traditions or become one big homogenous "melting pot" for racism to end. That will never work. We must do something much greater. We must evolve our culture to be one that has an even *better equipped* immune system to hold competing ideals—one that has practices, knowledge, and systems in place that make it hard for racism to show up; and when and if does, *the immune system of our culture* is strong enough to handle it. *You are what creates that culture.* The conditions in this new culture are set such that we are capable of handling racism in a way that does not leave us in shambles, more distrusting of one another, or more divided in the aftermath of racism rearing its ugly head. In this way, we're not resisting racism but rather creating the conditions for it to end. We *embody* the conditions required for it to end. *We—each* *of us, individually—are the end of racism.* When racism touches you, it ends. If enough of us learn the skills needed and take them into our individual areas of influence—with all of our fields of expertise, into all of our circles, into all of our interactions, and into all of our relationships—we will end racism, together.

Repairing Our Old House

A metaphor we often like to use in our workshops, which is from Isabel Wilkerson's book *Caste*, is that living with racism is like inheriting an old house. When we inherit a one-hundred-year-old house and realize the pipes downstairs are rusted and the foundation is sinking or the support beams are starting to crack, we don't walk into the house and say, "Well, I'm not responsible for fixing any of this stuff because I'm not the one who built it. The people who built the house one hundred years ago need to fix it since it's their fault it wasn't built correctly." Yet this is what we often do as it relates to our history. But if this world is the old house that we all inherited and we are the ones living in it, there's no one else to repair it but us. Yet we often find people spending so much energy laying blame to who caused it and pointing fingers at who should be responsible for repairing it. It's time we stop waiting for somebody to show up to fix things and realize that we are, in fact, that somebody. Each of us is. It's time we all step up to do the work that is each of ours to do within our specific fields of influence and expertise in the corners of the world that only we can reach. If you've already been stepping up, we hope this book supports you to make an even bigger and more significant impact. Wherever you are along your journey, if you picked up this book, we know you are ready.

The Journey

What you will find in these pages is a carefully curated and integrated voice that combines decades of our work (which builds upon centuries of work by others, as well) to create one unified "we" voice that seeks to prop up the collective vision for a future without racism. There are times throughout the book that we share our individual stories, but for the majority of the content, you will see a voice that models exactly what we are hoping to teach you—that we are stronger when we come together, that *we all* (you and us, white and Black, People of Color, Americans and the global community at large, all of us!) have work to do to end racism, and that it *can* be done together.

While we have both been teaching for over four decades combined and have taught and researched the conditions that allow rapid, large-scale change to transform a culture, we have also both personally been deeply impacted by the existence of racism. Justin grew up in a biracial family that disowned his mother for marrying outside of her race but learned to come together and find a unity and love that defied the odds of the time. Shelly was raised in a culture that taught her to fear and hate a perceived "enemy" from a different culture, but she now advocates and fights on behalf of the rights of the so-called enemy population. It is because of our experience not just in our professional lives but also in our personal lives that we know racism can end.

The vision we are setting forth is that we can all create a reality where our descendants will look back in history upon this era of racism the same way we look back now on many things humans did before that seem nonsensical to most of us today—from human sacrifices, to murdering young children and the infirmed elderly who couldn't keep up with their tribe or required too many resources, to even more recent (and perhaps relatable) examples of smoking cigarettes on airplanes or riding in cars without seatbelts. One day humanity will reflect on this historical timeline and scratch their heads, saying, "Can you *believe* people did that?! Why on earth would people separate themselves because of this made-up concept called 'race'?!"

That's our North Star. That's how you'll know we've made it.

We've synthesized the teachings from our workshop into eight distinct pillars for you. *How We Ended Racism* is the amalgamation of all the most effective tools that we've gathered from well-researched teachings, experiences, and proven methods—including techniques for inner healing, talking across divides, shadow work, forgiveness, calling one another forward instead of calling out, and much more. The eight pillars are designed to help you move beyond simply "hoping for" the end of racism and instead have you *become* the end of racism. These conditions don't arise spontaneously out of the ether—*they must be consciously cultivated.* For this reason, we've provided a special set of additional resources to support your journey. You can find those resources and others we mention throughout this book—such as audio guided practices, printable guides and worksheets, podcast episodes, and ways to connect with our global community—at HowWeEndedRacism.com/resources or by scanning the QR code on page 9.

It's important to note there are entire research institutions and books specifically devoted to the topics presented in each of the pillars, so we don't want you to think that each chapter is the be-all and end-all guide on every concept introduced. Rather, we aim to teach you just what you need to know to start taking action now. We believe that the concepts, skills, tools, and techniques that we present are prerequisites for the possibility of ending racism as evidenced by our research and work—that racism will never end without them. But we also understand that these are not the *only* skills that can be learned to help. We are hoping that as you engage in the inner work and start to change the conditions in your own life, you will find additional pillars to build an even stronger foundation for our "old house" and you'll do your part to bring them to the world.

We need for each of you—the policy makers, teachers, Republicans, Democrats, activists, artists, parents, students, politicians, executives, nonprofit leaders, young and older folk alike from every generation and every identity—all of us—to show up and build upon these foundations a stable, safe house that we can all enjoy living in together. We hope you do, and we hope you share them with us as well. This is what it means to cocreate.

Last, we want to thank you for entrusting us to take you on this part of the journey. We—a Black queer millennial and a white Jewish Gen Xer—came together just like it's been done throughout history, to model for you what it looks like for two regular people to join hands and take a stand for a brighter future. We began this journey by placing ourselves in the future, in a world where racism has ended, just as we will to teach you to do, and we asked, "It's the year 2050 and racism has ended—what *did* we do *today*, in the earliest part of the twenty-first century, that would've *caused* this outcome?" This book is our contribution to creating that world. By the time you're done reading this, you will be equipped to ask this same question of yourself, and when racism arises, you will have the tools to end it—not because of what we teach you but because of who you chose to *become*.

Let us all come together to realize a new possibility in one generation. This is our time. This is the moment. It's time to end racism.

The 8 Pillars of Possibility

- We Anchored into a New Vision
- We Agreed on the Truth
- We Owned Our Emotions
- We Became Intraconnected
- We Did Shadow Work
- We Practiced Forgiveness
- We Had Big Conversations
- We Took Action

Resources

For all the resources we mention through this book visit HowWeEndedRacism.com/resources or scan this QR code.

Pillar One

we anchored into a new vision

1

∞

Creating from the Future

It dawned on us several years ago that almost every piece of work or literature that we've read on racism has one assumption in common: *it cannot end.* Or, at best, that it will be a "lifelong fight" we may contribute toward advancing in our lifetimes but that we are destined to hand down to the next generation, and they will hand the remainder off to the next generation, and the next, and so on; that every generation will struggle for lifetime after lifetime until the end of time in the fight against racism.

We understand that this is, indeed, the struggle *of a lifetime,* but we also believe that it is possible for us—collectively—to end racism *in a lifetime.* As we invite you to anchor into this vision of the future with us, we are not minimizing the centuries of incredible work done by civil rights leaders from Dr. Martin Luther King Jr. to Congressman John Lewis, Rosa Parks, Harriet Tubman, and more, nor are we ignoring the countless known and unknown individuals who suffered and sacrificed for us to arrive at this moment. Without them we would never have the opportunity to even *consider* the possibility of ending racism. We believe, in many ways, that together we can all build upon their work and dreams as we try to advance the torch toward a defined finish line. The current work toward equity, inclusion, and diversity has *real impact*—it's *improving and saving lives.* So is the current work and research on racism and the tireless work that has been done by our ancestors for generations. It's creating systemic change and it's bringing us together, and we understand that *these things matter*—tremendously.

But through our research we have noticed that much of this work continues to be created from a place that automatically assumes (whether subconsciously or consciously) that racism is *unlikely to ever end*, and we believe that if *that's* our starting point, if that's the plateau from which we're writing our books, creating our podcasts, and creating our movements for activism and social change, then we're missing a big opportunity here—*one that this generation is specifically prepared for.* We want you to imagine what our work to create a better world would look like if it came together with a different context: What if our work to end racism was not approached as "a lifelong fight" but instead with a common united goal to *end racism in this generation*?

In order to lean into this vision, we need to shift our thinking by understanding the fundamental difference between *creating from our limitations* of the past and present (which is what we normally do) and *creating from the possibilities* of the future. You can spend your entire life looking at the past. There's no end to going to the past. You can learn every aspect of why the past unfolded the way it did yet still not have this understanding make any tangible difference toward the future. As we're seeing in the world today, history *does* repeat itself in many forms. That's because going to the past can be helpful, certainly—and we do not ignore the harm of the past or the lessons that can be learned from it in this book—but what we can definitively share with you after working with thousands of people from all over the world is that creating from the future is where the kind of transformation required to end racism occurs.

Let us be clear: this book will not *ignore* or deny the past, but we must look to the past only so that we can learn and free ourselves from it, to start creating from the future. We simply can't create a new future if we're constantly looking backward; we can't drive forward by only looking in the rearview mirror. *Creating from our limitations* looks like this: we stand in the middle of the problem while throwing our hands up and asking, "How did we get here?" or "With everything going on in the world, what can we even do as individuals to make things better?" Sound familiar? *Creating from the future* beckons us to ask bigger questions. Creating from the future requires that we ask: "If I am standing in the future looking back at this present moment—the now—what *did* I do *today* to produce the outcome that I'm standing in?" This graphic should help you understand the concept more deeply.

Problem Solving, Creating from the Future

PROBLEM SOLVING

What **SHOULD** I do now
to make this vision come true?

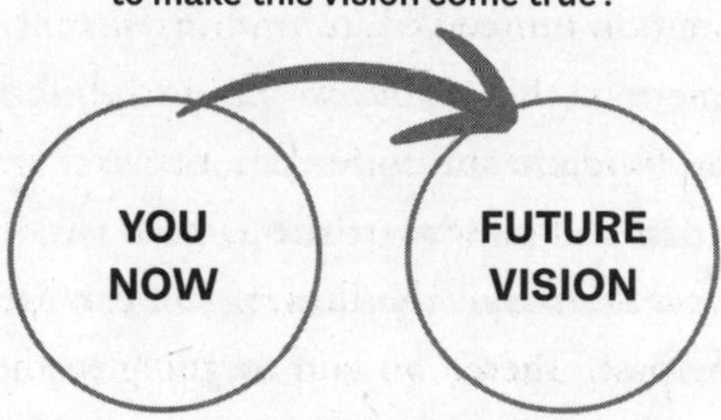

CREATING FROM THE FUTURE

What **DID** I do now
to make this vision come true?

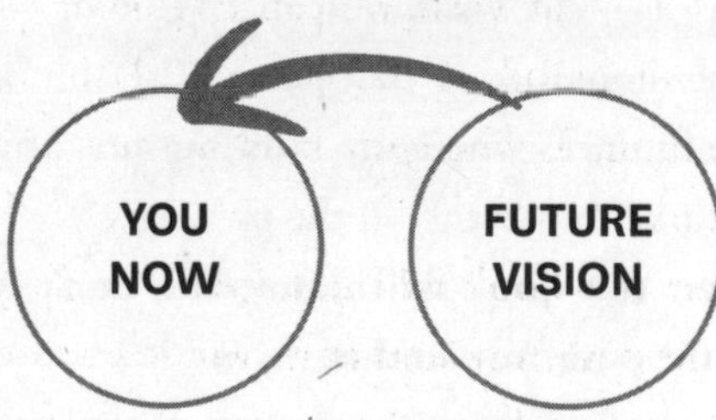

With problem-solving, we are standing in the limitations of our circumstances and asking, "What *should* I do?" With *creating from the future*, we look back from the perspective of the future fulfilled and ask, "What *did* I do?" If this vision were to come true, we're asking, "What *would I have been required to* do now to make it happen?" Problem-solving begins with limitations because it begins with the circumstances of our present state and then tries to improve upon them or make them better. *Creating from the future* goes beyond those circumstances to create *new possibilities* altogether. Although this may seem like a subtle shift, it makes a profound difference in the outcome. By the time you're done reading this book, you'll learn how to embody this perspective shift so that it can reorient the way you go about creating changes in every part of your life.

It's important as we make this distinction that you understand that we are not suggesting that problem-solving is wrong or that *reacting* to the problems that are present in our lives or in the world is unnecessary. Nor are we saying that it's less valuable than creating from the future. We need both. But as we looked around at the current acumen of curriculum about ending racism, *creating from the future* is what wasn't getting enough attention in the conversation.

You'll notice that you can insert the same question into both the *problem-solving model* and *creating-from-the-future model* and come out with entirely different ideas. Creating from the future leads to different solutions because instead of asking "What's possible?" it asks us "*What needs to happen* and *who do we need to become* to make what seems impossible, possible?" As author Jim Selman, who played a big role in inspiring us to write this book, so perfectly shared with us, ***"The future is nothing but a possibility in the present."*** Ending racism is a *real* possibility. To get there, we must center ourselves in the possibility of its fulfillment and base all of our actions from that point. The only way we will ever create a world without racism is by standing for a bigger possibility, otherwise we'll just be improving on the present.

Let us be clear: **You don't fix racism. You don't improve racism. You don't make it better. You end it.**

It is from this place of possibility that we created the foundations of the book and this first pillar. Science has proven time and time again that future visioning is not just a fun parlor game.[1] Future visioning helps us make new choices.[2] It prepares us for different actions. It helps us create a reality worth living for, one where we can thrive. Future visioning reduces our anxiety and stress because we have something to walk toward instead of just focusing on what we're running away from. With a future vision, we can finally come together in service of something greater because the difference now is that we are *fighting for* something rather than *fighting against* something.

Here's a visual representation of what *fighting against something* looks like:

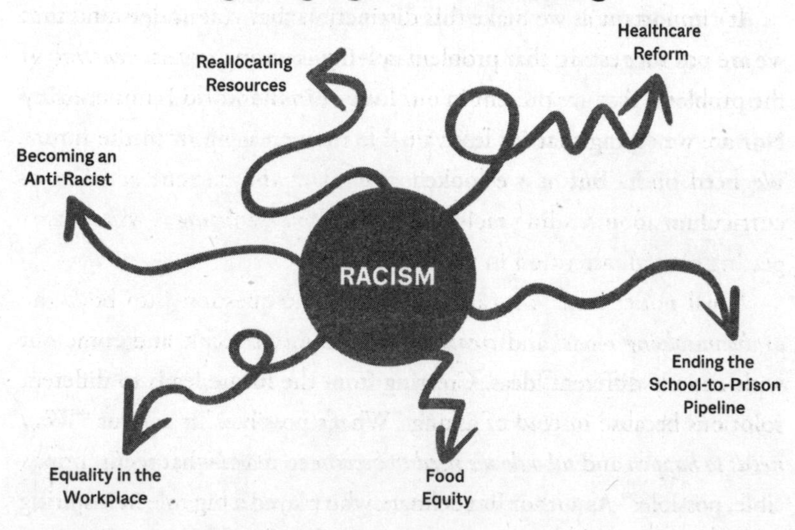

And here's a visual representation of what *fighting for something* looks like:

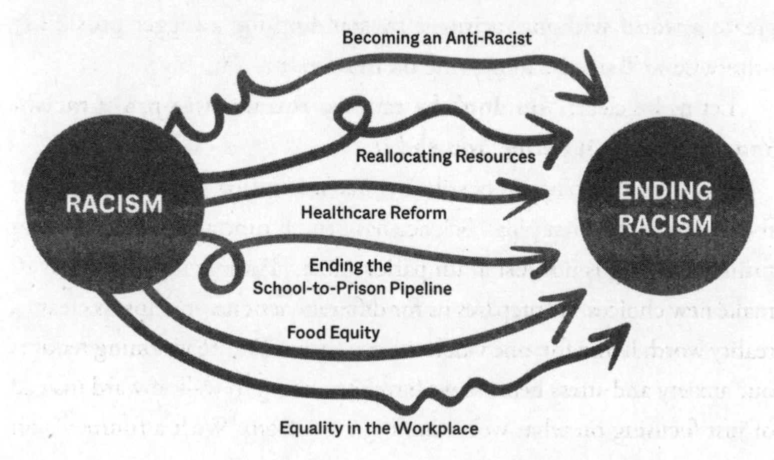

Notice how when we are fighting *against* something, we often become even *more* disconnected from one another than when we started because our only tether to one another is the problem itself. In fighting against that problem, it's only a matter of time before we end up fighting each other, arguing over whose way of fighting the problem is better or more important. In this case, which is modeled many times throughout history, the persistence of circumstance prevails and we end up torn apart. Using the contrasting model, however, we create a future vision that clearly defines our "why" and keeps us moving toward something new. Although we may have different ideas on how to get there, the vision is our anchor.

Inner Work

In every chapter, starting here, we will use a simple integration technique to help apply each concept to *you*. We refer to this as "inner work." Doing the inner work is important because we won't end racism by just reading about it. We must also integrate these teachings into *our lives*.

Your task now is simple: Take a moment to imagine you are in the year 2050 and racism has ended—imagine a *future world without racism*. What comes up? What do you notice? Don't worry if you have some trouble with this to start—imagining a world without racism isn't something most of us are accustomed to. Your ability to arrive in this vision of the future will strengthen as you learn the eight pillars in this book. We'll come back to it again at the very end of our work together and you can see for yourself what's changed. For now, just slow down for a moment and imagine a future world without racism. Get as clear of an idea as you can, even if it's fuzzy, blurry, or incomplete. Be with whatever arises for you for a few extended moments.

Now using whatever arose for you, finish the following sentences. Don't worry about your answers being "wrong" or "right"; this is just for your personal processing. Answer them with the first thing that comes to your mind.

- The main thing I noticed in my vision of a world without racism was ________________.
- What excites me most about the vision is ________________________________.
- For this vision to come true, what I need to cultivate in my life now is ________________.
- For this vision to come true, what I need to release from my life now is ________________.
- For this vision to come true, who I need to become is ________________.
- I am on a journey of ________________ and ________________.
- I am *fighting for* ________________.
- I am ________________.

When we first did this exercise, the main thing we noticed in our vision of a world without racism was a sense of *safety* and a sense of *camaraderie*. People were safe to move, live, and be anywhere they wanted, in any city, and in any town or venue without any worry of anyone causing harm to them. In our vision, people in a diverse group were truly *enjoying* one another—people learned to love each other again. This allowed all of us to dedicate our energy to creating solutions that enhanced society's well-being rather than drain so much of our energy fighting, arguing, and being angry with one another.

But creating this vision wasn't just about "those people" "out there." *We needed to become* more of a safe space for people who had different opinions than us. *We needed to become* less judgmental. *We needed to learn to listen more* and talk less. *We needed to let go of our preconceived notions about people* and stop placing people into large generalized bias boxes, especially based upon the extreme fears the media were inserting into our minds about them. Overall, we needed to become *welcoming*. We needed to go on a journey of becoming more vulnerable and less afraid, and believing in a bigger vision than we first thought was possible. Does any of this sound familiar? We had many of the same fears, doubts, and questions you may have when we began this journey. But one thing was clear: we are *fighting for* not only a better tomorrow for future generations but a better *now*—for all people of all backgrounds and all beliefs. This is the journey we are on together, and now that you are on this journey with us, we are excited for what's to come.

In a culture where it's become commonplace to be "anti-[fill in the blank]," it's easy to forget what we're striving *for*. A step in our collective evolution may have needed to swing the pendulum to becoming "anti-everything," *but we can't stay where we are now* because being "anti-" something only focuses on what we're fighting against, and it fails to tell us anything about the future we're *fighting for*. "Anti-" is beating something down. But once you've destroyed and beat down everything you hate, what are you left with? ***What's the vision for what comes after something's been dismantled?*** This is a key question that we will reach for together, and that we believe has been forgotten as an essential element to unlocking a future without racism. We are standing at the doorway of possibility as the ancestors of this age with the ability to look forward and backward and to dream a bigger dream.

Dr. Martin Luther King Jr.'s treasured vision inspired us to dream of a promised land that may have seemed like a utopian fantasy at the time but provided us with a clear vision of a future to aim for. Dr. King was not just a visionary activist; he understood that every vision required a practical road map, too. He understood the importance of doing the inner work, of showing up as whole and present as we can, rising to meet the moment required. Despite the pushback from the naysayers, Dr. King continued forward, always looking toward the dream of what was possible. He was able to envision a future outside of the circumstances of the time, and he understood that it required the eradication of the "three evils" of society, as he described it—racism, poverty, and war. He was able to frame in a context that made the impossible seem *possible*. He helped to paint a vision that was bigger than society was ready for at the time. We believe that we are ready for that vision now. This is our time. We must all carry on the legacy of our ancestors and ignite the torch with tools, skills, and a dedication to the inner work, so that we can be the generation that carries the world forward through the remaining dark hours and toward a new dawn, and so that Dr. King's dream is not just a memory of a proud moment in history but a reality that we are living in together. This is how we will *end racism*.

2

The Skeptic in All of Us

The American author George Jean Nathan once wrote that "the path of sound credence is through a thick forest of skepticism."[1] We are well aware that many of you are skeptics. We were, too. That is both normal and in fact productive to this movement.

Take a moment now to notice what thoughts or emotions come up for you when you read the phrase "How we *ended* racism."

Next, notice what thoughts or emotions come up when you read the phrase "We ended racism in one generation."

Do you feel hopeful? Cynical? Pessimistic? Are you thinking to yourself, "Who do these people think they are?" Perhaps you are waiting for a detailed plan?

Regardless of what came up for you, before we dive into the work that needs to be done to *end racism*—both systemic and internalized—it's important that we have a shift in our mindset. This chapter will be a bit more theoretical than the chapters the follow. The mindset shifts offered in this chapter are part of the foundation of the important personal work to come, so pay close attention.

The first step is acknowledging what makes racism *persist.* Just as we wanted to shift the context from fighting against something to fighting for something, and from creating from limitations to creating from the future—once you've been working on the same recurring problem over and over to no end, it becomes equally important to shift from "What is the problem?" to "Why does the problem *continue to persist* in the first place?" In part, these five shared yet individual assumptions are what we have found to be the most common assumptions that may be causing racism to persist:

1. Racism is unavoidable.
2. Race matters.
3. "Those people" will never change.
4. Real change takes a long time.
5. We don't know how to end it.

Before we can explore each of these five assumptions directly, we must own and acknowledge that all of us, as individuals and as a collective, see things through a certain lens or perspective. If enough people agree on a certain perspective, then that perspective becomes our collective reality and belief. This is what we mean by "shared yet individual assumptions." We aren't talking about a spiritual "law of attraction" here but rather *perception* and *belief* in the most tangible of ways.

As a quick example—and we will go deeper into this throughout the book—throughout much of ancient history, it was widely believed that the earth was flat. People literally thought if they traveled far enough, they might fall off the edge of the earth into an abyss of nothingness. Ancient civilizations from Greece and Egypt to Asia all believed this to be true, so they created a reality based upon that belief. We see it depicted in art, stories, religion, and ultimately their shared beliefs about the world. Now we know you might be thinking, "We've evolved beyond that sort of foolery," but let's look at another untrue yet harmless shared perspective that we all maintain today: our belief that the sun "sets."

There's a shared *perspective* that the sun sets, but the sun doesn't *really* set. Think about it. Would the sun appear to *set* from the perspective of an astronaut who is far away from Earth's orbit? No. Earth would be turning on its axis as it circles around the sun. Yet from our *shared perspective* here on the planet, there's an agreed-upon belief that the sun sets. On the foundation of this belief we've created our reality, the structure of our lives, and our world. This leads us to an important point: our world is created upon shared beliefs, even if those beliefs aren't necessarily true. Therefore, to *end racism*, we must first own and acknowledge that we, as individuals and as a collective, see things through a sometimes-faulty lens. We must also agree that if enough people *choose* to see through the same faulty lens (for example: Black people should be slaves; women are inferior), then that chosen perspective becomes the framework in which we live our lives. In essence, if enough people share the same socially perceived illusions, those illusions cause a certain "way of life" to persist.

Now, with that in mind, let's dismantle the five faulty perspectives that might be causing racism to persist.

1. Racism Is Unavoidable

It's been proven by neuroscientists and psychologists that racism is *learned*—it's not some automatic human condition that we're born with.[2] It's not something that "just happens" as a result of putting a bunch of diverse people on a planet together. This is not our idea or opinion. It is widely respected and proven by science that racism itself is *not* "a given." It's not unavoidable.[3]

What *is likely* unavoidable, however, is the fact that we create what's called "in-groups" and "out-groups" to keep ourselves safe. Terror management studies show that we tend to treat people in our in-group kindlier and people in our out-group more harshly. Yet even with this scientific knowledge, the idea of using *race* as a way of defining our in-group and out-group is something we can eliminate—if we try.[4]

But *we the people* are funny creatures. When we can't figure out a quick solution to something, most of us label it as "unavoidable." Inevitable. Unfortunate even, but unlikely to change. Yet the idea that racism is unavoidable would be like saying the Holocaust was unavoidable or that American slavery was unavoidable or that refusing the LGBTQIA+ community the right to marry was unavoidable.

There's a real danger in saying something is unavoidable because we immediately absolve ourselves of taking *responsibility* to change it.

We throw our hands up in the air and say, "Welp, can't do anything about *that*."

> We can't do anything about slavery.
>
> We can't do anything about LGBTQIA+ rights.
>
> We can't do anything about equal pay for women and minorities.
>
> We can't do anything about immigration reform.
>
> We can't do anything about racism . . .

Until somebody does.

As Confucius said in this famous Chinese proverb, "The person who says it cannot be done should not interrupt the person doing it." People will try to disrupt our work; and you, too, will have doubts arise about ending racism even while you are doing it. You must simply commit to continuing to anchor in the shared vision for the future. We'll explore moving beyond this doubt later in the book. For now, keep reading.

2. Race Matters

We are going to say something that's sometimes hard for people to truly face: *Race* is a complete fabrication of the human mind that's used for power and control. It's a social construct, a delusion, and a harmful imaginary truth that we've *all* continued to build our lives and civilizations upon. To quote the professor and novelist Toni Morrison on this matter: *"There is no such thing as race. None. There is just a human race—scientifically, anthropologically."*[5]

To be clear: We don't want you to think for one second that we are saying the *effects* of racism aren't real. The trauma, the deaths, the lives lost, the impact of racism, and the persistent *collective belief* in the idea of "race" has had *very real consequences*. It has created wars, dismantled countries, pitted religions against one another, and taken innocent lives for generations. Racism has caused incredible harm and trauma, which cannot be minimized. Nor are we suggesting that we put our cultures, values, and traditions into a blender to make a "we are all one" raceless smoothie. Again, we don't need to give up our culture, values, and traditions or become a homogenous "melting pot" for racism to end. We have the opportunity to do something far greater than that.

While this can be triggering or hard to stomach, we need to agree once and for all that *the concept of race is literally IMAGINARY*. Someone created it to gain and maintain power and control. And now we use it to control ourselves.

Race is not real.

Heritage is real.

Culture is real.

Tradition is real.

Appropriation is real.

Skin color is real.

Trauma is real.

But race—not real.

Or . . . *it's as real as we make it.*

Skin color is a biological fact. Race is a cultural/historical interpretation. Race is not a fact.

3. "Those People" Will Never Change

There is a commonly held belief that "those people" will never change. Yet all throughout life, we can point to and tell stories of people who have changed—and not just "people out there" but people in our lives and family line. For us to collectively anchor into the vision, we need to agree that the statement "Those people will never change" is not a fact, because people are capable of change and do change. These instances are not rare. We are willing to bet that you can point to at least one person in your life who has changed—your once-racist family members, your formerly unaware coworkers, your used-to-be homophobic relatives, and the ways in which you've personally grown over the years.

People's beliefs can change. Racists are not exempt from this.

For us, the main question we are interested in asking is *What causes people to change?* This book aims to provide you with the tools needed to create a model for ending racism where those conditions for real change can be met and met quickly.

4. Real Change Takes a Long Time

One of the greatest sources of doubt about ending racism in one generation comes from the assumption that *real and enduring change* must always take a long time. But let's look at some examples of big changes in recent human history. The "start" and "end" dates that follow represent unmistakable widespread shifts. Keep in mind, a generation is typically considered to represent a period of between twenty to twenty-five years.

- (1973) The first phone call made on a handheld cellular phone. (1995) Widespread global use of mobile phones = **22 years.**
- (1991) Creation of the World Wide Web. (2001) Total widespread use of the internet = **10 years.**
- (1981) First documented case of HIV in the US. (1995) Ability to detect, treat, and live with HIV = **14 years.**
- (2004) First US state legalizes same-sex marriage. (2015) National legalization of same-sex marriage = **11 years.**
- (1831) First knowledge of slaves escaping through the Underground Railroad and the start of abolitionism. (1865) End of the Civil War = **34 years.**
- (1903) Wright brothers take first flight. (1920) Widespread commercial airline travel begins = **17 years.**

- (1929) Start of the Great Depression. (1945) End of the Great Depression = **16 years.**
- (1933) Hitler's first position of leadership and the formation of the Nazi Party. (1945) End of the Holocaust = **12 years.**
- (1957) First satellite launched into space. (1969) Humankind lands on the moon = **12 years.**

Given what you just read, let's ask ourselves: Does meaningful change *really* have to take a "long time"?

We recognize that *every* change in human history does not fall into this timeline. We also recognize that there were years of unrewarded labor that came before the cited "start" dates. Our intention is never to minimize the generations of work that have come before us but to help you notice that once the ground has been prepared—which it is now—real change *can* happen. And it can happen *quicker than you might think.*

5. We Don't Know How to End It

There is a strong assumption held by many that we "don't know" how to end racism, which assumes that there are no solutions. People often say, "If we knew how to end racism, it would've ended already." That isn't the case at all. In fact, there are *plenty* of real, tangible, and proven solutions that can contribute to ending racism. These ideas and models were created by researchers, scholars, universities, and entire college campuses dedicated to the cause. Experts have created models, systems, structures, and written *New York Times* bestselling books—all of which could end racism. We aren't waiting for "better solutions." Rather, as a society, as individuals, and as a collective, we need to be *willing* and *ready* for our solutions to work. We must become people who are ready to receive the world we are asking for.

These five shared yet individual assumptions are what we have found to be the most common assumptions that may be causing racism to persist, but we want to uncover anything that's left inside of you before we move forward. It's okay to be skeptical, but get it out on the table now so you can see and be responsible for your own assumptions rather than have them run you from the background.

Inner Work

Complete the following sentences to explore your relationship to your own assumptions.

- What makes the end of racism most unlikely or impossible is ______________________________.
- The reason I believe this to be true is __________ ______________________________________.
- Of the five assumptions shared in this chapter, the one I think is the hardest to overcome is ___________ ______________________________________.
- Because ______________________________.
- If racism were to end, the most important thing that would have to happen is _________________ ______________________________________.
- Racism is ______________________________.
- In order for racism to end, I will need to become more ______________________________________.

The key to any major shift in the world has always been the same: getting enough people to believe not only a cause "matters" but that change is *possible*. Researchers from the University of Pennsylvania and the University of London discovered in a 2018 study that it takes the support of just 25 percent of people to make a major social shift in the world. While we believe that currently more than 25 percent of people *want* racism to end, more than 25 percent of people believe racism is *wrong*, and more than 25 percent of people think the fight against racism *matters*, we don't think that these same people believe that racism can *end in one generation*. We don't think that 25 percent of people have actually *considered* that they could personally be instrumental in *ending racism in this generation*. We don't think that 25 percent of people think it can start with us.

It's time to change that. Our call now is simple—to get people to believe and anchor in this collective vision for the future. First, *we must believe it is possible*. Then we must commit to a timeline. There's a crucial difference between saying something will happen "someday . . ." and a concrete plan. For example, imagine you're in the supermarket and you bump into a friend that you haven't seen in a long time. You both say, "Oh, wow, it's been so long, we should totally get together sometime." We all know how likely that is to happen. That statement is very different from "Do you want to have lunch on Tuesday?" A timeline puts a plan in motion because it requires a yes or no. A timeline requires a commitment. A timeline turns dreams into reality. Without a timeline, things remain a pipe dream—a "what if." One of our favorite quotes is **"The difference between a dream and a plan is a timeline."**[6] The actions we take to end racism by 2050 are very different from ending racism "someday." The title of this book isn't "How We Ended Racism Someday" but *in one generation*. So let us bring our skepticism with us and march on to the next step with a timeline in place and a new type of commitment that has the power to change humanity. This is how the new reality of a world devoid of racism will finally emerge. Are you with us?

Pillar Two

we agreed on the truth

3

∞

The Truth about the Truth

If we stand together in the future in the year 2050, looking back at today, and ask, "What *did* we *do* back in the earliest part of the twenty-first century that led to the end of racism?" we'd learn that the first thing we did was learn *the truth—but not in the way you might expect.* "Truth" is one of the most challenging concepts of our time. Ironically, it almost always leads to controversy. What is truth? Who or what decides it? Can something that is true change? What happens if *your* truth is different from someone else's? Or what if *your* truth contradicts what is widely considered to be true? In that case, is it still the "truth" or are we talking about something else altogether? These are the fundamental questions and concepts we are exploring in this chapter because if we are to end racism, we must first come to understand, tell, and be with "the truth" much differently than we're used to.

Here's the thing about the truth: It's more than about honesty. It's also more than about being "right" or "wrong." Real truth-telling requires that we dig deeper to understand what's going on with us and within us. It demands that we walk into the emotional shed and get out the seldom-used tools to begin an excavation that may yield artifacts that terrify us. Yet a commitment to the truth keeps us digging anyway. There is a deeper truth you must be able to access and understand if you want to create any transformation in your life, in our world, or toward our shared mission to end racism. Without tapping into *that* truth, it will be impossible for us to make any real progress toward the vision.

In this pillar, we will provide you with the tools to dig for your truth. We will help you tell your truth, show you how to atone for the parts of your truth you are not proud of, and help you commit to a path laden with truths that you can feel aligned with and that will move you forward. Shifting your relationship to the concept of truth will light your pathway to ending racism. Uncovering these truths may not always be pleasant, but if you commit to pressing pause on any shame and blame that comes up in the process, you will reveal a pathway for a new possibility. You may have heard the phrase before that "the truth will set you free," but the truth does more than that—*it also sets others free.*

The most important thing to know about truth is this: there is a difference between *assessments* and *assertions.*

For example:

> Assertion: Justin is five feet ten inches (178 cm).
>
> Assessment: Justin is tall.

-or-

> Assertion: It's 65°F (18°C) outside.
>
> Assessment: It's cold outside.

Assertions are *facts.* Assessments are the *subjective stories* we create. Assertions are verifiable by multiple sources, measurable, often unchanging, objective, and can be labeled as true or false by a commonly agreed-upon standard. Assessments, on the other hand, can never be verified as true or false because they come through the lens of a subjective experience. *We create assessments from our own perspective.* In other words, a height of five feet ten inches and a temperature of 65°F are measurable and practically inarguable; they are simply data points. They can be labeled as true or false. Those data points are *facts.* But while one might consider Justin, who stands at five feet ten inches, to be "tall," in some cases he might also be considered "short." This would be the case, for example, if Justin was standing next to someone who is six feet eight inches or if he was hanging out with a team of professional basketball players. "Short" and "tall" are assessments about the assertion of Justin's height. Similarly, to someone who's spent most of their adult life in Los Angeles or Miami, 65°F is usually considered chilly weather, but to someone living in upstate New York or Montreal, Canada, 65°F can warrant wearing a bikini or inspire tanning if the sun is out. The "truth," in these cases, changes depending on the circumstance, subjective perspective, and experience. But in general, "the truth" should be unwavering, right?

Here's the important thing to remember: With assertions, the main data points always stay the same, regardless of who's looking at them. Assessments, on the other hand, require an opinion or judgment, which is *always* subjective. Two people can experience the exact same assertions yet create contradicting assessments based upon how they interpret and internalize that experience.

This work on assertions and assessments is based on the writing of Chilean computer scientist and coaching expert Dr. Fernando Flores and his speech acts theory.[1] He states that human beings are hardwired to be assessment-making machines. We make assessments every single day, such as "*Those people* are dangerous," "She's not very competent," or "I can trust this person." Yet all assessments are not created equally. An assessment, or story, can be grounded or ungrounded. "Grounding" is the act of finding reason for your assessment beyond your subjective preferences, which usually includes a rigorous standard to measure your assessment up against. For many people, their standard is based upon personal preferences and "how they feel." But preferences and "feelings" don't give rise to well-grounded assessments. We must be more rigorous than that. For example, you might say, "Chocolate tastes good." But when you understand the nuance between assessments and assertions, you know that the chocolate *itself* does not taste "good." *You may think* chocolate tastes good, but the important distinction here is that chocolate tasting "good" is not something that can ever be proven as verifiably "true" or "false" from any sort of objective standard. This example might seem simplistic, but we chose it to show how this concept can apply to any area of life. When we learn to ground our assessments, we recognize them for what they are—opinions.

Grounding your assessments relies on applying them to standards and supporting them with assertions. There are many standards you can use to ground your assessments, including *history of past action(s)/events* ("The fire cannot continue beyond that wall. We know because it worked to prevent a fire from spreading in the past."); *agreed upon metrics, standards, theories, or schools of thought proven by rigorous study* ("This food is healthy. I know because I read the ingredients and nutritional information."); or *clear evidence based on assertions* ("There are a lot of mass shootings in the United States. I know because I compared it to the metrics of mass shooting occurrences in other countries.") There's nothing wrong with making assessments. In many ways, assessments have saved us as a species and ensured our survival—for example, "I'm safe here" or "Mountain lions are scary." But learning to *ground* your assessments is essential. If you don't, the advantages provided to you by making assessments can become your downfall. You'll risk continually churning out assessments about yourself and others that may not be true and then base your decisions—and subsequent actions—on ungrounded assessments.

Collectively, if we don't take the time to understand the difference between assertions and assessments and whether they are grounded, we end up pointing the finger of blame at one another and arguing over whose assessment matters more or whose "truth" is correct, instead of standing together and dealing with the *assertion* that's causing the problem in the first place. This is how we end up on opposite sides of the aisle from one another. We believe that this conundrum is one of the biggest problems facing society today. We must become people who make assertions and *grounded* assessments. We must become people who don't mistake our opinions for facts. This is our first step to transforming our culture—and it has to start with you.

Ve is a young Vietnamese student in our program who realized she held the unconscious assessment that "Black men are dangerous." She was so ashamed of this that she could barely say it aloud. She said, "Growing up, I never had a dangerous personal experience with a Black man, but my parents always told me I needed to stay away from them." This was primarily because Ve's mom once heard a story about a Black man who robbed a mutual friend's restaurant at gunpoint. Ever since Ve's mother heard that story, she instilled a fear of Black men into her children. Although Ve has Black coworkers and interacts with a few Black men daily, she tenses up a little bit every time she sees Black men, especially if she's alone. She says, "I've built up this incredible fear that I feel so ashamed of."

When Ve started to further explore the origins of her assessment, she realized that the standard she was using to make her assessment was based on two things: first, the story she heard from her mom; and second, the things she's seen in movies and on the news. Upon further investigation, Ve realized that she personally never experienced any of this herself, nor has she ever met anyone who has. We asked Ve to try further grounding her assessment and what she realized after doing some research was that Black men did not account for the majority of violent crime in America. In the US, Black people account for less than a third of violent crime, while white people account for more than half.[2] This revelation shocked her. She said, "I was so afraid to upset my mom that I was willing to let go of what's really important to me, and I'm so ashamed of that." We asked Ve to drop the shame. As soon as she did, she saw the lesson: that she was holding on to an assessment that was harming her ability to interact with life in a way that was in alignment with her values. Ve stepped into a truth that was uncomfortable for her to admit to, but it was the starting point for her to begin working toward transforming this area of her life.

Aaron, a traditionally raised Jewish American man in his midforties who enrolled in one of our first cohorts, was courageous enough to share his assessment that he "could never be friends with a Muslim." He admitted at one point that he "feared all Muslims" because he believed all Muslims thought that he, as a Jew, had no right to exist. He said, "This fear runs my life, but I don't even know where it comes from." As he explored his belief further, he found that the reason he harbored this fear was because of the narrative he was taught growing up, in Hebrew school and in community spaces like his synagogue, about the Palestinian-Israeli conflict and acts of terrorism enacted by certain Muslim people throughout history. Aaron never had a Muslim friend or even acquaintance, neither as a child nor in his adult life. Anything that he knew about Muslims—from the religion to their culture—primarily was knowledge he acquired from his teachers and family when he was younger or consumed through mass media. His fears, as an American, were largely based on a broad belief that Muslims in the United States sympathize with terrorists and that Muslims do not share Western values.

Upon further discussion with us, Aaron realized that he had never personally had a meaningful interaction with a Muslim. Thus Aaron's fears were based on indirect experiences, history lessons that were often presented through a specific lens, and secondhand knowledge or stories. When confronted with that assertion, Aaron realized that he had to start *grounding* his assessment. Aaron began with primary sources, starting with the Qur'an, where he learned that there is nothing in the religious text or in the Prophet Muhammad's example that supports hatred of the Jews.[3] He then began to delve into the history of past empires and regimes under Muslim rule and learned that Jews actually flourished under such leadership in parts of North Africa, Jerusalem, Persia, and Spain.[4] Then he started to learn about organizations in the United States and even in Israel where Jews and Muslims are working hand in hand toward peace and tolerance. Since he lived in a major metropolitan area, Aaron realized through his research that there were several "common ground" groups right in his town. Aaron said to us, "This whole time, I was only looking at one side of the story, and I had it all wrong."

Aaron decided to attend a few of those common-ground gatherings, and by being in proximity to Muslim people in a safe space for discussions and connection, he began to befriend several of the organization's members. Aaron stepped into a truth that was uncomfortable for him to admit, but by being open to exploring the possibility that perhaps his "truth" was not well grounded and that he was applying a broad stereotype based upon the actions of a few, he was able to ground into a truth that allowed him to find friendship and community he might never have known otherwise—one that has now become one of his primary sources of friendship and connection. Anyone who has ever gone through a transformational experience understands that the first step to any type of healing is facing the *truth*.

Inner Work

Now it's your turn. Complete the sentences below to do some excavation of your own and explore your relationship to truth and what might be ready to shift.

- An assessment I've made about myself or others as it relates to the concept of race is ______________ ____.
- What I might be trying to prove, gain, or protect by making that assessment is ______________ ____.
- The reason I think this assessment matters to me is ____.
- The standard I am using to make this assessment is ____.
- From as unbiased a perspective as possible, the *assertions* (verifiable facts) related to my assessment are ____.

  (This may require a few minutes of research.)
- Having gone through this grounding process, what I now realize is ______________________.
- The way this assessment has affected me in the past is ____.
- Knowing what I know now, the way I would prefer for this assessment to affect me in the future is ____.
- What I will do next time this assessment comes up in my mind is ______________________.

As you learn to claim your truth, please remember: your *assessments* are *never* true or false. You're never right. Regardless of how grounded they are, your assessments are *still* your perspective. That's a hard pill to swallow sometimes, especially when we believe in something strongly or that something "should" be a certain way. Grounding your assessment is never about proving your accuracy; rather, it's about *revealing your thinking*. With enough evidence, you can make a case for any side. That's why it's fundamental you understand WHY you're making an assessment in the first place. Why is the assessment that you're making important to you? Is it taking you forward toward the future you want? Is it in alignment with your values and beliefs about what you want for the world? What are the motivations and true intentions behind the assessments you make? If your reason is "to be right," then there's no amount of information that could ever be presented to you that could change your mind. That is fundamentalism. But if you understand that regardless of how much data you have to support your claim, your assessment is never anything more than a personal opinion with evidence, then there is room for nuance and thus room for conversation beyond the binary way of thinking. This is the road to ending racism.

Excavating, standing in, and voicing our truth can be incredibly difficult. It takes a level of personal responsibility that isn't standard in today's culture. But similar to what is taught in most addiction counseling, the first step toward recovery is "admitting that we have a problem." It can be challenging for many reasons: First, we have been programmed since we were born to look at the world in a binary way—in other words, black or white, good or bad, right or wrong. Second, we have been rewarded our entire lives for subscribing to the herd mentality in that if we challenge that binary way of thinking, it can make life more challenging for us, and in some cases, it can even cause us to be rejected by our loved ones or peers. In some communities, challenging long-held "truths" can even cause us to be excommunicated or killed. In *this* community—the one taking the steps toward ending racism—we hold space for thinking beyond the binary, because that's where the real truth can emerge.

As you go throughout the rest of your day, pay close attention to the ways you and others speak about "truth" and how often assessments are mistaken for facts. Listen for statements of right and wrong, good and bad—phrases such as "The truth is . . . ," "The fact is . . . ," or "What they should've done . . ." Anytime you hear or say phrases like that, check to see if an assessment is at play.

It is important to also understand that we are *not* saying assessments are bad. Assessments matter tremendously. Throughout this book, we will make many assessments. Assessments are what individually (and collectively) shape our world. But we use caution because we understand that assessments can become prejudice when they are committed to intensely. Prejudice is simply a *prejudgment.* Prejudice is based upon the *assessments* we make about people and their association with certain groups. As we mentioned in the introduction to this book, for racism to end, we don't fantasize that one day the whole world is going to wake up suddenly unprejudiced. Instead, we must *become aware and then responsible for our prejudices.* Sure, we all have prejudices, but it doesn't mean those prejudices have to control us. When we know our assessments are nothing more than assessments, it frees us from their bondage.

Returning to our story about our student Ve, if she continued to be under the illusion that her assessment about Black men was "truth," she would spend the rest of her life in fear every time she encountered a Black man. Once she became aware that her fear was based upon ungrounded assessments, she could watch the fear arise when she encountered Black men and let it pass because she knows it is based on an old story that is out of alignment with her desire to create a more loving and compassionate world. Today Ve has several close Black male friends whom she loves dearly that she met through our program. This wouldn't have been possible if she was lost in the hypnosis of her ungrounded assessments.

We believe that when it comes to *ending* racism, it's crucial that we are rigorous about understanding when we're making assessments or assertions. When we're moving toward freedom, and building our stories and strategies for change, they must not be based on hearsay or ungrounded assessments. In every instance, at every turn, and in every moment of our lives, each of us is allowed to have different assessments. For this reason, it's important that the assessments we build our future upon are grounded and solid, because when we build our world on a shaky foundation, it inevitably falls apart. The next time you realize you're making an assessment, whether it's about race or not, stop and ask: *Why am I making this assessment in the first place? What am I trying to gain, prove, or protect? What is my assessment grounded in?* And most importantly: *Is it taking me forward toward the future I want?*

This will set you free.

Pillar Three

we owned our emotions

4

∞

Describing How You Feel

The pathway to ending racism is deeply emotional. When we stand in the future and ask, "What *did* we do today?" one of the foundational things we did was learn to *connect*. Humans cannot connect without being in touch with our *true* emotions and expressing them properly. The reason we are teaching you about emotions is because we want you to use them to deepen your connection to yourself and to others. We want you to learn how to speak across divides, and you cannot do that without first connecting with yourself. We want you to notice your old patterns and programmed reactions that are affecting your behaviors and responses—whether subconscious or conscious. Emotions lead to vulnerability, vulnerability leads to connection, and in that space of connection is where we will find a deeper, more nuanced truth about ourselves and others—the kind of truth required to end racism.

In the previous chapter, we articulated how emotions don't give rise to well-grounded assessments. That reality, however, doesn't mean that your emotions don't matter but rather that you simply need to understand the *role* and function that they both play in your life.

In this chapter, we will give you a different way to relate to and understand your emotions so that intense emotions don't have to derail you from your growth or from connecting with others. You will also learn how to speak about your emotions differently than you may have been programmed to. Your emotions can work *for you* instead of against you if you learn to speak about them more accurately.

First and foremost, you must understand that emotions don't lead to *truth*. How could they? One moment you're happy, then sad, then depressed, then tired, then you're joyful again—and that can all be in the course of the same day. Emotions are like your internal weather. If you tether "truth" to what you feel, then when a storm comes (anger, sadness, rage, depression, or something terrible happens in the world that upsets you), you will lose sight of who you are, what you believe is possible, and thus what you're committed to. In this book, we are asking you to make a fierce commitment to a new truth about humanity: that the possibility of ending racism is here, that the time is now, that we're the ones responsible for ending it, and that we must come together across divides to make it happen. But if that commitment wavers like the weather, how will you stay committed when hard times come, when extremists take center stage, or when something happens in the world that you don't want?

Jake, a student of ours, is deeply committed to the path of ending racism. But every time he sees a story on the news about a racist hate crime, Jake abandons the mission, and we don't hear from him for several weeks. The story is always the same. He says things like "When I saw the news last week, I felt so hopeless. What's the point? Nothing is ever going to change." Many of us have felt this way. But the truth is, if we tether our commitment to ending racism to "hope," then it will never end. Hope, just like any other emotion, is fleeting. *Hope is not a strategy.* You cannot let your emotions dictate your commitment to your path.

Still, you don't want to ignore your emotions. They are important. As researcher, professor, and author Dr. Brené Brown's research has proven, we like to think we are cognitive beings who, on occasion, feel. We are not. We are *emotional beings* who, on occasion, think. Our emotions impact everything we do. So instead of pushing our emotions deeper into our subconscious or letting our emotions control us, we must learn to *be responsible* for what emerges. Our emotions can open the doorway for connection. But to do that, we must first learn how to be responsible for them.

How does one take responsibility for their emotions? Well, saying things like "*He made me feel . . .*" or "*That made me feel . . .*" is always a sign you're on the wrong path. Being responsible for your emotions means if someone says something that triggers you, you understand that no one is "making you" feel anything. Though you may be personally impacted, you understand that *you've been activated.* Regardless of what's happening on the outside, you understand that your emotions are happening *in you.* Of course, people may say and do terrible things, but ultimately your response is happening *inside of you,* so *you* are the only one who can be responsible for your response to any given moment. If we are not responsible for our emotions, they control us. We end up saying things we regret and doing things we wish we hadn't. The more uncomfortable we are with an emotion, the deeper we bury and avoid it. We're more likely to be reactionary when confronted with that emotion or to place the responsibility on someone else for "making us" feel a certain way.

Your comfort level with your emotions often has to do with your emotional history, which is based on an amalgamation of the family you grew up in, your culture, social norms, and of course, your trauma. Some of us grew up in families where we were taught that it is acceptable to experience joy but not to experience power. Others grew up in families where anger was given space for expression but not trust or love. How was yours? Becoming aware of your emotional history will help you identify the emotions that are more challenging to feel or express. Your emotional history plays a large part in dictating which emotions you have the capacity to feel and express and which you don't. Once you become aware of that history, it no longer has to control you.

Right now, pause for a moment, and if you are able, place your hands over the center of your chest and take a couple deep breaths. Now answer this question: *What emotion(s) am I experiencing right now?* Come up with at least one word that describes the emotion that is arising in this moment. Jot down what comes to you; we'll be coming back to it in a few moments. Go ahead, do this right now as you are reading this.

The first step of enhancing your relationship to your emotions has everything to do with language—learning to name and communicate what emotions arise for you. Many people are at a loss for words when asked to specifically describe or identify their emotions. In fact, studies have proven that on average, most people can only identify a range of three emotions as they're feeling them: happy, sad, and angry. Yet studies have proven that the *words* you use to describe what you're feeling can induce you into experiencing that emotion.[1] For example, if you say, "I feel sad," it actually prompts your nervous system to feel sad, even if you were never feeling sad in the first place. On the other hand, if you say, "I feel grateful," you are more likely to find the silver lining in even the most challenging situations. **The words you use to describe your emotional experiences matter tremendously because if you don't have the language to describe what you're feeling, you have no way to understand what's actually going on inside of you. It will be nearly impossible for others to understand what is going on, either.** As the philosopher Ludwig Wittgenstein said, "The limits of my language mean the limits of my world."[2]

We want to help you expand your world using a tool that is backed by science and incredibly useful: the emotions wheel. There are many versions of this wheel, but we will show you one created by the psychotherapist Dr. Gloria Willcox that we've redesigned. It is a visual aid that equips us with the language we need to identify and communicate our emotions.

The wheel is composed of an inner circle with six primary emotions: sad, mad, scared, joyful, powerful, and peaceful. The two outer circles describe secondary and tertiary emotions that relate to the primary emotions at the center. These rings will help you define your emotions more clearly. For example, dropping her son at college for the first time, Diedre felt many emotions. After driving away from the campus, Diedre sat in her car and put her hands on her heart to help her understand what she was feeling. Looking at an image of the wheel that she saved on her phone, the word *scared* resonated with her. She then moved outward toward the second ring of words and realized that she was also anxious.

Feelings Wheel by Gloria Willcox

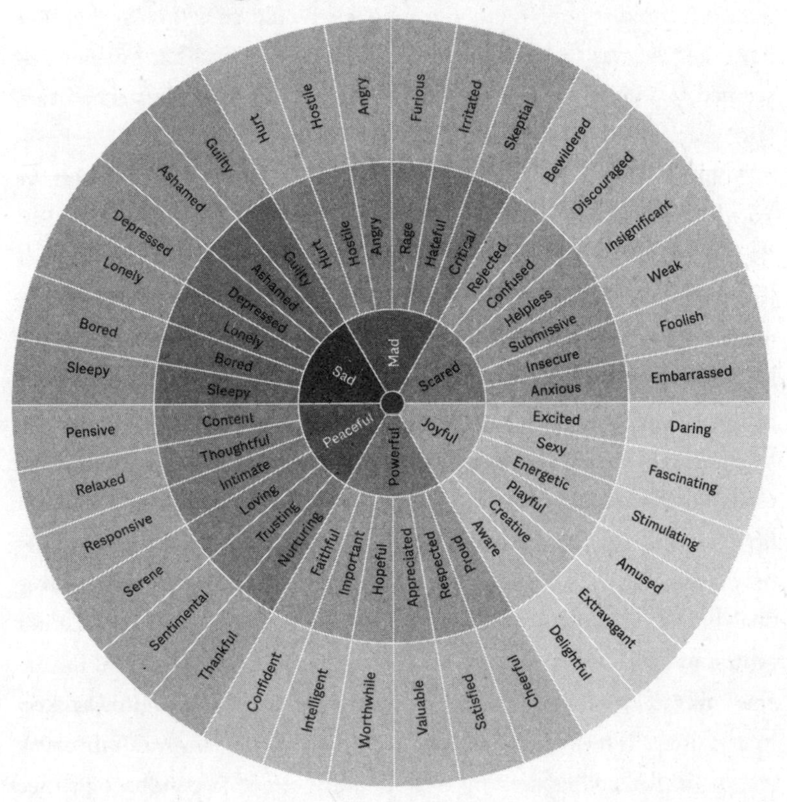

Then moving farther outward, she understood that her anxiety was a factor, in part, of feeling insignificant and no longer needed by her now independent son. Understanding this emotion more deeply helped her begin to add more quality and distinction to the word *scared* and begin to explore the roots of her emotions as she steps into this new version of her role as a mother. This allowed her to begin to ask more effective questions, with her emotions as the messenger.

The purpose is to help bring language to the nuance of what you're experiencing inside. Once you have the language, you can begin to work more directly with your emotions. But if you can't identify what you're feeling, you can't treat it. For example, Jon was noticing at work that every day for two weeks he was feeling sluggish and tired. His creativity was limited, and he just couldn't get inspired. He kept falling asleep at his desk but couldn't quite figure out why. He would go to his car and take naps, and he was sleeping at night the way he always did, but nothing seemed to solve the problem. He started reading books on exhaustion and sleep. He asked his doctor to check his thyroid to see if there was a problem. The doctor found nothing. Finally Jon came to us, and we asked him to answer the question, "How are you feeling at work?" and then look at the emotions wheel and circle every answer that felt resonant. Right away he noticed that *sleepy* was under the *sad* category. But he also noticed he felt other emotions on the wheel, too. He felt apathetic, inferior, critical, frustrated, and irritated at work. Based on those responses, Jon realized that he was "sad" and to his surprise, "mad." We asked Jon to close his eyes, and we asked him to complete this sentence: "What I'm really upset about at work is __________." Right away he talked about how a month ago, his boss shut down a big idea Jon had been working on for months. When it happened, Jon convinced himself it wasn't a big deal, but he realized now he was hurt by this. Jon wasn't just "tired," he was angry and sad. Even though he convinced himself into thinking he was "over it," his emotions were a messenger. All he had to do was drop in and listen. If he hadn't, he may have gone off on a tangent of drinking energy drinks, taking sleeping pills he didn't need, or continuing to see doctors for a problem he never had. Jon went to have a heart-to-heart with his boss. The next day, his creativity returned.

Now it's your turn. Pause for a moment and check in with how you feel. Now use the wheel to identify the primary emotion at the center that you most associate with, based on the question we asked you before: *What emotion am I experiencing right now?* Notice if anything shifts from your original response by using the wheel this time. Now begin to move from the inner circle to the outer ones, choosing as many words as you'd like. Use the whole circle; you do not have to stay in one quadrant—you may notice you are feeling more primary emotions than you realized, or multiple primary emotions at the same time. You may also choose to go the other way around—starting with the outer circles and working your way to the inner.

Here's an important tip: Most people answer a seemingly simple question—"How do you feel?"—with a sentence that starts with the words "I feel *like*. . . ." But an answer that starts with "I feel *like* . . ." leads down the wrong path—one that avoids vulnerability. It usually means you are heading into a *narrative* instead of a description of a real emotion. This narrative isn't an effective way to get in touch with your emotions or communicate them to others. Instead, it describes the *story you are telling yourself about why you are feeling the way you feel* rather than the actual emotion you are experiencing. The wheel helps us use clearer and more precise language. A good way to answer the common question "How do you feel?" is to reframe the question itself, starting your answer with the words, "The emotions I am experiencing right now are . . ."

Why is it important for you to be able to answer this question so precisely? First, you can't heal what you don't feel, and what you don't heal, repeats. You will keep repeating the same cycles and patterns that may not serve you if you don't learn how to name and take responsibility for what you feel. Naming your emotions opens the door for healing toxic cycles. For example, if you can identify experiencing shame, simply being able to name it can give rise to the ability to cultivate self-compassion ("It's okay to make mistakes, I am human") and work toward changing habits ("I can learn from this and do it differently next time") or patterns of thought ("I am not defined by this one experience, and it doesn't need to define me forever"). But without being able to name the emotion, the doorway to healing remains locked.

Second, language is a portal to connection. You cannot experience connection to others if you can't communicate your emotions properly. This is science.[3] The emotions wheel is a tool that helps us hone this power by simply giving us greater access to vocabulary to build intimacy. Soon we are going to teach you about having big conversations and how to talk across divides, but first you must recognize and label what you're experiencing inside of your own self so that you can share and communicate those true emotions with others.

Inner Work

Let's continue our excavation by learning more about your emotions. Complete the following sentences to understand more about your emotional history and patterning.

- The emotion that's hardest for me to experience is ______________________.
- Where I imagine I learned or acquired this pattern from is ______________________.
- The emotion that's easiest for me to experience is ______________________.
- Where I imagine I learned or acquired this pattern from is ______________________.
- The emotion I hide most from others is ______________________.
- The emotion I suppress or hide most from myself is ______________________.
- The way I typically handle anger is ______________________.
- The reason I handle anger in this way is because ______________________.
- The person or thing that taught me to handle anger in this way was ______________________.
- Something I want to shift about the way I handle my emotions is ______________________.
- My first step might be ______________________.

Now that you better understand your emotional history and have the emotions wheel as a tool to help you more accurately describe your emotions, it's important that you bring this tool into all areas of your life, but especially as we continue through this book. It can be used in the moment when you sense an inner shift or heightened state of emotion, before or during a conversation, or as a contemplative tool to track your emotions throughout the day or at the end of the day. Tuning in to your emotions isn't hard, but it does take commitment and awareness.

Here's a simple practice that you can use when you feel a shift in your internal weather.

First, pause. Next, place your hands over the center of your chest, one over the other.

Then take a deep breath and ask yourself, "What emotion am I experiencing right now?" Often, you may find that you do not have the right words to answer. This is why we've provided a downloadable version of the emotions wheel for you to keep on your device:

HowWeEndedRacism.com/resources.

Look at the wheel and choose two or three words to identify how you're feeling in that moment. You'll notice that over the course of just a few days, your access to the vocabulary you need to describe the nuances of your emotions will expand significantly. We've prescribed this practice to people all over the world, so we know it works. You'll also have more opportunities to practice this throughout the book.

We'll be invoking this chapter on emotions throughout the rest of this book. In the coming chapters, we are going to teach you about conversations across divides, forgiveness, setting boundaries, and more. All these topics require you to be in touch with your emotions, so bookmark the page with the emotions wheel or be sure to have your digital copy handy as you will likely come back to it often throughout our work together.

Shana is a tough and successful young activist who has no issue expressing anger and frustration. In fact, anger and frustration are how she's learned to get her way. But while working with us, she realized that even after months of marching and protesting for a particular outcome, and having that outcome achieved, her primary response to everything would be "This is not justice. We are not done yet. There is still much work to do." When we gave Shana this inner-work exercise, she looked at the wheel and realized she has massive trouble expressing celebration, satisfaction, joy, and peace—especially in relation to her work toward justice. After a victory, she would feel joy and happiness arise, but she would immediately push these feelings down. She didn't realize this until she did this practice.

Shana began to explore the roots of her inability to express joy. She said that for her entire life, she has always had to worry about what was coming next. Even as a child, she was the youngest and smallest in her family, and she always had to worry about being teamed up on by her siblings if she was to win at a game or succeed in school, so she learned to downplay her victories. When she began working in activism, every victory seemed to be overswept by another immediate issue. To her, it seemed no matter how good things got, she always had to be on guard about what was coming next. This caused her to teach herself that experiencing joy would always come with some sort of punishment. This exercise helped Shana realize that joy was indeed *trying* to arise in her, but she was conditioned to push it down. And while there would always "be more work to do," we explained to Shana that giving space to celebrate her victories—with joy, happiness, peace, and rest—is essential to her healing. You cannot sustain activism without joy and celebration because joy and celebration create fuel for the work ahead.

When we stand in the future, looking back at now, and ask, "What did we do that created the end of racism?" learning how to take responsibility for our emotions is an essential pillar. It is from this pillar that all the rest of our work is born.

5

The Emotions of Race

Let's turn inward, starting with a question inspired by the author and leader Rev. angel Kyodo williams: *What is your very first memory of realizing there was a thing called "race," that a certain group of people were to be treated differently based upon their racial identity?* Describe the story and, most importantly, identify how it made you *feel.* As you recount the story in your mind, what words from the emotions wheel can you use to identify your emotion(s)? If you're having trouble tapping into an emotion right now, see if you can remember how this moment made you feel back then. Flip back and use the emotions wheel if you need to. Go ahead and pause and give yourself a moment to do this now.

Racism has impacted all of us. To end it, we can't just point outward toward others; rather, we must enter in through our own lived experience—through the heart.

Thus far, you've gained a deeper understanding of truth and the difference between assessments and assertions. Then we dove deep into the role of emotions and how to name and begin to communicate them. But in the real world, assertions, assessments, and emotions aren't compartmentalized in neatly packed chapters—they exist together, comingled and sometimes in a messy fashion that can confuse us. The reality that we must embrace if we are going to take on a commitment to ending racism is this: if we can't differentiate between the *truth* and our *emotional response* to the truth, we may end up pushing the truth away simply because we can't handle the emotions that arise with it.

The primary purpose of the rest of this chapter is to exercise *intersecting* truth and emotions, and to practice everything we just learned in a context specifically related to race. We will make no assessments in this chapter, only assertions. This will help you practice relating to what emotions arise for you as you read difficult truths—some that might surprise you, and others you may know—about the history of racism.

This is a practice for the real world. However, there are a few important disclaimers we need to make. First, reading this chapter and doing these practices may be challenging or triggering for some (especially while reading alone), so please take care of yourself by pausing or stepping away and coming back as you need to.

Second, although this practice primarily uses the racial context of the United States, you can apply what you're learning here to any part of the world. Third, you might notice much omitted from the brief history we share. That's because in every country, racial context varies dramatically, and if we were to write an extensive history lesson on race, this would be an entirely different book. The purpose of this practice is not to give you an extensive history lesson on race but rather to help you practice *feeling your emotions without pushing them down* and *naming your emotions* as you experience truths about race.

This chapter isn't here to teach you about race; *it's here to teach you about you.* You will learn how *you* react emotionally to challenging truths about race. What you find may surprise you. Do you get angry? Sad? Ashamed? Disconnected? Do you freeze? Get defensive? Do these emotions sway your desire to end racism? You'll learn a lot about *yourself* in this chapter. Even after giving all these disclaimers, when we teach this practice in our workshops, someone will inevitably get upset and ask, "Why didn't you include [fill in historical moment of your choice] in this section?" If that type of question comes up for you, use it to notice how a *narrative* might be creeping in to convince you to point a finger of blame at us to distract you from *feeling something challenging within yourself.*

Fourth and finally, we want to be clear that this section is not a Black Lives Matter conversation, nor an All Lives Matter conversation; it's not a Democratic or a Republican conversation, nor a liberal or conservative conversation. We understand and hope that people of different backgrounds and with different beliefs from different ends of the spectrum are reading with us. **All beliefs—even the ones opposing yours—are needed at the table if we are going to end racism.**

We will provide special callouts to help you track your emotions properly throughout the chapter. Notice the subtle changes as you follow along. Be sure to refer to the emotions wheel on page 53 and do your best to go beyond just naming your initial surface-level emotion because, from our experience, that emotion is usually rooted in something deeper. Tapping into that something deeper can take a great measure of courage. Use every sentence, question, and emotion that arises as an entry point to your heart.

We will now take you on a journey of exploration of your emotional responsiveness, using United States racial history as our reference. We will only use *assertions*, allowing us to ground into the same truth. Even if you think you already know much of this history, no matter what level of historical context you already have, *track how you feel.* There may be truths here that surprise you.

Let's begin: "It was here in the United States, not that long ago, that Native Americans were occasionally skinned and made into bridle reins. Andrew Jackson, the U.S. president who oversaw the forced removal of indigenous people from their ancestral homelands during that Trail of Tears, used bridle reins of indigenous flesh when he went horseback riding."[1]

This is not-so-ancient history. This quote from Isabel Wilkerson's *Caste* exemplifies how present-day Americans tend to view themselves as far-removed from barbaric traditions of yore. Yet it was here in the United States, not too long ago, that Native Americans were skinned and fashioned into bridle reins for horseback riding—even by the president of the United States himself, Andrew Jackson, who founded the Democratic Party.

☑ Emotional Check-In

Identify how you feel after reading those paragraphs. Take a moment to sit with and digest what you read and try to feel into it with your heart, not just your head. Use the emotions wheel to name one or more emotions that are arising and see if you can sense where in your body you physically feel the emotion. Does your chest feel tight, are you clenching your stomach, are you holding your breath? Place your hands on your body where you feel any sensation arising in you and take a few deep breaths.

Let's continue our exploration in the year 1619. That was the year that the first African people became enslaved in the newly established colonies in America. The descendants of those enslaved people were not freed until after the Civil War in 1865, *nearly two and half centuries later*. Sit with that for a second. Nearly *250 years* passed during which an entire population of humans were not allowed to be educated or own any assets, engage in trade or participate in the economy, or have autonomy over their own bodies. The enslaved in America were viewed as property. Six-year-old children were assets that could be bought, sold, and traded and were often placed on chopping blocks, naked, in front of their parents and family, with their genitals being examined by the fingers of dozens of white men to assess the value of their fertility and offer a price for their sale. If their parents dared shed a tear or did anything other than smile, they were lashed with a whip for showing signs of weakness.

☑ Emotional Check-In

Take a moment to sit with and digest what you read and try to feel into it with your heart, not just your head. Use the emotions wheel to name one or more emotions that are arising and see if you can sense where in your body you feel the emotion like you did earlier. Place your hand on that body part and take a few deep breaths. Don't stop reading if you get uncomfortable. You can sit with discomfort. This is where the growth happens.

When these enslaved individuals were freed in and after 1865, they had few resources and few to no advantages to help them succeed in their new reality. Most did not know how to read or write or have any funds of their own—not because they didn't have the capacity but because they were not allowed to. Yet enslaved people were told "You're free now." Since many of the now-freed enslaved people had no resources, education, money, or property of their own, as reparations, the United States agreed to offer every male that was a descendant of an enslaved person forty acres of land and a mule. However, most enslaved people did not receive this reparation, and most who did eventually had it taken away. To be specific, forty thousand freed men had been settled on four hundred thousand acres of land, but the reparations order was overturned in the fall of 1865 and the United States returned the land along the South Carolina, Georgia, and Florida coasts to the planters who had originally owned it. The land given to Black families was rescinded and returned to white Confederate landowners.[2]

☑ Emotional Check-In

Pause now. Be with the reality of what you just read. Try to imagine yourself in this position. Be with your heart. Be vulnerable. Don't judge the feelings arising. Use the emotions wheel to identify your emotions and place a hand over the part of your body where you feel the emotion arising. Again, take a few deep breaths. You are building your capacity. Sit with these emotions. We are with you.

As the newly freed began to build cities, businesses, and search for better lives, many previous enslavers did not accept the new realities that came with the end of American slavery and began to threaten to burn the new Black communities down, destroy property, and kill their inhabitants. The situation become so hostile that from 1865 until 1877, federal troops were stationed throughout the Southern states to keep the peace and make sure white citizens did not illegally force slavery back upon the Black inhabitants of the South.

For context, you may recall when federal troops were stationed in many American cities during the unrest happening at the same time as the COVID-19 pandemic of 2020, with guns and tanks on street corners—that lasted for just a few months. Federal enforcement of the end of slavery with the use of federal troops lasted daily, for twelve years, and is an era known as the Reconstruction: a period where the new anti-slavery laws were enforced by troops, allowing Black Americans to successfully build bustling cities, businesses, and communities. Within this period, former enslaved people built their own Black Wall Street in Tulsa, Oklahoma, and they founded Black colleges. The formerly enslaved were beginning to build a new society, learning to read, write, and engage in trade as others had been allowed to.

However, in 1877, soon-to-be President Rutherford B. Hayes was faced with a scandal that could've caused him to lose the upcoming election. To keep the scandal from becoming public and ruining his chances of winning, he accepted a bribe from white Southerners, who controlled the vote. The bribe: white Southerners would keep the scandal quiet so long as the president withdrew all federal troops from protecting Black people's rights in Southern states. The bribe was accepted, and federal troops were then ordered to leave the South. Immediately, many of the Black businesses and communities that the formerly enslaved had spent twelve years building were, with no hyperbole or exaggeration, destroyed or burned to the ground.

☑ Emotional Check-In

Take a moment to sit with and digest what you read and try to feel into it with your heart, not just your head. Use the emotions wheel to name one or more emotions that are arising and see if you can sense where in your body you feel the emotion as well. Place your hand on that body part and breathe into that feeling. We're almost to the finish line. Let yourself be with these emotions. We'll explain why soon.

This new circumstance—a South with no federal troops, white confederate Southerners having few consequences, and the unrest of Black people whose communities had been destroyed—spawned violence and opened the path to the passage of laws that were created to "keep the peace." Known as Black Codes, these were "restrictive laws designed to limit the freedom of African Americans and ensure their availability as a cheap labor force after slavery was abolished."[3] An example of a Black Code in South Carolina: Black people were prohibited from performing any type of labor other than farm or domestic work. Here is the verbiage of an actual law on record in the United States: "No person of color shall pursue or practice the art of trade or business of an artisan, mechanic or shopkeeper, or any other trade, employment or business besides that of husbandry or that of servant under contract of labor on his own account and for his own, until he shall have obtained a license from a judge, the district court, which license shall be good for one year only."[4] The license cost one hundred dollars annually, which would be the equivalent of $1,500 per year in the twenty-first century. Of note, this license and annual fee was only required of Black people; white citizens did not have to obtain one or pay such a fee. Additionally, even if a Black person managed to obtain the funds to pay for said license, they would now be required to get the license approved by a white judge in a white-run justice system that created the law in the first place.

To put this entire story in context, imagine for a moment that you were a once enslaved person who learned to read and became educated to be a pharmacist in Tulsa, Oklahoma. You built a thriving pharmacy to support your Black community only to have that business burned down while you were asleep at night, your legal ability to rebuild taken away from you by the government (due to Black Codes), and the only viable option available to you now was to return to serving a white family in order to support your family.

☑ Emotional Check-In

Take a moment to sit with and digest what you read and try to feel into it with your heart, not just your head. Use the emotions wheel and name one or more emotions that are arising and see if you can sense where in your body you feel the emotion. Be with these emotions. You can do this. Take a few deep breaths.

The concept of "race" itself was invented in the eighteenth century. The idea of "whiteness" (as one homogenous race) is an ideology that is actually less than a century old. Prior to that, people classified themselves by tribes, kingdoms, religions, socioeconomic status, and a myriad of other identities. Although people, of course, could identify differences in how people looked—short or tall, light-skinned or dark-skinned, red hair or brown hair—there was no concept of race. But during the eighteenth century, scholars started to classify people into groups (that eventually became "races") based on physical attributes such as eye color, skin color, and even skull dimensions. One of these classifications came from Johann Friedrich Blumenbach, a professor in Germany who developed "varieties" of humans based on skull measurements and then created a scale (from ugly to most beautiful) based on *his own personal preferences* (assessments) of beauty. In his "ugly skull" category were skulls that were African and Asian. In the "most beautiful" was the skull of an Eastern European woman who was a native of the South Caucasus. This is what later inspired the terminology we still use to this day: *Caucasian*. It hailed from one professor's assessment.

By the 1930s, this new concept called "race" to dehumanize an entire group of people had become so effective that the Nazi Party in Germany, under Adolf Hitler, became fascinated by the global leader in codified racism—the United States of America. So much so that Nazis sent spies to the United States to understand how the dominant caste in America was able to succeed at dehumanizing an entire group of people based upon something as seemingly irrational as skin color. It is historically known that the Nazi regime, its laws, and the extermination of millions of Jews was built, learned, and inspired by American racism.[5]

☑ Emotional Check-In

Take a moment to sit with and digest what you read and try to feel into it with your heart, not just your head. Use the emotions wheel to identify one or more emotions that are arising and see if you can sense where in your body you feel the emotion as well. Your feelings might be intensifying now, but just continue to feel and name them. You got this. Place a hand over the part of your body where the emotions are most noticeable and take a few deep breaths.

As we look to more recent history, there are still laws governing the United States today that began in a racialized context. For example, if you want to attend a school with more resources, you have to move or get a new home address in the district you want to be enrolled in. This is because in many states, more than 30 percent of the funding for public-school systems is based on property taxes collected within a specific region. In other words, in most states, schools in communities with a lower income—and thus a lower tax base—get less money allocated per student, fewer teachers, and less resources and supplies.

In the areas with more money, schools get more resources and supplies. While this may have become a norm for many in the United States, no country in the entire world relies on property taxes for education more than the US.[6]

Although some do not view laws such as this to be overtly "racist" —attributing them purely to wealth and economics—the truth is that this law and many others like it were created during the Jim Crow era as a response to segregation for one reason: to ensure that white communities' tax dollars were not being spent to support Black students. With the wealth disparity that never healed from the rescinded reparations, the end of the Reconstruction, and Black Codes, White communities benefited from higher-funded, higher-performing schools. This is the exact same system the United States is governed by today. Thus, even though the desegregation of schools occurred in 1964, this law, which was created to perpetuate inequality, was kept mostly intact and is still what American families are living with today.

☑ Emotional Check-In

Take a moment to sit with and digest what you read and try to feel into it with your heart, not just your head. Use the emotions wheel to name one or more of the specific emotions that are arising and see if you can sense where in your body you feel the emotion. Place your hands on that part of your body, if you can identify it. Take a few deep breaths. You got this.

There are many more stories that could be included here, from other People of Color and indigenous folks in America, along with the stories of Italian, Irish, and white Americans who faced many struggles of their own—not with an intention to *compare* our struggles but with a nod to the fact that in many different ways, the concept of race has impacted *all of us*. We end our brief practice on emotions here.

This practice wasn't easy. Take a moment to acknowledge that you just took a big step in learning how you react emotionally to challenging truths about race. What were your emotional reactions? (Feel free to use the emotions wheel.) Perhaps you felt sad, angry, ashamed, or shocked. Certain emotions may have even surprised you. But the more we tap into our emotions, the more we'll understand them and anticipate how they sway our decisions and influence our actions.

Inner Work

Use the following incomplete sentences to reflect on your experience and ground into what you learned about yourself. It might be useful to pause, close your eyes, and scan your body and emotions for each prompt.

- The emotional reactions I feel to reading all of this are ____ .
  (Use the emotions wheel.)
- Where I feel these emotions most in my body is ____ .
- My comfort level with experiencing these emotions is ____ .
- What I typically do when these particular emotions arise in other areas of my life is ________________ ____ .
- What I typically do when uncomfortable conversations about race arise is ____________________________ .
- What I realize now is ____________________________ .

Many people in our workshops feel shocked and saddened when they read this history. Others feel confused or apathetic, or they dissociate; others feel a blend of emotions that are hard for them to describe. Whatever you are feeling is valid, but we want to challenge you not to accept the answer of feeling "nothing." Feeling "nothing" or "I already knew this" after reading this means there is some disassociation occurring, which could also be a trauma response. Feeling "nothing" is the gateway to disconnection. We know that for many, the response of "feeling nothing" is a well-trusted armor. To end racism, we must start taking off that armor. Vulnerability is going to be our greatest power.

We know going through this practice can stir up a lot of emotions, so take a moment now to come back to the present moment. Glance around the space you're in to see what's around you. Take a few deep breaths. Remember that there are millions of incredible people in the world doing great things to move us forward. The fact that we live in a world where a book called *How We Ended Racism* can even exist is a miracle. You are here now. We will continue to rise together.

This very brief history gave you practice with tapping into your emotions, trying to locate them in your body, naming them in relation to challenging truths about race, and staying with them instead of pushing them down. If you'd like to continue this practice in a more personal way, we encourage and invite you to spend even a few moments now learning about what history has happened in *your* corner of the world. That could be the sometimes-hidden racial history of your country, city, workplace, or even your family or culture. You now have the tools to face it. When you finish reading this chapter, spend a few moments doing a quick online search or talking to a safe family member to see what you might find. Be present with your emotions as you discover what's there. As you research, don't just research with your head. Allow your emotions to arise without pushing them down, just as you practiced here. This is a skill to cultivate as best you possibly can.

In order to end racism, you will need to build and strengthen the capacity to sit with uncomfortable emotions. You will continue to learn about and hear challenging truths for the rest of your life, but now that you have had some practice, you know what emotions might arise, because you've learned about yourself. The next time you learn or hear something difficult that relates to race—or to anything challenging, for that matter—notice how your response may or may not be similar to what you experienced today. With this practice we hope that you can learn to expect what might arise within you so that you aren't blindsided when difficult things come up and so that you have a better chance at *staying present in a situation* when you're hearing someone else's truth or a new truth about the world. We'll be exploring more about this when we talk about forgiveness and having conversations across divides. In each moment, we are creating new history. We must be present with all that is—even the hard stuff—because whatever we push away will continue to haunt us.

Pillar Four

---

we became intra-connected

6

∞

Becoming Mwe

When we stand in the future, at a point where racism has ended, and ask, "What *did* we do today that brought forth the end of racism?" the answer is a centering truth that's at the heart of the movement to end racism. This centering truth is fundamental to the underlying conditions needed to end racism. But before we get to that centering truth, we need to break down a few commonly held misconceptions, starting with what we call the *Two O's*.

An idea that's often touted by people looking to create global change is the idea that "we are all one." While it may be true that we are all "one" human race, we believe the phrase "we are all one" often causes more harm than good. First, it's often used as a way to ignore the very real and dire differences and inequities in the world. We hear people with great privilege shouting "we are all one" from the mountaintops, but what they don't see are the eyerolls from the many who live in the margins.

Second, "we are all one" asserts that we are all the same, and clearly we're not. On the opposite end of the spectrum from "oneness" is complete differentiation, which we refer to as "othering." These are the Two O's. Oneness focuses on us being the same; othering focuses too heavily on how we're different. Othering is when we place people in in-groups and out-groups depending on our personal preferences, background, beliefs, and the like. Neither of these Two O's are accurate—we are not "one," *and* we are not "other." The truth we'd like you to ground into is much more nuanced than either of those perspectives.

Dr. Daniel J. Siegel—a good friend of ours, a pioneer of interpersonal neurobiology, and the author of the book *IntraConnected*—taught us a concept that he calls "**intra**connection," not to be confused with the usual way we see and use the word ***inter**connection*. The difference between the two words can be described like this:

- **Inter**connection: The connection between separate parts.
- **Intra**connection: The connection between something that is *already whole*.[1]

Interconnection is the wrong word to use to create a reality without racism because it refers to the desire to connect "separate parts," which automatically infers an assumed and inherent *disconnection*. This language sets up a false reality that each of us is "separate" rather than inviting us into the *truth*, which is that we are a part of one larger collective ecosystem with each component affecting another. This is not "woo-woo" spiritual stuff; this is proven and widely accepted science. The prefix *inter-* itself requires that we start with the assumption that we are inherently disconnected. But science has confirmed that the idea of separation is a delusion of the modern mind.[2] Scientists (and mystics!) call this "the illusion of the separate self."

One of the greatest wisdom teachings from many indigenous cultures is the understanding that we are not just *connected* to all things but rather that *we are all things*. Don't confuse this idea with "oneness." What we are suggesting here is greater than oneness—it's *wholeness*, which posits that even in our individuality we are part of a wholeness. This is why the term ***intra**connection* (rather than ***inter**connection*) makes such a powerful distinction. **Intra**connection considers the fact that the "self," the "I," the "me" that we describe as ourselves, is part of a whole, intricately connected to a larger network of other individuals and the planet.

With **intra**connection, we take a different stance on connecting "across divides": we are seeking to create deeper and stronger bonds within something that is already whole, even when others seem to believe or act "differently" than we do.

Thus, to do this work, we must be operating from a place of wholeness instead of oneness and othering to understand that we are all *already* more than connected; that we are part of the same system and the same whole. We must move *beyond oneness and othering* to wholeness. Ending racism is not about putting all our cultures, values, traditions, and differentiation into a blender to create some "we are all one" raceless, homogenous smoothie. We must honor our differentiation. Wholeness allows us to do that. Oneness does not. Think of your living, breathing human body. Your body comprises differentiated organs that each evolved to serve a specific purpose that helps to keep you alive. Each of these organs on their own serves no purpose; it is only when these organs work together in one larger, whole, intraconnected fashion that they thrive and serve their intended purpose. Yet at the same time, they are differentiated and need different nutrients, care, and support.

If we acknowledge the truth and live as if the whole is *already* a part of us and that we are a part of the whole, and that other human beings *are also a part of this larger organism that we are also a part of*, then the perspective for our work will shift completely. Instead of working so hard to "try" to create connection with other human beings who are different from us or who live on the other side of a "divide" from an assumed disconnection, *we must focus our work on strengthening the inherent connection that is already there*, even if that connection is weak, has gone unnoticed, or has been damaged for decades or generations. *You have connections with people who seem to be across a divide.* Moving society forward is not about just addressing what we perceive as weak or filling a void but rather expanding what already exists, and there is much more that exists than meets the eye or what divisive media might suggest.

As long as we human beings continue to believe that we are separate entities rather than parts of a whole, we will continue to live in the midst of collective trauma. And if more of us don't learn the tools to connect across all of the seeming divides that we have made up—across Black Lives Matter and All Lives Matter, Republican and Democrat, conservative and liberal, pro- and anti-anything—it is easy to see where we're headed. In society, the danger of excessive othering is that when it happens, the human brain shuts down what Dr. Siegel calls "mindsight circuits." He says, "When mindsight circuits shut down, human beings treat other human beings like a piece of dirt."[3] We've seen this in colonization, in Nazi Germany, through slavery, and in many other cases throughout history. **This terrible capacity of human beings to excessively differentiate to the point of not seeing one another as human is a vulnerability of our brains.** However, the intraconnection vantage point beckons us to ask, "If I am part of a whole, how could I possibly dehumanize people with different beliefs than me, people with a different skin tone, or people of a different political party affiliation, when in fact these people *are* me? How could I destroy the planet when in fact the planet *is* me?" It is no different from you deciding that your heart is too differentiated from your other organs to be in your body. If you remove it, the other organs die. Your heart is you just as much as your liver and your lungs are you. Your body is one whole connected system with differentiated parts. Humanity is one whole connected system with differentiated parts. The planet is one whole connected body with differentiated parts.

We know seeing other people as a part of you is a challenging stance to take when you believe that group is causing harm to you or the people you love. (We'll teach you more about that later.) But the people in our research who learned this were the most impactful in their work and in the world. We learned in our research that to move the world forward, to enact visionary activism, this is the type of truth we must call each other toward—that we are whole as one human family with many differentiated unique members. We are already whole (whether we fight each other or not), and it's time for a group of us to be equipped and ready to deepen the connections in society. You are a part of that group.

To embody this idea of intraconnection, Dr. Siegel coined the term "Mwe," which admittedly at first sounds like a silly word but is quite profound. Many personal and societal growth books suggest that we move from "me" to "we." But all science proves that's a terrible suggestion. Scientists agree that living in a me-centered state (where you focus primarily on the self) causes excessive differentiation; similarly, moving solely to a we-centered state (where you focus primarily on the collective and don't honor the individual) also does not create a healthy society. Thus, we should not aim for a dissolution of self but an *expansion* of self. It's not about moving directionally from me to we. Instead, it's about creating a relationship between me and we—a unified front where we get to honor, respect, and love the me and, at the same time, care for, love, and do the best for the we.

Me + We = Mwe

Mwe is a word we will sometimes use throughout this book (a weird word, we know, but you'll get used to seeing and using it) to remind us that we are all connected, inextricably in relationship to one another. Not living from Mwe consciousness is like the hydrogen and oxygen atoms of the ocean fighting over whose identity is more important without realizing that they must be separate but also bonded for the entire ocean to exist—both essential in their differentiation and connection at the same time. Or like firefighters trying to distinguish between redwoods and pine trees during a forest fire to decide which ones are more important to save. Even though redwood trees are known to have fire-resistant trunks (you can call this a "privilege" in the forest), telling a firefighter to "ignore the redwoods" because of this privilege would cause the entire forest to burn down. We are currently on fire, yet here we are, fighting one another, arguing over whose suffering is more significant. Instead of fighting the fire itself, we are trees fighting trees while a fire is raging. Instead of swimming in the ocean, we are molecules taking sides. It's time to unite to become water—and put the fire out.

Inner Work

We are, indeed, differentiated individuals but part of the same united system. *Intraconnected.* Even in our differences, we are whole. Use the following prompts to explore your relationship to intraconnection and wholeness.

- A group who I often view as "other" is ____.
- When I look a little deeper, what I might have in common with this group is ____________________.
- A group that I feel "others" me or my culture is ____________________.
- How that makes me feel is ____________________.
- When I am "othered," the emotion(s) that arise in me are ____________________.
- The way I typically react when I am "othered" is ____________________.
- How that makes me understand other people's reactions, even when they have different values, beliefs, or opinions than me, is ____.
- What I really want for the world is ____.
- What I can shift about myself to be more in alignment with what I want for the world is ____.

As we continue to expand the core concepts and define the conditions that need to arise in our mission to end racism, **it's important to understand that you do not have to lose the parts of your individual culture, traditions, values, or beliefs that are important to you to get to the finish line—as long as they don't harm the collective or compromise the health and wholeness of the human ecosystem,** they can help contribute to the mission. You get to keep the things you love about your differentiated me, all the while understanding that it all exists in relationship to a larger we. Everything about your culture—its music, food, clothing, customs, and even religious and spiritual beliefs—are born out of a reaction to or through a relationship to another.

Modern Mexican food was derived from the fusion of ancient precolonial civilizations dating back to 7000 BCE fused with Spanish, French, and Italian influences, while some traditional Black American food is rooted to the horrors of slavery. American country music was deeply rooted in African American jazz and blues but also blended with Celtic and Irish fiddle songs. Gospel music has African roots but is also connected to white enslavers. Christianity is related to Judaism, Judaism is related to Islam, and so on. Thus, none of the things that you might think of as "my culture" really exist in as much of a silo as people often think, because they wouldn't exist outside of the context of their relationality to something else (or *many* other things). There would be no self to identify with without the relationality of other selves. Without differentiation, there is no self. But without others, no differentiation is possible. You cannot be you without the rest of us.

The human mind is prone to create in-groups and out-groups. It's a foundation of humanity. But it doesn't have to control us—if we all understand excessive differentiation to be part of the human condition, then our job is not just to do what we normally do and dismiss the tendency as "this is just what humans do" while continuing to live in warring camps. Understanding this inherent vulnerability gives us a greater responsibility because we realize that the work we're doing goes beyond ending racism. **We are here to help evolve our species.** This is what it means to literally *move humanity forward*. The way we are going to do that is through *connection*.

One of the practices that we love to teach at workshops and also personally engage in ourselves is called "Just Like Me." It's a meditation practice that was originally developed by the spiritual teachers Ram Dass and Mirabai Bush.[4] As we ready ourselves for this practice together, reflect first on this quote from His Holiness the Dalai Lama: "Realizing that the other person is also just like me is the basis on which you can develop compassion, not only towards those around you but also towards your enemy. Normally, when we think about our enemy, we think about harming him. Instead, try to remember that the enemy is also a human being."

The "Just Like Me" practice is easy. It involves repetition of a handful of powerful phrases, using the same but a slightly modified version of the script taught by Ram Dass and Mirabai Bush. Before you begin to read through the phrases, though, we want you to think of someone you love. Go ahead and do it now. Think of someone you love dearly. Now read the following phrases with them in mind.

This person has a body and a mind, just like me.

This person has feelings, emotions, and thoughts, just like me.

This person has in their life experienced physical and emotional pain and suffering, just like me.

This person has at some point been sad, disappointed, angry, or hurt, just like me.

This person has felt unworthy or inadequate, just like me.

This person worries and is frightened sometimes, just like me.

This person has longed for friendship, just like me.

This person is learning about life, just like me.

This person wants to be cared about and experience kindness from others, just like me.

This person wants to feel safe from harm, just like me.

This person wants to be free from suffering and pain, just like me.

This person wants to feel like they belong, just like me.

This person wants to feel comfortable in their own skin and happy with their physical form, just like me.

This person wants to be content with what life has given them, just like me.

This person wishes to be happy, just like me.

This person wishes to be loved, just like me.

Now, allow some wishes for well-being to arise:

I wish for this person to have the strength, resources, and social support to navigate the difficulties in life.

I wish for this person to be free from pain and suffering.

I wish for this person to be happy.

I wish for this person to have peace.

I remember that this person is a fellow human being, just like me.

Now, take a moment of pause. Put your hand on your heart. Now we are going to do the practice again. But this time bring someone to mind who you are having a challenge with, maybe even someone with whom you are dealing with racism, discrimination, othering, or bias or racial harm of some sort. When choosing your person, don't pick a person you are *most* challenged by, though. On a scale of 1 to 10, with 10 being the most challenging, pick someone at a 5 or 6. Okay, let's do it. Go back to the top of the statements and read them again, but this time with a challenging person in mind, then continue on and explore the following questions:

How did you feel when you brought the person to mind? Was it easy or difficult? What kind of emotions did you feel? Can you identify them?

If any distracting thoughts arose, what were they? Were there any common themes between your thoughts?

What was the most difficult part of the process? What was the easiest? Did you find that as the practice progressed, that the qualities of your feelings changed? Did they become more intense? Less intense?

What kind of feelings and sensations arose after you wished this person kindness, safety, and health?

To understand why this practice may be difficult with people that we may have biases toward or individuals that we have attached narratives to, we must consider that patterns of thinking and behavior are like the deep grooves that get carved into a rock by the repeated passage of running water. The deeper the grooves, the more likely the water is to continue flowing through them. This is why we tend to have the same argument repeatedly with certain people, or we find ourselves unable to free ourselves from the familiar scripts. Compassion-based practices, including "Just Like Me," improve our ability to see those grooves more clearly, to lift ourselves out of them, and to intentionally choose a better, more intentional pathway.

Sometimes when we teach this practice in groups, we ask participants to sit in pairs, facing each other. We have them do this practice with multiple partners, over and over again, to emphasize the point that every single person is "just like me." However, this beautiful practice can also be done alone by bringing to mind any person you choose to think about. It can be a person you love, a person who is an acquaintance, or even someone you may not personally know (for example, a political figure). This practice can also be used when meeting someone new, and it is particularly useful when we find that judgment or fear of—or some other aversion to—another person is arising. This potent reminder that even that person is also "just like me" is powerful and helps us reframe and reset, instead of going down the well-worn pathway of acting or reacting unconsciously.

When we acknowledge our very real and sometimes unfair differences, we have three choices. We can ignore and pretend "we are all one," we can build walls and call people "other," or we can look one another in the eyes and ask, "How can I better understand you? And in doing so, better understand me?" The third choice is the pathway of *connection.*

We know what you might be thinking. Is this approach too *idealistic*? No. *It's strategic.* Standing for our wholeness doesn't mean we always have to be mild, meek, timid, agree with everyone's opinions, or condone harmful actions. But it does mean we have to aim for *connection* in our work with everyone. *Connection* cannot be forgotten; it must be integrated into everything we do, even in our anger. As the saying goes, the high road can be narrow and bumpy, but the view is magnificent. The high road doesn't mean we're better than them. The high road means we stand for a higher state of integration, that we don't fall for the delusion, that we live from the space of Mwe, standing for the truth of our **intra**connection to all things.

Oneness is not the greatest virtue needed to end racism. Connection is. You cannot connect with something you're already one with. When we project into the future, where racism has ended, and ask, "What did we do?," we believe what we did now, in the earliest part of the twenty-first century, was to learn to intra*connect.* We must begin to understand that a world free of racism means that when we bear witness to an atrocity happening somewhere in our community or country or in the world, we don't see it as happening "to them" but rather as something that reflects on all of us. It starts with the fundamental vow and belief that all human beings are deserving of compassion and kindness. It begins with the internalized understanding of this line from a poem that is engraved at a genocide memorial in Rwanda: "If you knew me and you really knew yourself, you would not have killed me." This knowing requires wholeness.

We ask you now to make a vow: to begin to see the world through a lens of intraconnection and to use your assessments, assertions, and emotions in the name of expanding connections in humanity. That you will start now with everyone you encounter. That you will process your emotions so that you can open the door for deeper connection. That you will honor the truth that we are different *and* whole, and that even when it's hard, you will aim with your whole heart—to seek connection, above all else. Moving forward throughout this book, *connection* is our underlying thread. Connection is what will move us *forward.*

Pillar Five

we did shadow work

7

∞

What's in Your Shadow?

When we stand in the future, in the year 2050, where racism has ended, and ask, "What *did* we do today that brought forth the end of racism?," we discover the next phase of our journey together: *shadow work.* Shadow work is deep; and as its name implies, it is about engaging the hidden parts of yourself—the parts that you typically want to turn away from or that are easy to keep hidden in the dark as you live your life. However, ignoring the shadow doesn't mean that it isn't there. As you do the work to transform yourself and move toward a vision for humanity without racism, your shadow will often meddle with your plans and sabotage your life from the background without you even realizing it—that's why it's called the shadow. By committing to engaging with and understanding your shadow, you free yourself from the stronghold of your habits and patterns—especially those that are subconscious—so they no longer control your destiny. Doing shadow work liberates you. It frees you from living on autopilot and allows you to begin making new choices that aren't steeped in the hidden traits and motives that are influencing you.

Some people are afraid to engage their shadow because they don't want to face what they may find. It may be painful or unearth a bevy of emotions that are uncomfortable to experience. Some use the excuse that they are being of service to others as a reason to not engage in this work. We see this often with educators, activists, social workers, community organizers, and members of corporate diversity teams who skip over their personal work because they "want to focus on helping others" or "don't want to be selfish." However, skipping over the inner work means we can never authentically show up in the outer world as the best version of ourselves. The best version of the world starts with the best version of us. A world without racism requires the best version of us to show up. **If we don't commit to doing our personal shadow work, our efforts to make the world a better place will get colored by our unresolved wounding.** Being a "good" person, a person who is a helper and already of service to the world, doesn't absolve us from doing this work. In fact, we are required to do it even more because many times, the brighter your "light" in the world, the darker your shadow. We cannot create lasting shifts in the outer world if we don't first create shifts in ourselves. Committing to shadow work helps us ensure that our good work in the world is not sabotaged.

Topics related to racism often trigger us into reacting and acting from our shadow. Do you ever get upset and say things that are out of alignment with who you know yourself to be? Or find yourself spinning in anxiety because you're afraid to speak up, especially when you see something that you know is wrong? How about wielding or yielding to unhealthy power dynamics? Or having trouble setting boundaries? Or even getting taken over by anger? Do you find yourself frozen and stuck in perfectionism, afraid to take action when it's needed? Those are just some of the cues that your shadow is in control. Similarly, if you find yourself in a continuous cycle of undesirable situations again and again despite your efforts to grow or change, you can be certain that your shadow has a strong hold on you. Although other people may play roles in the challenging situations that can arise in our lives, shadow work signals us to ask, ***What is the role I am playing that's causing these problems to persist?*** To end racism, the future beckons us to stop reacting from our shadow, especially in conversations related to race. You cannot have challenging conversations or make connections across divides if you get triggered and operate from your shadow every time something upsets you. You cannot experience atonement or forgiveness or create new solutions if your shadow is always in control.

Now that you've built your understanding of how to sit with challenging emotions, you're ready to dive into the cave of your shadow with us. Once you understand your shadow, it can't creep up on you. When it's in your awareness, your actions can come from a truer, more authentic place. It's as if you are awakened from a trance.

So, what exactly is the shadow? When we ask our students, they often respond with answers like:

- trauma
- our past
- everything we don't want to deal with
- our dark side
- what we don't see about ourselves
- victim consciousness
- anything we hide, repress, or deny
- bad habits
- ego
- limiting beliefs
- what we run from
- chaos
- negative thoughts

Contrary to popular understanding, doing shadow work is not just about unearthing bad, painful, or traumatic things. While painful or traumatic things can be *in* our shadow, they do not *define* the shadow. For the purposes of our work together, our definition of shadow is based upon what we learned from the speaker and teacher Sianna Sherman. We will define the shadow as *anything in your life or in our world that you have not cast your light of awareness onto.* It's important to note that *the shadow* and *shadow work* are two separate things. Everyone has a shadow, regardless of whether they choose to work on it or not. Shadow work, though, is the conscious choice to lean into what's unknown and uncomfortable. It's having the courage to grab a flashlight and investigate the unconscious and hidden parts of your life to see what's there so it can stop controlling you and sabotaging your efforts for transformation. We must not demonize darkness.

Historically, demonizing darkness has created harm. (You may notice how a fear of darkness in preference for light parallels skin-color-based racism.) When we demonize darkness, it causes people to run away from and fear that which is dark. But darkness is intrinsic to the process by which we birth ourselves into a new state of being. As the activist and author Valarie Kaur writes, darkness does not have to be a tomb or signal the end but rather it can be a womb and signal *the beginning*. So, while going into the shadow can sometimes contain painful, traumatic, or embarrassing things (which may lead you to wonder why we would want to uncover them), the reason we go into the shadow is simple: *without uncovering our shadow, we cannot unlock our greatness.*

Emily, one of our students, came up to us after a workshop and said, "I have a confession to make." We both looked at her, perplexed. She continued sheepishly in a whisper so that no one else in the room could hear her: "I don't have any big trauma. I grew up in a loving family, with a lot of privilege. I went to a great school, I have a loving marriage, my parents were emotionally available, and I'm almost embarrassed to say this, but I really don't have any huge trauma. Does this mean I don't need to do shadow work?" Most people, like Emily, equate shadow with trauma. But if trauma were equated to shadow, then people who've experienced the least amount of trauma would be the most enlightened. Obviously this is not the case. In fact, sometimes people with less trauma have a hard time digging deep into shadow work because they've had less to work through in their lives. In all cases, trauma and shadow are not the same thing. What we are looking for inside our shadow is much deeper. What we're looking for is our *conditioning. Conditioning is our inner culture*. It's what our mind says about "the way things are."

As we learned from the author and shadow work expert Robert Augustus Masters, conditioning gets created in many ways—through our families, life experiences, relationships, societal expectations, and, of course, traumas and beyond. Conditioning can be programmed in us at any point in our life, from childhood to elderhood. It's important to know, however, that while *all* conditioning isn't bad, the conditioning hiding in our shadow is often the most harmful because it subconsciously makes choices and dictates the actions of our lives without our realizing it—while we think we're "free." Think of yourself like a marionette puppet who appears to have free agency but is really controlled by a puppet master with invisible strings. Your puppet master is your shadow. The invisible strings are the conditioning. Shadow work is not "cutting the strings." *Shadow work is befriending the puppet master.* When we're under the unconscious control of the puppet master, we end up becoming stuck in the same cycles, individually and collectively, over and over again. We're constantly treating the symptom while thinking we're making different choices, yet we're never able to find our way out of our circumstances. When this is the case, the shadow is in control. This cartoon, captioned "The Illusion of Free Choice,"[1] published in 2010, is one of the best examples to help you understand conditioning:

Illusion of Choice

Regardless of how many entry points are added or which choice the cow makes, it will end up in the slaughterhouse. For us to change the outcome of the cow's fate, the cow must be placed in a new circumstance. In other words, without different conditions available to it, the cow's choices will always result in the same outcome. **For our choices to produce a different result, we must change the condition in which those choices exist.** That's the purpose of shadow work—it changes the *internal conditions* where our choices are made. The same applies to the collective. There is no hope for ever changing the external conditions of our society if we don't commit to changing the internal conditions where those choices are made in the first place. *In order to have any hope of changing the external, we must commit to changing the internal.* When we do collective shadow work—healing as a group, company, culture, or nation—conditions transform, and we are then presented with new choices that were not available before.

Our conditioning can show up in so many ways. For example: always choosing to play small because you were the oldest child and had siblings who were jealous of you; not speaking up because you got shamed for using your voice as a child; getting erratically angry because you learned this pattern of communication from your parent; thinking someone from a particular race is lazy because that's what you learned as a child; or having porous boundaries because you saw one parent be submissive to your other parent throughout your childhood. The list goes on.

While the goal of the type of shadow work we're doing in this book is to deeply understand our individual and collective conditioning, we don't want to get lost in it. Journaling, meditating, praying, conducting rituals, going to therapy, or doing antibias trainings to learn more about your shadow are great resources but, alone, they will not help you transform your life or the culture. You can attend diversity trainings, go to therapy for years, understand every aspect of how your conditioning came about, *and still never break free from the conditioning itself.* Shadow work makes you understand the mechanics and motivations underneath the choices that you make. The goal of shadow work is to make you self-aware enough to be able to coexist with the shadow *while empowering you to make different choices.* Let's be frank: Every person, family, collective, country, and nation will *always* have a shadow colored by its history. For better or worse, we cannot make the past disappear. However, we can take control individually and collectively by choosing to face our history so that we can heal the wounds caused by it and so that it doesn't control us anymore or have such a dramatic impact on our future.

Kim, a Black woman in her forties, grew up in a home with two older half sisters who were half Black but who presented as white. Kim's sisters were several years older than her and often ganged up and looked down upon her, sometimes even poking at her physically as they teased her. Kim was convinced it was because of her dark skin. The only way Kim could stop them was when she finally screamed, yelled, and got violent with them. This installed a *conditioning* for Kim that said, "If you don't show 'your size' and yell and scream with aggression to stand up for yourself, people will walk all over you, especially if you're darker skinned." In her adult life, screaming and yelling was Kim's modus operandi, her inner culture—it's just "how she was." Although she knew it caused many problems in her life, she had constant problems with anger.

If someone even dared to glance at her the wrong way, she would snap at them. It would happen in grocery stores, coffee shops, concerts, and events. It would even sometimes be aimed toward her friends and coworkers. In every circle, Kim earned the reputation of "the woman you didn't want to mess with." Her conditioned reaction was especially bad toward white people. Because of the situation with her white-passing sisters, compounded with societal conditioning, if a white person looked at Kim in a way that made her upset, she would immediately adopt a story that they were racist and begin to yell and get aggressive and combative in situations where, Kim says, "it was absolutely uncalled for." This created problems for her at work, and after each occurrence, Kim would vow to never act this way again. She said, "It was like I get put in a trance"; it seemed that she just couldn't help herself. This is a sign that the shadow is in control!

One day, a woman working the checkout at Kim's local grocery store was tired and having a bad day after a double shift, and she was less than polite to Kim. Kim got so upset with her that she reached across the checkout and pushed the woman. This nearly got Kim arrested, which scared her enough to finally commit to doing something to transform this pattern. When Kim joined our program, she discovered that her conditioning said, "If I'm not tough, people will walk all over me"; "Violence and aggression are the only ways to get people to respect you"; and "All white women think I'm less than." It didn't matter what the *real* situation was in front of her. Kim would continue to make every situation in her life model her conditioning. The lens from which she viewed the world always led her to a self-fulfilling prophecy. This lens is conditioning.

Even a tired woman in the grocery store took on the unhealed wounding with her sisters. Instead of wearing rose-colored glasses, Kim was wearing *shadow glasses* with conditioned lenses that dictated her felt and seen experience of the world. She recognized that her conditioning often blinded her from seeing each situation in front of her for what it was. Instead, it made it *all about her*, which led her to choose the same options again and again. Like the cow in the cartoon, it didn't matter what data point (fact) entered Kim's narrative, her shadow story just kept choosing the same outcome, reinforcing her ideas about the world and "the way things are." Once she woke up from the trance, Kim said although she couldn't confirm, she's pretty certain very few of the situations in which she'd been aggressive actually had anything to do with race or that anyone even had bad intentions toward her.

When we don't do our shadow work, we don't see the world as it is. We see it colored by our wounding. Kim didn't keep having this problem (and almost get sent to jail!) because she "wanted to." She just couldn't stop. This begs us to ask the question: What part of Kim was making her choices? Her highest consciousness didn't choose to be violent and aggressive. Her conditioning did. Even after her best efforts, her shadow was sabotaging her and making choices for her. For things to change, Kim needed to become conscious of the glasses she was wearing and understand that there were other glasses available to her that would change her worldview and thus her actions and outcomes.

Our conditioning paints how we experience the world. It is the lens through which we see the world and interpret what is happening. It can control what we do, what we're attracted to, who we choose to hate, who we choose to love, and so on. Until we engage in shadow work, we cannot see the world as it really is. All we can see is our conditioning reflected back to us. By doing shadow work we are learning to see clearly. This is true mindfulness. Seeing beyond our conditioning is one of the primary purposes of our work together here and the groundwork that must be laid in order to end racism.

Exercise: Learning from Your Reactivity

Take a moment now to answer this question: *What types of situations make you the most reactive?* (Note: *reactivity* can show up in many ways—anger, shutting down, disassociating, becoming passive-aggressive, defensive, and more.) For example, when someone ignores you or talks over you; when you think someone is mad at you or you don't know where they stand; when someone says something racially insensitive; when someone is narcissistic; when someone gives you critical feedback; when others show their anger; the list goes on. After thinking of a few scenarios, choose one—pick just one particular type of scenario where you tend to get the most reactive. Now answer these questions related to that scenario: (1) What do you tend to do automatically when you get reactive? What exactly happens? (2) Where do you feel it in your body? (3) If you can imagine yourself in that situation now, *how old* does the part of you feel that's choosing to react this way? (4) What's your first memory of feeling this way? (5) What would the fully conscious, mature adult version of you say to this reactive part of you if it were to give it some wisdom?

Often our reactivity can teach us a lot about what we value, our unresolved traumas, and where we need more healing. In this way, our reactivity doesn't have to control us—it can instead be our teacher.

Inner Work

What else hides in your shadow? Let's continue to explore. Use the following incomplete sentences to get a peek into the hidden conditions that might be driving you.

- What I hide about myself from others is ______________________________.
- A part of my personality that I don't like about myself is ______________________________.
- The way that this part of my personality shows up in my life is ______________________________.
- What I'm avoiding in my life right now is ______________________________.
- The real reason I'm avoiding that is ______________________________.
- The *story* I'm telling myself about why I *can't* end racism is ______________________________.
- Other areas of my life where this same story plays out is ______________________________.
- Where this pattern began in my life was ______________________________.
- How these patterns might be impacting my ability to step into my vision for my life and the world is ______________________________.
- What I really want for my life and the world is ______________________________.
- I am ready for ______________________________.

Shelly often teaches and writes about how her lack of self-worth remains one of her biggest areas of struggle that she is consistently working on. It shows up for her in the form of this question: Am I worthy? While she can intellectually understand that she is worthy, as she often describes it, "there is an invisible pull—in my cells, in my DNA—that convinces me that I'm not." To understand the origin of this pull, Shelly had to delve into her shadow, and what she found there was the collective history and thus the collective shadow of all the women in her family for generations, her ancestors. She began to understand the intergenerational trauma that can be passed down when someone comes from a lineage of refugees, multiple times over. In her family's case, over generations, they would make a home for themselves and then be uprooted because they were not wanted or were at risk in their home country. Through research on her family's history, deep conversations with older living family members, journaling and regular therapy, Shelly had to lean into the encoded conditioning that results from being oppressed for hundreds or thousands of years—in her case, as not just a Jew and a refugee but also a woman.

Some of the specific prompts that Shelly used to delve into her shadow as it pertains to her self-worth include:

- One negative thing I often say to myself is ____________.
- This pattern of unworthiness can be tracked to my family or lineage in this way: ____________________.
- The root causes or things my family/lineage might have had to face that caused this thought pattern might have been ____.
- How this pattern crept its way up to me is __________ ____.
- The specific instance(s) where I diminish my self-worth most is ________________________.
- The next time this pattern arises, I can commit to replacing it with this phrase or action instead: ______________.

In Shelly's case, she was able to identify that her grandmothers' paths were dictated by the confines of a stringent interpretation of religion and the cultural norms in the Middle East during their lifetimes—conditioning that made them incapable of believing that they were worthy or had a voice that deserved to be heard. Her mother's path, Shelly learned, was dictated by conditioning that her voice needed to be quieter than the men's around her and that her dreams and desires came last. Shelly's own conditioning, as an immigrant to the United States, had her looking through a lens that told her she would never belong. While there were many narratives welling up, all the stories from her matriarchal lineage were pointing to a lens that said, "I'm not enough." Thus, it was no surprise that she has always struggled with finding her own worthiness.

This residue from your ancestors' struggles is real and scientifically proven to affect your conditioning, often showing up in multiple ways. While some conditioning is certainly encoded in our shadow through our own life experiences (nurture), the trauma of our parents can alter the ways that our genes function. This explains why the experiences of our ancestors can endure in us long after a threat is gone, and we end up seeing some of the traumas of our parents expressing themselves and attempting to be healed through us.[2] Dedication to practices learned in shadow work is what allowed Shelly to heal. The same opportunity is available to you. You are healing generations forward and backward.

Justin avoided shadow work for quite some time, primarily because he thought there was no point in digging into the past because he had worked so hard to "grow beyond it." His perspective when he was younger was "I've moved beyond that mess, so I don't need to return to it—all I need to do is focus on sending love and light." But one day, after complaining to his friend and teacher Sianna Sherman about the toxic patterns in his relationships, Sherman said to him, "The bigger the light, the bigger the shadow." Simply put, when a person is a big light, they cast a big shadow. The more you build your light, the more skilled you must be at getting to know your shadow. If not, your conditioning could well end up sabotaging your efforts. This is the reason we see so many world leaders, celebrities, politicians, and spiritual gurus involved in big scandals exposing huge shadow aspects of their personalities that seem totally incongruent with who they present themselves to be to the public. These scandals, committed by some of our icons, leave us perplexed, wondering, "*How?*" If you are to take on the task of doing good and creating real transformation in the world, your family, your workplace, or your community—if you want to *be a light* unto others—then you must also be deeply committed to taking responsibility for your shadow. Without shadow work, you can become the antithesis of the change you want to see in the world. This is why we mustn't simply "look past" or "move beyond" the blatant, abhorrent, and publicly acceptable racism that occurred historically, even though times and laws have changed for the better in many places. As Justin learned, you don't turn to your past just to dig up the past but rather to stop it from impacting your future. Here are a few more prompts that will allow you to explore what you might be trying to avoid.

- A past experience in my life that I often try to avoid thinking about when it arises in my mind is ___________.
- The story I tell myself about why I *cannot* or *should not* think about it is ___________.
- What I imagine might happen if I allowed myself to think about this more is ___________.
- What I'm afraid of is ___________.
- What often triggers this past experience to arise in my mind is ___________.
- The connection between this past experience and what's happening in my life now is ___________.
- If I could allow myself to be more intimate with this experience, I might ___________.
- If I could free myself from the fear of this experience, how it might impact my life in a positive way is ___________.

The shadow work we did in this chapter lays the pathway for all of the work to come. The next time you see yourself acting or responding in a way that's out of alignment with the vision you have for your life or the world, pause. Take a few deep breaths. Then ask yourself this question: *Which part of me is making this choice?* The pause gives you the opportunity to get to know your shadow in-the-moment and center back into your true vision. Remind yourself in these moments what's important to you, what you stand for, and the future you are committed to creating. It's important that you *acknowledge* and *thank* the shadow part of yourself because at one point in your history, it likely created that response and pattern to help you—to protect you. But you may not need it anymore. This time, *you get to choose differently*. You get to choose to act from a place that's aligned with who you *really* are and who you want to be. Your shadow can guide you into understanding your unresolved wounding and the patterns that were created to protect you and your gifts. But it does not have to control you any longer.

Your shadow is not separate from you; it's *part of you.* You don't get rid of it; you *understand it.* You befriend it. It is by creating an alliance with your shadow—not fighting it, banishing it, or beating it—that your shadow stops controlling you and instead becomes a ground for a greater state of integration than has ever been available to you before. This is how darkness becomes the womb of creation, the cave that holds the jewels and treasures you seek. By breaking free from your conditioning, new choices become available to you that were impossible to see before—this is a part of what we mean by making the impossible *possible*. But that's not all. By learning to face your own shadows, you will be closer to understanding the shadow that exists in others, too. This connection will help you find compassion and understanding, see across divides, forgive, and create connections where it seemed there once were none. When you take off the lenses of your past conditioning, you can start to see clearly. You can connect the inner work to the outer world. You can stop repeating the same patterns that cause racism to persist in the first place. You can begin to end racism.

8

Intergenerational Change

As we mentioned, if you don't do your personal shadow work, then what you haven't resolved in yourself gets projected into the work you're doing for the collective. The opposite of this is also true. If you don't look at the *collective shadow*, then the shadow of your environment seeps into your personal growth and self-care practices, causing spiritual or emotional bypassing, limiting results on the healing journey, and a self-serving focus that keeps perpetuating the same cycles and patterns you're trying to end. To end racism, we must look at both the personal and collective shadows. When we stand in the future and ask, "What did we do today?" the answer is that we stopped pretending that the collective shadow doesn't exist and instead tackled it head-on.

Getting to the root of our collective shadow allows us to address what's causing our biggest problems to persist in the first place. What is lurking in the shadow that influences people to repetitively choose their own suffering over a new possible path? Why is it that people continue to prefer separation over integration? What conditioning causes us to vote for laws, leaders, and policies that are clearly against our own best interests and contribute to our own suffering and that of others? If we don't dig into what lies underneath the symptoms, which appear in the form of politicians, policies, and laws, we will just keep recreating the same "solutions" over and over again, oppressing and marginalizing a different group while convincing ourselves things have gotten "better," when for another group, they've gotten worse.

Remember, we weren't here to "make things better." There is no such thing as "better" racism. *We arrived at this moment with the goal to end racism.* There is a difference.

There are several ways we could approach the topic of collective shadow and how it has affected our individual opportunities to heal, but the most profound approach might be to discuss the phenomenon of intergenerational trauma as studied through the science of epigenetics. There is nothing more appropriate to the topic of shadow than our "unseen" DNA coding that influences so much of our lives and the way we "are."

Now, we are going to get science-y with you for a moment, so bear with us. The new and emerging field of epigenetics is the study of how environmental influences can impact our genes. Epigenetic studies in recent years show that we can inherit stress or traumas that we have never directly experienced and that this can affect the expression of our individual genes—in other words, how much or how little of a specific gene is expressed. These studies also show that too much stress in utero can cause a fetus's brain development to be affected. Thus, what we've learned is that, to a certain extent, we are more than just an expression of our ancestors' genetic code; we're also expressions of our most recent ancestors' experiences.[1] Simply put, generational trauma and the environment you're in after birth can affect the expression of your genes.[2]

First, we need you to understand the concept of intergenerational trauma, meaning trauma that's passed down from one generation to the next. For example, a trauma experienced by your birth parent can affect the genetic material you inherit at birth. A trauma you experience in early childhood can also change the way your genes are expressed, rearranging what's called your epigenome, which can determine how little or how much of the genes you inherited are expressed. In simplified terms, gene expression is a process that allows for a cell to respond to its changing environment. Think of the gene-expression process as an on/off switch that ultimately affects the final way that a gene shows up tangibly in us. Our gene expression is the way our visible and invisible "characteristics" are expressed in the world.

Trauma is created when a stressor or experience is not able to be properly integrated. Cortisol is a hormone that gets excreted into the body when we are in a situation of stress (or trauma). When we excrete too much cortisol, it starts to get stored in our bones, our blood, and if we are pregnant, in the amniotic fluid (the fluid in the womb holding a baby). Thus, the trauma experienced when a person is pregnant (that may even be unresolved trauma from a time prior to their pregnancy) enters the fluid with which they then give birth to the next generation.[3]

So when we're talking about the transmission of intergenerational trauma, we can go directly to the womb. Amniotic fluid, a part of what creates new life, is one of several ways trauma gets passed from generation to generation. If we think about the amniotic fluid as a life-giving broth that an innocent child is marinating in, then the way that the parent responds to certain situations of stress adds ingredients to the recipe, directly affecting the genetic makeup of the child. At the genetic level, there are different chromosomes that are turning on and off inside of the baby, in the womb, in response to hormones inside of the amniotic fluid. The building blocks upon which that child is developing are being guided by the stress hormones located in the actual fluid, and this can continue to pass through a generation.

Before science finally caught up in the field of genetics, the popular belief was that DNA was unable to be altered after birth; the genetic code you were born with was "set in stone." However, new emerging studies in this field of epigenetics are finding that the conditioning *and* conditions—nature and nurture—continue to work in early childhood development to modify our genes. The different experiences that children have in early childhood can alter their genetic expression, even if they were in adverse and stressful environments while in the womb. This explains why genetically identical twins can exhibit different behaviors, skills, health, and achievement—the way they express their genes is based in part on nurture, not solely nature, as once thought. This is huge news because, yes, trauma is passed down genetically, *but* those genes can express differently based on our environment and experiences. Yet our society rarely changes unless we've changed our inner world. In other words, you must understand that conditioning can be changed when we change conditions and that conditions can change when we change our conditioning.

We find this emerging research to be incredibly hopeful. Where we once thought that the genetic conditioning that we inherited at birth was what we got "stuck" with for the duration of our lifetime, it's actually not the case at all. Recent research demonstrates that we can reverse negative changes to the way that genes express themselves and actually restore healthy functioning to those genes *after we are born*. The epigenome can be altered by things such as positive experiences, supportive relationships, and opportunities for learning. Knowing this, we can begin to understand why the work we are embarking on now—together—is even more important. We are working to ensure that what we pass on to our descendants is positive for their development.

Learning the tools and developing the resources to do the inner work required to reverse effects of genetic trauma can begin to shift our trajectory. It starts with each of us. **We are doing the healing our ancestors were unable to do, so that those in the future will no longer be stuck in the same cycles and inherit the effects of our trauma.** The other reason this research gives us great hope is because we now know that even if we have no plans to give birth (or perhaps we gave birth a long time ago and our children are grown), we can help reduce stress in the environment and support positive relationships in our communities. Just as Dr. Isabelle Mansuy, a professor of neuroepigenetics at the University of Zurich, has stated, "The effects of trauma which can be transmitted to the offspring can be reversed by a positive experience."[4] In this way, we each have the opportunity from where we stand to heal generations forward and backward.

Sara, a student in one of our retreats, never met her father, and now that her mother has passed away, she had very limited knowledge about him. As we began to do collective shadow work with her, she was curious about how to understand the intergenerational trauma that might have come from her father's lineage without more information. As we prepare for the next exercise, it's important to know that many people fall into this category or something similar—where there's some gray area in their understanding of their biological history. So, here's an idea: when we use the word *ancestors*, don't limit your frame to a biological lineage. The epigenetics of your personal biology are important, but so are the collective intergenerational traumas of what we call *identity ancestors*—the ancestors of your social group and other identities.

For example, if you identify as queer, you might consider someone from the LGBTQIA+ movement to be an ancestor. Or you might connect with a civil rights leader, suffragette, or people of a certain spiritual community as ancestors. Justin, for example, often thinks of Oprah Winfrey as an identity ancestor, with her personal healing impacting the descendants of millions. While you may not know all of your biological family history, it can be helpful to focus on what you *do* know instead of what you "don't know" as you fill in your ancestral knowledge gaps. For example, Sara not knowing her father was at first seen as a void of knowledge, but we encouraged her to remember that she was connected to a long lineage of others who grew up without a father, and the pain caused and resilience gained from that. This gave her a new identity group to explore. No matter what you perceive to have been taken away, there's a long lineage before you who have dealt with similar issues. What might you learn from them?

Your Infinity Lineage-Visualization Exercise

Adapted from a practice by Dr. Sará King. To listen to the audio guided version of this exercise, go to HowWeEndedRacism.com/resources.

Imagine for a moment the many generations of ancestors that came before you, fanning out one by one by one in rows—stretching out into infinity behind you. From wherever you are now, imagine leaning back into this long line of ancestors, feeling yourself being supported by them.

If you're in a comfortable place to do so, you can actually lean your physical body back now. Lean into those who came before you.

At the same time, imagine the many descendants—familial, social, or identity-based—that will be impacted by you in the future, fanning out one by one by one in front of you. Feel yourself now situated in the center of infinity, right between this infinite group of ancestors behind you and infinite group of descendants in front of you. You are the connection point between them.

Keep this vision of infinity in mind and ask yourself these questions:

1. If there was one message your ancestors had for you, what would it be?
2. Do you have a message for your ancestors?
3. What message do you want to share with the generations of the future?
4. What message does the future generation have for you?

Right here where you are—standing at the center of infinity—is where the transformation begins.

Inner Work

Use the following incomplete sentences to reflect on how the collective shadow has impacted you. It might be useful to pause, close your eyes, and come back to the infinity visual from the visualization. As you consider the following incomplete sentences, remember "ancestor" can be used to identify a biological or identity lineage. Explore one or both.

- The message my ancestors might have for me is ________________________________.
- What I know about the lives of my ancestors that could be affecting me today is ________________.
- The intergenerational trauma that my ancestors might have experienced was ____________________.

- As I think about my ancestral lineage, the specific kind of harm my ancestors may have caused in the world is ____ . (Be specific. Don't know? Take a moment to look it up.)
- A way I might be perpetuating that harm, even in my family or social circles, is ______________________ .
- The resilience and strength we gain from our ancestors is often hiding in the shadows. What my ancestors have been through that has given me the resilience I have today is ____ .
- How I might use that strength to help me in my life is ____ .
- How I might use that strength to help me continue to end racism is ____________________________ .
- The message I have for the future is ______________ ____ .

Although we focused heavily on trauma and stress in this chapter, remember that stress can be motivating. It can create a push for us to move forward. Post-traumatic growth and resilience are factors that our ancestors experienced from all their trials. Remember, inside the shadow lies our greatest gifts. **Don't only think about your past as a source of pain; think of it as a source of power.** This is how the light and shadow come together to create great wisdom.

In order to end racism, we must become aware of the conditioning and programming that is inherited from our ancestors, as well as external conditioning that many of us have chosen to accept as "the way things are." This impacts everything we create for the future. While you are not beholden to the traumas in your past, nor those in your ancestral history, you can become beholden to whether or not you choose to ignore the shadow and continue making choices from an unconscious place.

The key to creating a more equitable and just society starts with understanding where our biases come from in the first place, so that we can counteract them.[5] What we know for certain is that unresolved trauma and harmful belief systems are handed down generationally, perpetuating racial and social injustices and cycles of violence. We cannot control what gets handed down to us, but we *can* control two things: what we do with what is handed down and what we hand down to our own descendants. They say "the children are our future." The less junk we hand down to them, the freer their hands will be to stop needing to fix things from the past, and instead the children can create a world anew.

9

∞

The Big P

Thus far we've laid out a clear understanding of truth and how to discern facts from the subjective stories we create derived from those facts. From this place of truth we've provided you with an abridged foundation of the history of race in America and practiced noticing, naming, and taking ownership for what we feel. We've understood the importance of journeying into the dark cave of the shadow and connected to what we usually hide, uncovering some of our hidden conditioning while connecting to the resilience and strength that comes from our ancestral lineage. We've affirmed our role in the conscious healing of our lineage and for future generations, starting with us, right here at the center of infinity. It is essential that everyone in the awakened culture we are cocreating possess and begin to use each of these skills. When we reflect back on what conditions needed to arise in order for racism to end, these tools are the pillars that laid the foundation for us to arrive at the finish line. While the previous chapters focused on the awareness and skills we need to strengthen, the final few chapters of pillar 5 will focus on what we need to release. We start with what we call *The Big P*. The Big P is *Privilege*—surely a concept that you've heard about before (and that is often overused in concepts about race), but we promise to orient this differently than you might expect. Read closely.

In one of our online workshops, Marsha, a Black woman, expressed to Anna, a white woman, that she felt frustrated that, generally speaking, white people didn't understand how privileged they are. To provide more context, Marsha gave an example of how much fear she felt every day when she was driving her young Black son home from school through a predominantly white neighborhood. As a Black woman, she felt fear for her life and the life of her young son, especially when she would see a police officer driving behind her, which she said happened often because she lived in a community overpopulated with police officers relative to neighboring communities. She expressed her frustration to Anna, saying that "I don't think white people will ever understand how hard that is."

Anna, eyes welling up, responded, "I work in a manufacturing town with a factory that shut down several years ago. My husband left me for a woman in another city where he went to find work. I now live in a trailer, alone with my five-year-old white son, in a community that is succumbing to the opioid crisis. My town is all boarded up and has no police presence at all. There are literally no police here." Anna paused, tears now streaming down her face, and said, "I sleep with a shotgun next to my bed to protect me and my five-year-old son from people trying to break into our home. I've had to use the shotgun twice because of attempted break-ins this month alone. Please don't call me privileged."

Marsha and Anna sat in silence, in a heightened emotional state, both keenly aware that they were standing at a crossroads. At that seminal moment, a conversation like this could go one of two ways: The two could continue to compare stories of whose suffering and situation were worse and thus argue about who had more or less privilege, or they could lean into the possibility of finding the inherent connection in their stories. Instead of fighting against each other, they could find common ground against the systems that are oppressing them both.

Anna and Marsha share a narrative of being dedicated and tenacious single mothers in adverse circumstances who are doing everything they can to care for and raise their young sons, to provide them with opportunities for a better life. These two very different women have an opportunity in front of them: They can choose connection and band together to find strength or they can continue to widen the perceived gap and focus on their perceived differences. It is precisely because of the work we're going to embark on next that Anna and Marsha were able to take the high road. Although Anna may still be privileged enough to be able to trust in law enforcement while Marsha does not, that which connects them eliminates the façade that causes what we've come to call the "Oppression Olympics," which only causes further separation.

The Oppression Olympics is a game that forces people into a war comparing whose suffering is more significant. In this game, there are no winners; one group is constantly trying to out-prove their suffering to another, with the goal being to be acknowledged for the "worst" trauma. This game is a distraction preventing us from coming together to **realize that instead of comparing our suffering, we can join together to change *the systems that are causing the suffering in the first place.*** Trauma and suffering are relative—and they always will be. Our workshop, which we cocultivated and comoderated, provided a safe space for Anna and Marsha to have honest, difficult—but nonjudgmental—conversations that allowed them to work through and find their points of connection. Most of the time, in the "real" world, we tend to recoil from continuing such conversations or even having them in the first place. However, when we commit to practicing the tools we've been learning in this book, we can break through the discomfort. What tends to happen is that the perceived great divides between us that seem unbridgeable are not as wide as we think. Sometimes there isn't even a divide there in the first place.

Six months after our workshops, we usually hold follow-up focus groups and surveys. We learned through this process that Anna and Marsha have forged a deep and authentic friendship—born from their pain and struggles. Where they still have differences, they don't see them as insurmountable chasms but rather as conversation points to explore. The pair is now working together across party and state lines to learn how to assist efforts and political candidates who are supportive of strategies to make their communities better and safer for everyone. They no longer waste their time defending their suffering to each other or, for that matter, identifying other individuals as having it "better" or "worse." Does Marsha and Anna's connection end *all* racism? No. But can racism ever end without a connection like Marsha and Anna's? Absolutely not. We are all Marsha and Anna. We must wake up from the façade of our disconnection and tit-for-tat suffering wars so that we can come together to release and dismantle the systems that cause all this suffering in the first place. That's the only way racism will ever end. Incrementally. One person at a time. It starts with you.

Given the context of the United States today, when most Americans hear the word *privilege*, they instantly think of "white privilege," but we want to expand your thinking beyond this.

Regardless of how you typically think of privilege or where you're from, take a moment now and look at the Privilege Scale below. If you had to place a pin that represented your privilege on this scale, where do you imagine it would fall?

Privilege Scale 1

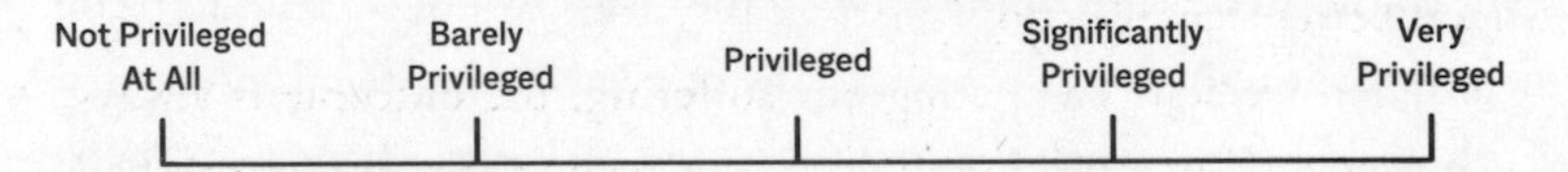

Keep your answer in mind as we continue the journey.

Our entire perspective of the concept of privilege shifted when we heard this quote from the activist Janaya Future Khan:

> Privilege isn't about what you've gone through, it's about what you haven't had to go through.[1]

Take a moment to read that statement again: "Privilege **isn't about what you've gone through**, it's about what you **haven't** had to go through." Understanding this perspective of privilege is essential in our movement toward ending racism. As we mentioned, in the culture of Oppression Olympics, people are pitted against each other to compare their suffering and trauma. One party accuses the other of being privileged, and when the other party gives a rebuttal, it can sound something like, "But my family went through the Holocaust . . ." or "But I'm queer . . ." or "But my family had to immigrate here . . ." or some version of "Don't call me privileged; my family had to work really hard for this!" or "My status in life didn't get handed to me!" or "I've had trauma, too." ***When we compare our suffering, we reinforce our limitations and sabotage our capacity for connection.***

The truth is that every human being on this planet has experienced or will experience suffering at some point in their lives. Every person that has ever lived before us and every person that will ever live after us will experience suffering or trauma in some form. It is a guaranteed part of the human experience we all share. Most of us are born into families and recent ancestral lines that have been through challenging times, and yes, some families have been through more challenges than others. That is expected and what we need to collectively acknowledge. *Everyone has been through things.* Saying that someone shouldn't be sad because of a trauma or deep wound because someone else (or you) has it worse is like saying someone shouldn't be happy because someone has it better than they do.

When we start comparing our suffering, the outcome is always resentment, disconnection, anger, or a feeling that we are pushed further away from each other. The walls go up. Where walls go up, bridges can't be built. This is the opposite of what we really want, which is connection, empathy, and feeling that we are valued. Everyone wants to know that their stories matter. Everyone wants to feel heard and seen. This is why Janaya Future Khan's approach to privilege is so important.

Read it again: "Privilege **isn't about what you've gone through**, it's about what you **haven't** had to go through." This approach looks at privilege as a function of what we *haven't had to suffer* and transforms the Oppression Olympics into an exercise in compassion, where we can look at another's suffering and say, "I can't imagine what my life would be like if I had to endure that."

The Privilege Test

Our next task is to take the Privilege Test, a tool that we adapted from a popular exercise called the "Privilege Walk," which can be easily found online by searching its title. In the well-known video showing participants engaging in the exercise, each person is invited to take a step forward, stay put, or take a step back based upon their answers to specific questions about privilege. In our modified version, we can engage in the practice by taking a scored test. Some view this test as harmful because people who are less privileged get used as examples, but we are going to land this exercise quite differently so you can see how it transforms the comparison of suffering into connection and agency.

As you engage in this exercise, please keep this in mind: For every "step" you take, there is always someone who's stepping in the opposite direction. Really feel that. It's easy to focus on "what I've been through," but let's instead look at this exercise through the lens of *what you haven't been through*. As a bonus, do this exercise with a partner or in a group, but it's also effective if you do it alone. In all cases, feel into your emotions as you read through each statement.

The Privilege Test

For a printable version of this exercise, go to HowWeEndedRacism.com/resources.

Directions: Score each of the thirty-three statements with your personal responses:

+1 for a step forward or -1 for a step back (if the statement applies to you)

0 for no movement (if the statement does *not* apply to you)

We will do the same. At the end of the test, tally up your numbers. Then we'll tell you what to do next.

1. If your parents worked nights and weekends to support your household, take one step back.

   Shelly Tygielski (ST) = 0, Justin Michael Williams (JMW) = -1, You = _____

2. If you can go shopping alone and be pretty well assured that you will not be followed or harassed, take one step forward.

   ST = +1, JMW = 0, You = _____

3. If you are able to move through the world without fear of sexual assault, take one step forward.

   ST = 0, JMW = +1, You = _____

4. If you are cisgender (meaning your gender identity corresponds to your birth sex), take one step forward.

   ST = +1, JMW = +1, You = _____

5. If you can show affection for your romantic partner in public without fear of ridicule or violence, take one step forward.

   ST = +1, JMW = 0, You = _____

6. If you have ever been diagnosed as having a physical or mental illness/disability, take one step back.

   ST = -1, JMW = 0, You = _____

7. If the primary language spoken in your household growing up was not English, take one step back.

   ST = -1, JMW = 0, You = _____

8. If you have ever tried to change your speech or mannerisms to gain credibility, take one step back.

   ST = -1, JMW = -1, You = _____

9. If you can go anywhere in the country and easily find the kinds of hair products you need and/or cosmetics that match your skin color, take one step forward.

   ST = +1, JMW = 0, You = _____

10. If you can pass as heterosexual, take one step forward.

    ST = +1, JMW = 0, You = _____

11. If you were embarrassed about your clothes or home while growing up, take one step back.

    ST = 0, JMW = -1, You = _____

12. If you are rarely asked to speak for all the people of your racial group, take one step forward.

    ST = +1, JMW = 0, You = _____

13. If you can legally marry the person you love, regardless of where you live, take one step forward.

    ST = +1, JMW = 0, You = _____

14. When asking to talk to the "person in charge," if you are pretty certain you will be facing a person of your race, take one step forward.

    ST = +1, JMW = 0, You = _____

15. If you or your parents have ever gone through a divorce, take one step back.

    ST = -1, JMW = -1, You = _____

16. If you felt like you had adequate access to healthy food growing up, take one step forward.

    ST = +1, JMW = +1, You = _____

17. If you are reasonably sure you would be hired for a job on the basis of your abilities and qualifications, take one step forward.

    ST = 0, JMW = 0, You = _____

18. If you would never think twice about calling the police when trouble occurs, take one step forward.

    ST = +1, JMW = 0, You = _____

19. If you can see a doctor whenever you feel the need, take one step forward.

    ST = +1, JMW = +1, You = _____

20. If you have ever been the only person of your race in a classroom or workplace setting, take one step back.

    ST = 0, JMW = -1, You = ____

21. If you have a college education, take one step forward.

    ST = +1, JMW = +1, You = _____

22. If you took out loans for your education, take one step back.

    ST = -1, JMW = -1, You = _____

23. If your parents or guardians attended college, take one step forward.

    ST = 0, JMW = 0, You = _____

24. If you always get time off from work for your religious holidays, take one step forward.

    ST = 0, JMW = +1, You = _____

25. If you need legal or medical help and you can be sure that your race will not work against you, take one step forward.

    ST = +1, JMW = 0, You = _____

26. If you have ever traveled outside of your home country, take one step forward.

    ST = +1, JMW = +1, You = _____

27. If you feel confident that your family would be able to financially help/support you if you were going through a serious monetary hardship, take one step forward.

    ST = +1, JMW = 0, You = _____

28. If you have ever had to fight or advocate for the validity of your culture's customs, dress, or traditions in a classroom or workplace setting, take one step back.

    ST = -1, JMW = -1, You = _____

29. If there were more than fifty books in your house growing up, take one step forward.

    ST = +1, JMW = 0, You = _____

30. If you studied the culture or the history of your ancestors in grade school, take one step forward.

    ST = 0, JMW = +1, You = _____

31. If one of your parents was ever laid off or unemployed not by choice, take one step back.

    ST = 0, JMW = -1, You = _____

32. When you were growing up, if most of the toys, books, or visual media you had access to featured representations of people/dolls/characters who did not look like you, take one step back.

    ST = 0, JMW = -1, You = _____

33. If you have access to clean water, take one step forward.

    ST = +1, JMW = +1, You = _____

Before you tally up your score, please take a moment to pause. Place your hands over your heart for a moment. As we've done before, check in with how you feel emotionally. What emotions are present for you now? (You can even refer back to the emotions wheel on page 53.) Take a few deep breaths. Can you locate where you feel the emotions in your physical body? Now, what's your total?

You = (____)

Here's ours:

ST = (11)

JMW = (0)

Take a look again at the Privilege Scale and notice your placement with the scores now attached. Is it where you predicted that you would land or are you in a different position than you anticipated? Almost all of us are privileged in one way or another. Once we understand, in practical terms, how much privilege we have, regardless of our race, we can use it as a springboard to create authentic connection, which is the key ingredient to ending racism.

Privilege Scale 2

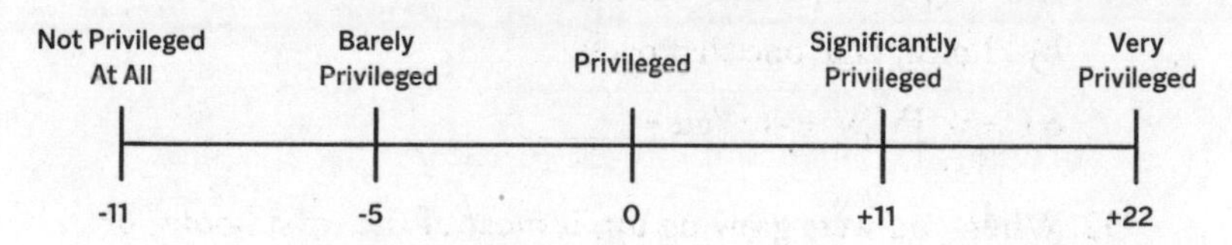

While doing the exercise, how well were you able to keep your focus away from *what you've gone through* and instead on *what you haven't had to go through*? The exercise we just did is just a model to teach you about yourself. So, what did you learn? What causes you to abandon compassion for comparison? How skilled are you at holding compassion for others even as you deal with your own struggles? This is an essential skill we must cultivate to end racism.

Inner Work

Use the following incomplete sentences to cultivate a deeper understanding of your relationship to our new definition of privilege: privilege isn't about what you've gone through, it's about what you haven't had to go through.

- The emotion I feel after doing this exercise is ____.
- Something that challenged me about this exercise is ____.
- My ability to keep the focus on other people's pain ("what I haven't had to go through") during this exercise was ________________________________.
- When I imagine other people who had to overcome many obstacles that I have not had to deal with, what I feel is ________________________________.
- My ability to find compassion for their pain while still acknowledging my own suffering is ____.
- What I recognized about my own suffering is ____.
- What I understand about privilege that I didn't understand before is ________________________.
- My key takeaway from this exercise is ______________.

For many people, doing this exercise brings up a range of emotions from sadness to gratitude and everything in between. Our student Lori felt sadness and shame for how much privilege she's had without realizing it, while Daveed was excited because he scored higher than he imagined he would as a queer Latinx immigrant. Sam did this exercise in a group and felt ashamed because she never realized so many of her close friends had dealt with so much, and she thought she was the only one. When we led Brian and his leadership team through this exercise, Brian had tears in his eyes. He said that although his score was one of the lowest compared to his coworkers, he couldn't help but notice all that he "hadn't had to go through." He realized that although he's been through major struggles in his life, there was still so much he had to be grateful for that he often overlooked.

One of the more nuanced (and probably the most important) emotions that we want to address is one that arises for many but that people are often afraid to admit: ***defensiveness.*** For some, a wall goes up after doing this exercise. Their wall is usually built out of statements like "But why didn't Justin and Shelly mention anything about [insert your challenging situation here] in the test?" or "How come the scale isn't balanced?" or "This was confusing because my life now is very different from when I was younger, so I wasn't sure how to answer some of them." Did any of those types of questions or concerns arise for you? If so, good. If not, still read carefully because understanding this subtle defensive response will be critical for you if you hope to help others as we shift our culture.

Think about it this way: If after journeying this far through the book, you *still* feel a wall go up after a simple privilege exercise, *imagine how other people feel when they get shamed, blamed, and accused of being "too privileged" in their real lives,* especially if many of them have never done the depth of work that we've done together. If you, a person conscious enough to pick up a book with this title, can still feel defensive, perhaps you can have more compassion for how others might feel this way, too. It's no wonder people tend to have walls go up. They would rather run away from the topic. Noticing (and admitting to) our own defense mechanism is a portal into allowing us to find understanding and compassion for those around us who get defensive when we try to attune them to their privilege. When defensiveness arises, it's important for us to acknowledge it so it doesn't run the show (from the shadow). We must also recognize that any feeling of defensiveness is based upon the old model of privilege: comparing what we've gone through and then shaming and blaming those who have more privilege. That's the old culture's game. We're playing a new game now.

Our privilege is not something to be ashamed of or silent about. We see it as our most authentic entry point to connection. If you are lucky enough to get out of a burning house before the fire department arrives and there are still others trapped inside the flames, your responsibility is to grab a hose and start dousing the house with water. Having privilege gives you the opportunity to hold more hoses. But most of us have been so ashamed of our privilege that we choose to hide it. Thus, instead of getting out of the burning house and helping to douse the raging fire, we play small and pretend that we can't hold anymore hoses because we don't want to "look too privileged" or "make it all about us." In the meantime, the house is burning down with people trapped inside.

Another way to help you understand this new perspective on privilege is cross-generationally. We—Justin and Shelly—have worked our asses off to create better lives for ourselves and our families. Thus, if our children (real or imagined) were to take this test, *we would anticipate that their score would be much higher than ours*. We wouldn't want our kids to be ashamed of that, because we worked hard for them to be able to score higher. As the bestselling author Adam Grant writes, "Too many people spend their lives being dutiful descendants instead of good ancestors. The responsibility of each generation is not to please their predecessors. It's to improve things for their offspring. It's more important to make your children proud than your parents proud."[2] Although we believe it's possible to make *both* your children proud *and* your parents proud, here, our task is to raise our children into a culture that is actively ending racism so they can be the first children to never question whether they should hold hoses when they see a burning house. They will inherently understand that they have a moral responsibility to hold as many as their privilege allows them to hold, and they would take pride in helping as much as they can. By taking this compassionate approach, we reorient our relationship from thinking privilege is something "negative" or something we should hide or be ashamed of and instead see it as a springboard to use our privilege, regardless of how we got it, as an access point to being of greater service.

Finally, understanding our privilege helps us learn our "language of loss." Let's pretend for a moment that your score on the Privilege Test was 21 out of 22 points and that the *only* thing you'd experienced from the test was that you were scarred from enduring the terrible divorce your parents went through when you were younger. With the old model of privilege, where we compare our suffering, someone with a 21 score would be told to keep quiet about their hardships, that their sharing could "risk causing more harm" and that "so many people have had it worse than them." But this mindset goes against every scientific finding about successfully creating connection and uniting. The truth is, people who speak the same *language of loss* have a shared context that connects them beyond their differences. For example, Shelly has been working for many years with organizations that provide trauma-informed healing tools to survivors of gun violence so that when another mass shooting occurs in a community, the first people on the scene to comfort grieving families (other than first responders, of course) are other parents and families who have also lost family members to a shooting. What's been proven through years of doing this work is that the most effective person to talk to a mother who must survive the horror of losing her child in a school mass shooting is another mother who has lost her child in a school mass shooting. It doesn't matter if the mothers have nothing else in common—whether they are Black or white, financially well-off or struggling, who they voted for in the last election, or what part of the country they are from. Shelly has watched people connect across what seems like uncrossable schisms through sharing this unspeakable loss. For example, a white mother from the upper-middle-class community of Parkland, Florida, whose son was murdered, connected deeply with a Black mother from a lower-income community in South Side Chicago, whose daughter was murdered. While these two women come from different religions, cultures, races, ideologies, sensibilities—when they met, they were immediately able to understand each other based on their shared traumas—their *shared language of loss*. Many years now after the shootings, the two women are still friends.

When we share a language of loss, it's easy to find compassion for another person's struggles because *you know* what they've been through. This shared language of loss is proven to shatter the ridiculous barriers we place between us. We all have a shared humanity. We don't need to have shared trauma to access it—but the trauma can be used as an access point to help us get there. This is the space we must seek to get to as often as possible to end racism.

The story we shared of the two mothers is just one very specific, drastic example of the interpersonal science of connection. There are many more examples of how this works in other places in society. What the Privilege Test allows us to do is not only practice finding compassion for the things we haven't been through but also find the easy connection points using the things we *have* been through. We're learning to hold both.

Now go back through your Privilege Test. Look at the things *you have* been through from a whole new perspective, using what you've been through as a gateway to connection instead of a point of comparison. Perhaps even think about the things you may have experienced that were not mentioned in the test.

Now, here's an invitation. Many people often ask us: "What's my most authentic entry point to help this movement for change?" Now you found it. Don't ignore what you've been through in fear of "making it all about you." Instead, use that energy to connect to others in your community who are experiencing that same pain, a familiar suffering—the access point. Look up an organization that supports those who speak your language of loss or any other access point language you can tap into. For example, if your only hardship was enduring a difficult divorce that left your family in shambles, then your language of loss is clear. You can look up an organization that supports children and families who are healing from broken homes and dealing with the aftermath of divorce. Why you? Because you've been through it, so you can connect more deeply with others.

This is your pathway, and understanding your privilege is your gateway in. This is how you can turn your pain into purpose and hold compassion for others' suffering while inspiring others to do the same. The main questions you need to rest with are: What are the most significant things you *have* gone through? What is your language of loss? Who in your circles of influence and community may be able to benefit from your wisdom and experiences? What national or local organizations or groups are doing work to support people who have that same language of loss?

Often our privilege hides in the shadows and creates a condition that keeps us—and others—stuck. It's time to claim your privilege while holding a wide-open space of compassion for yourself and others. Your privilege is the pathway through.

10

∞

Supreme

As we continue our excavation of the shadow, there's another topic we must explore and reorient our conditioning toward in order to move forward on the path of ending racism. Next up: *supremacy*—but not in the way you would expect. *Supremacist* almost stings when you say it. Like a stove that's too hot to touch, people don't even want to utter the word, let alone identify themselves with it. When you hear the word *supremacist*, what's the first thing you think of? Most people immediately think of "white supremacy." But to end racism, we must expand our understanding beyond "white supremacy" to the larger concept of *supremacy* itself to see how it extends into each of our lives, because the truth is ***we all have a relationship to supremacy, regardless of what color our skin is.*** Most people are surprised about their relationship to this this topic.

Let's begin with the word ***supreme***, meaning "situated above" or "highest." For something to be *supreme*, it must be considered the best. Everything else must measure up against it and automatically rank below it *regardless of what's true*, because supremacy itself is an *assessment, a story* (not a fact, like we covered in chapter 3). We believe that *supremacy*, along with any type of prejudice, is not as often derived from hate as one may think but rather from the pervasive human need for positive self-regard: a desire to make ourselves feel good about ourselves. We want to feel good about ourselves and the groups that we identify with. If you're a male, for example, you want to feel good about being a man; if you're a trans man, you want to feel good about being a trans man. Most people want to feel good about their identity, like it matters and is significant. Often people also want to feel good about being a citizen of their country—patriotic. Unfortunately, one of the easiest ways to buttress our sense of worthiness, competence, and belonging is to compare ourselves to others.

This often creates a hierarchy, where we perceive other groups as somehow inferior. As an example of how we can use our nationalism to feel supreme to another nation, we might say something like, "I'm so glad I'm American; we're better than the Europeans." The reality is that even if we may be sensitive enough to not say these things aloud, we often still think and feel them. This need for favorable social comparison—to feel that we're better than others—hides in the shadows, and from that place it fuels the fire of prejudice and supremacy. We all do it. But if we are to end racism, we have to get honest with ourselves about who we think we're better than. Generally speaking, people are not against you as much as they are for themselves.

Here's how supremacy works. To make any sort of determination about something within a given culture—whether it be your family culture, work culture, or collective culture—everything must be measured against an agreed-upon standard. For example, for something to be considered "too hot," we must have a standard for a baseline "room temperature." The same standard is required to determine if something is "too cold." In this case, the baseline "room temperature" is the *standard* that you are holding everything up against. In the case of culture, we have many of these standards that allow us to rank things as "good or bad," "appropriate or inappropriate," "valuable or unvaluable," "acceptable or unacceptable," "just or unjust," and so forth. To make any sort of determination or valuation of any kind, you must have a baseline standard. *Supremacy* takes whatever is considered "supreme" by the culture and makes it the standard.

As aforementioned, in America, white supremacy is the most commonly mentioned form of supremacy. White supremacy, as with any other supremacy, makes whiteness the standard to measure everything else against. For example, phrases such as "Those people are too loud,"

"That hairstyle is inappropriate," "That outfit is not professional," or "My butt is too big" are statements you can make regardless of the color of your skin, yet in each of these contexts, there is a *standard* being measured against to make these valuations and determinations.

To figure out what form of supremacy is being applied when using a phrase like "That hairstyle is inappropriate," you simply have to ask, *"Compared to what?"* In this case, and in all of the previous examples, the determination is being made compared to the standard of whiteness: white social cues, white hairstyles, Eurocentric clothing, white European body types, and the like. This is what creates a culture of white supremacy. For example, for much of modern history (and sometimes still today), Black children in America were often sent home from school for having their hair styled in box braids and what were known as dreadlocks. Why? Because it was considered inappropriate. How could something that is normal and natural to any culture be considered inappropriate? Because it's being forcibly measured against another standard. In this case, the standard is whiteness—hairstyles that white children are accustomed to. As a solution, many Black people learned to press their hair straight, cut their hair short, or wear weaves, wigs, and extensions in order to be deemed "appropriate" and achieve the socially acceptable standard.

You can apply this logic in any part of society. If, for example, you consider "formal attire" in many cultural communities, you'll see that European business casual is not the norm. In Mexican culture at a quinceañera (the traditional Latin American culture's celebration of a girl's fifteenth birthday, marking her transition to adulthood), or in India at a wedding, as with many other cultures of the world—if you ask people to "dress nicely," they would not dress in European business casual. You might instead see ornate dresses, colorful saris, incredibly elaborate jewelry, and beautiful hats and headdresses. But in the Western world, which often bases its standard of dress on white supremacy, diverse cultural clothing is not considered appropriate in most contexts. It gets dropped to fit the standard and is only allowed to arise in a protected cultural context where the gaze of supremacy is not present. In this way, the simple act of choosing what to wear can either uphold or oust whatever the dominant supremacist culture is. The important distinction here is that *you don't have to be white to uphold and perpetuate the harm of white supremacy*. You just have to be feeding into or compliant with the standards that create it.

Supremacy goes beyond race. Sometimes people feel some contention about this, but all of our research and focus groups (with people being unabashedly honest with us) has led us to understand that you can put any word in front of the word *supremacy*: Black supremacy, Latino supremacy, college-educated supremacy, rich supremacy, Christian supremacy, Jewish supremacy, heterosexual supremacy, spiritual supremacy, Democrat supremacy, Republican supremacy, and so on—all ultimately leading to a worldview that asserts that "we're better than everyone who isn't compliant with our standard, and if you want to be around us and be accepted, these are the standards that must be met for us to be comfortable with your presence." Although there are considerations about power, resources, and access that relate to supremacy, our point here is that many people subconsciously (or consciously) consider themselves supreme to others. This works against everything required to end racism. To end racism, we can't just focus on eradicating white supremacy; we must eradicate the concept of *supremacy* in general. The concept of supremacy itself creates othering and must be left behind as we step forward into this new future we are creating together. Let us be clear: This doesn't mean that you shouldn't celebrate your culture or affinity groups. Remember, this is not a binary conversation. It simply means that you cannot make your culture or affinity group supreme to any other, for any reason.

All of us, regardless of our race, must be honest with ourselves about our relationship to supremacy. Many of us consciously and subconsciously consider a certain group supreme without realizing it, even if that group is not our own. Those supremacies create our standards—as well as societal norms—and those standards separate us instead of allow us to exist in healthy relationships with others' differences.

Inner Work

Use the following incomplete sentences to excavate the shadow of supremacy. Take a moment to think about these, and be as honest with yourself as you can.

- If I'm really honest with myself, who/what I consider supreme is ______________________________.
- Until today, I didn't realize that or think about how I was subscribing to the supremacist standards of ______________________________________.
- The reason I am complacent with this supremacy is ______________________________________.
- What I'm afraid of is ______________________.
- A way I personally may be adding to the continuation of this supremacy is ______________________.
- A group that is sometimes considered more supreme than me is ______________________________.
- Things people might say who view me or my group as "less than" is __________________________.
- How that makes me feel is ____________________.
- What I could do about my relationship to supremacy moving forward is ________________________.

Lindon, a young African American activist, did this exercise and was shocked to realize how much supremacy he had within, from several different angles. Upon doing this exercise, he realized that in one respect, he believed Black people were a superior race, articulating this in one of our workshops by stating, "We even joke that we have superpowers, because deep down we know we have to be stronger and better than everyone else to have survived all of this." What he realized is that he wanted to honor and value the Black community for all they had been through and acclaim his community for the resilience and superhuman strength he felt they had. What he didn't realize was that he could do this without it being at the expense of another group. He could value, honor, and celebrate Blackness and what it represents without needing to place Blackness in a hierarchy, which just perpetuated the problem that he was often a victim of himself.

During the second half of our discussion around supremacy, Lindon realized something interesting: while he considered Black people to be supreme, he was also deeply engaged in white supremacy. This shocked him. He said, "I had no idea a Black activist could be a white supremacist, but I damn sure am!" Lindon discovered that even though it went against what was best for his success, he subscribed to the societal condition that "white people were better and more successful," and therefore he sometimes consciously and sometimes subconsciously believed that the more he assimilated into white culture, the better off he would be. You see, these two modes of supremacy don't exist in the binary—they can exist together, in one person. Lindon has been deeply committed to unraveling the supremacy that exists within him so that he can work toward his vision of creating an equitable world. Each of us can do this.

As a general practice for your life, examine the standards you live by at home, at work, and in your social circles. When something doesn't fit that standard, remember to ask yourself, "Compared to what?" This will illuminate more supremacies that are running your life from the shadows. As soon as you become aware of them, you have the power to shift them.

All of us have some form of supremacy programmed. **If you don't examine the supremacy that exists within, regardless of your race or identity, you risk a reality where the oppressed can easily become an oppressor.** This is why ending white supremacy alone is not enough. If we are to end racism, the concept of supremacy must end with it. **You are not better than anyone else, regardless of how "right" you think your beliefs are.** And just the idea of someone else feeling "You think you're better than me" adds to the disconnection we are leaving behind with racism. You are a unique expression of the whole. The connection of all of our beliefs together is what creates a healthy expression of Mwe and will light the pathway forward as we end racism—together.

11

∞

Doubt and Faith

Just after the protests erupted in response to the murder of George Floyd in May 2020, Justin engaged in a conversation with his father about what was happening in the world. He shared with his father how we were going to launch a program aimed at *ending racism*. As he talked through the curriculum we were planning and our mission, his dad's first response was, "Son, don't waste your breath. These white people ain't ever gonna change." Then he went on for about thirty minutes telling Justin why "white people will never change." Justin was shocked, especially because his father is normally so supportive of everything he does. How was it that Justin's father—someone who had personally *experienced* such a massive healing and transformation in his own family after his interracial marriage to Justin's mother—could be so cynical? Upon deeper investigation, it turned out his cynicism stems from his time working as a police officer. He told Justin that what he saw behind the scenes was more grotesque than anything imaginable, and that the idea of *that behavior* changing was a bigger battle than he wanted Justin, his son, to take on because he believed that it would be futile and that it would ultimately result in his loss of faith in humanity.

Doubt and cynicism are like needles to a hot-air balloon. As you stoke the flame of a vision to end racism, doubt and cynicism will puncture your ascent as you attempt to reach new heights. Thus, when we stand in the future and ask, "What *did* we do today that would have caused the end of racism?," we have to reorient our relationship to doubt and cynicism. Doubt and cynicism *must* be kept in check (and ultimately left behind!) as we move forward. Remember, conversations about transformation make the impossible *possible*. Doubt and cynicism keep things in the status quo—and fear is their common denominator.

If you closely examine the roots of any massive transformation that has happened throughout human history, it always stems from a small group of people who chose to **see beyond fear and instead stay steeped in faith.** Every successful social movement in recorded history has succeeded because someone chose to have faith in the impossible becoming possible. ***Fear and faith are the exact same thing: they each require you to believe in something you can't see and that hasn't happened yet.*** The kind of faith we are talking about here isn't limited to religious faith. We're talking about the dictionary definition of faith: *a confidence or trust in a person or thing [or as we like to say, complete confidence and belief in something or someone]; belief that is not based on proof.*[1]

Having faith is not a spiritual or philosophical idea. **It's a necessary strategy for transformation.** Faith has one promise: that your circumstances do not limit your possibilities. Faith asks you to look at every circumstance around you and say, "I am choosing to believe in something bigger, I am choosing to believe that things can change" or "I'm choosing to move forward without having the guarantee that it will." Some people will accuse you of having your head in the clouds, but being steeped in faith is no less "practical" than having doubt, cynicism, or fear. In all cases, you're choosing to believe in something you can't see and that hasn't happened yet.

If we're going to believe in something either way, then it is far more productive to choose faith, because *who we become* on the other side of fear is very different than who we become on the other side of having faith. The result of each one leaves us with two drastically different outcomes. Who we become when we come from a place of fear is, at best, a dilapidated and worn-out version of who we are now. But who we become when we choose to come from a place of faith is someone much greater and much more effective. Imagine if all the women in the past who did not have the right to vote, and were raised and often forced to believe they were the subservient property of their husband, chose to believe that their circumstances dictated the limits of their possibilities. For thousands of years, in many cultures, this was a woman's fate (and we recognize that it still is in some places). In the United States, this—with the exception of very few communities—has transformed. What would the world be like if enslaved people had looked around at their circumstances and said, "This is all we've got, might as well make the most of it." Imagine if the LGBTQIA+ community in countries that now have advanced queer rights said, "We're comfortable staying in hiding." The world does not transform without those of us who *choose* faith.

This is what we mean when we say that ending racism isn't just about shifting the content of the problem but the context and conditions in which the problem exists. *This is shadow work*. If you insert global issues into a culture that is governed by the shadow of fear, then regardless of what the situation *really* is, a fearful culture just twists the situation and perpetuates more fear and separation, which then breeds even more fear and separation, and so on. But in a culture that has faith, the insurmountable can be overcome. Such a culture creates an opening for a transformation of even the most challenging situations. So, when you hear someone say something like "Those people will never change," holding firm to your grounding in faith, you know a statement like that is not the truth. People *can* change. People *do* evolve. All throughout your life, you can point to and tell stories of people who have indeed evolved and changed. Looking inward for a moment, think about all the ways you have transformed in areas of your own life.

This teaching makes us think of Greg, a white man who attended one of our workshops. He grew up in Tennessee with a bunch of racist friends and family members who believed that "Black people were stupid and lazy." In one of our safe-space open forums he confessed, "I used to believe that if Black people were earning 20 percent less than whites, it's because Black people must be working 20 percent less hard or weren't as smart or capable. I even thought that something must be genetically different with them. Especially because I had always thought everyone had the same equal access to opportunity." Greg went on to say, "If I hadn't dramatically messed up my own life . . . if I would've still been working in finance, with a house on a lake and a bunch of 'toys' like many of the people I grew up with, I would definitely still believe those things. I was a proud white supremacist. I genuinely thought Black people were inferior."

But that's not the Greg that we got to know in our workshop. The Greg we met went through a massive transformation fifteen years ago when he struggled with alcohol addiction. After losing some of the most important things in his life—his marriage, for example—Greg became sober and began to consistently attend Alcoholics Anonymous meetings, where he unexpectedly was thrust into a group with several African Americans. In these meetings, participants share their trauma and difficult emotions. It was through the experience of proximity, connection, and sharing a language of loss that Greg began his transformation. Greg had never had any Black friends or neighbors growing up—and very few coworkers, for that matter. His entire narrative of being "Black in America" was formulated based on the opinions of those in his circle of influence and the media, using their lens and personal experiences to instill the narrative that Blacks are inferior.

However, getting to hear firsthand from the Black men in his group about the trauma and struggles they faced growing up in Tennessee and their road to becoming sober made him realize two things: first, that there is a lot they had in common (which surprised him); second, that there is a lot these men had to go through and continue to endure—while living in the same geographic area as him—that he never had to experience or consider. Realizing this, Greg came to our workshop because he wanted to gain the tools to ensure that his five-year-old son grows up on the right side of history. He didn't want to pass on the same conditioning that he grew up with, but he felt ill-equipped to ensure that outcome.

This story illustrates a massive transformation. Greg used to be a (self-proclaimed) racist and proud white supremacist and is now someone who cares deeply about his Black friends. He is committed to ending racism and to breaking the cycle of bigotry that had been passed down by his family. Greg's awakening didn't happen when he was twelve. It happened when he was thirty-five. Stories like Greg's are not rare (we can attest to that because we hear them all the time), but cynicism and doubt would have us think they are.

People transform their beliefs all the time. Point to your once-unreachable family members, your formerly socially unconscious coworkers, your used-to-be homophobic relatives, and the ways in which the people close to you have grown over the years. Racism is not exempt from this. The opportunities for transformation do not occur unless someone chooses to remain in a space of openness and connection with those who have differing and sometimes opposing beliefs, holding firm to a grounding of faith that things can and will transform. We need you to commit to being that person.

Inner Work

Complete the following sentences to explore your relationship to cynicism, doubt, fear, and faith.

- My cynicism and doubt around racism ending is ______________________.
- My most fearful belief about racism is __________.
- How that impacts my ability to make a difference is ______________________.
- The biggest shift in beliefs I've made in my own life around any topic is ______________________.
- This proves to me that ______________________.

- A personal shift I've made around the concept of race is ____.
- The *story* I'm telling myself about why I believe a shift around race might not be possible for "those people" is ____.
- "Those people" are ____________________________.
- How *my story* might be *contributing* to racism persisting is ______________________________.
- If I were to believe in a story that was centered in faith rather than fear, that new story would be ____.
- And that would lead me to ______________________.
- I am committed to ____________________________.

When you find yourself in a situation where doubt is bubbling up and you are having a hard time leaning into faith, it simply means that you're working toward something important to you. Experiencing doubt or fear is generally connected to vulnerability. Ask yourself, "What is my doubt and fear protecting? How can I shift to a place of *possibility, even while and if I am continuously experiencing harm*?"

Sometimes when we are in a space of openness, we feel exposed and like we are more susceptible to getting hurt or disappointed. We must remind ourselves then that it is perfectly normal for us to feel doubtful or to lack faith in an outcome. Then, being self-aware of what we are feeling, we must identify it (using the emotions wheel!) to help us become more present and bring us face to face with what's really arising so that we can return to a space of possibility.

From Doubt to Possibility Exercise

The next time you're feeling doubt, try this practice.

Place your hands over the center of your chest, one over the other.

Ask yourself, "What am I doubtful of?"

Then close your eyes.

Take five deep breaths, inhaling through your nose and exhaling through your mouth; make your exhales longer than your inhales. For example, inhale for three counts through your nose, and exhale for six counts through your mouth. This helps regulate the nervous system.

Then ask yourself these questions:

- *What emotion am I feeling?*
- *What is my doubt protecting?*
- *What future is possible if I flipped my doubt to faith? Envision it.*
- *How can I contribute to creating that future?*

Who you get to be when you believe in doubt is completely different from who you get to be when you believe in possibility. This is what our community believes in: to create a future where racism doesn't exist, we must stand in the space of possibility and hold the door open for people to step into a new possibility that's greater than what they believe is possible now. A future that is not limited by the bounds of what seems realistic today. A future that makes the impossible *possible*. That's the only future worth fighting for. Are you with us?

12

∞

The Other in Me

We've mentioned the concept of "othering" several times throughout this book, and that's because it intersects everything we are building toward. When we stand in the future and ask, "What did we do today to end racism?" *othering on the basis of race* is the primary phenomenon we are trying to eradicate in the human species. Human beings, for all of time, have created in-groups and out-groups. We know that this was—evolutionarily—a means for survival in the early days of the development of our species.[1] When this happens, we consider everyone in the in-group "like me" and everyone in the out-group "other." The "other" can be someone from an "other" religion, race, country, political belief, and so on. Othering is the opposite of integration. It's when we dehumanize or disconnect from the true vision of intraconnection—that we are all connected to and part of Mwe. Most othering is based on conditioning, stories, and ungrounded assessments instead of rational facts. We base our othering on the way we've been taught "things are" or "should be."

There are many types of othering, and many arguments and opinions about the difference between racism, prejudice, and discrimination. The definitions we will offer you here are as follows:

Prejudice is prejudging a person of any identity based upon negative stereotypes. Prejudices are the assumptions we make about people and their association with certain groups.

Discrimination refers to *actions, policies, or social arrangements* that disadvantage people based on the group to which they belong.

So, while prejudice is attitudinal, discrimination is behavioral and refers to the actions and policies that are created based upon prejudice.

Racism couples prejudice with power. It creates a system by which a dominant group is able to dominate over all other groups and negatively affect them at all levels—personally, systemically, and institutionally.

Each of these types of othering must be left behind to end racism. Having a conversation to differentiate or rank prejudice, discrimination, and racism is an example of the difference between having a conversation "about" something versus a conversation that *changes* something. Regardless of how we split the pie when we talk about or rank these differences, we fail to realize that it's irrelevant because the whole pie is spoiled. In many of the groups we teach, we hear people argue that discrimination is a more "acceptable" form of othering or one that is easier to look away from. When we ask people to delve deeper into this topic, they often discover that, if they're being honest, these arguments and distinctions are usually trying to excuse a minority group that is often on the side of oppression for their own discriminatory practices. Or they are trying to prove that People of Color cannot be racist or that racism is unique to white people. Sometimes a point on the opposite end of the spectrum is argued. The roots of this type of thinking get uncovered with good shadow work.

The point here is simply this: *Prejudice*, *discrimination*, and *racism* all describe forms of *othering* based upon the very social standards that we are leaving behind as we create a new future. All of it has to go to the same bin we put trash in if we are to end racism. Figuring out how to classify prejudice, discrimination, and racism perfectly is not even a conversation worth entertaining. A question that *is* worth wrestling with, however, is this: Regardless of whether you call it prejudice, discrimination, or racism, who/what group of people have you made it acceptable to *other*?

The answer often has to do with who you are being in the secret spaces of your life, when no one else is around, when you are with your trusted group of friends, or when you are in what you consider to be a safe space—where you think there are no consequences. We are all guilty of these behaviors, and thus the skill we must learn to end racism is not how to label and divide up a spoiled pie but instead how to track and eliminate all forms of othering when it shows up within us—especially in the secret spaces of our lives. Justin often tells a story in our online program that illustrates how to take this teaching and put it into action. When he was a child, his Uncle Michael was the first person in the family to hire a home cleaning service. The service would come to his home while he was away at work, without him ever needing to see or meet the people who were coming to clean. Although his uncle was told there would be different groups of people of all genders coming to his house to clean each week, he decided to call the cleaning service by the name Lupe, a common name of a woman of Latin descent. Anytime his uncle's house got cleaned he would call and say, "Thank God, Lupe came today!" Lupe was a recurring fictional character in Justin's childhood, to the point that when he and his siblings would leave a mess in the family room after a day of playing with toys, his mom would yell to clean up by exclaiming, "Who do you think I am, Lupe?"

Fast-forward to two decades later: It's 2020 and Justin's in the height of teaching his work related to ending racism. He walks into his friend Cristi's home, and to his surprise, her house is a mess. The first words out of Justin's mouth after seeing the mess were, "Girl, it's like a tornado came through here. *You better call Lupe!*" The moment he heard those words come out of his mouth he immediately felt shocked. Did he, the guy on the mission to end racism, just say that out loud? Did he just perpetuate a racist stereotype? Yes, he did. He felt shame right away, and Cristi looked at him confused. Unsurprisingly, she didn't even notice anything "off" about what he said. He paused for a few moments, took a few breaths, and then proceeded to explain to Cristi why he said what he said, why he stopped himself, and why it wasn't okay. He explained the story. He apologized for saying it. And he made an important promise to himself that day: he would do his best never to say that phrase again, but if he did, he would always, in every circumstance, stop and explain *why* what he just said was not okay. What Justin did in this case, while in conversation with Cristi, is a skill we want *you* to learn. Because we want you to understand that you're going to mess up. You're going to make mistakes. It's inevitable. It is part of being human. Your old shadowy conditioning is going to sneak in and that is totally normal and to be expected. It happens to the best of us. But shame, blame, and being silent aren't going to move us forward. What will move us forward is taking responsibility and committing to holding yourself accountable the next time you make a mistake, and turning it into a teaching opportunity for everyone around you.

This is how we start to shift culture. Not by calling ourselves and one another out but by each of us taking responsibility for our patterns of othering and becoming a ripple of transformation. Cristi was Justin's best friend, and he could've easily said nothing. *There would have been no consequences.* She didn't even notice anything was off. But that lack of responsibility is *not* what's going to take us forward. When we stand in the future in a world where racism has ended, we look back to see that we no longer waited for others to hold us accountable. We held ourselves accountable with compassion—and we showed others how it can (and should) be done.*

*You may be wondering what would have happened if Cristi did in fact realize that something was wrong with Justin's statement and how she could have pointed it out to him, compassionately. We get into this in great detail in chapter 16.

How can you recognize racism in all of its forms while it is happening, especially if you are the one perpetuating it, so that you can take the first steps, like Justin did, in tackling it? The first step is to start learning more about the differences between types of race-based othering. First and foremost (and likely most common), there are things that are "racially insensitive." There is a difference between being racially insensitive and being racist.[2] Racially insensitive remarks are out of touch, and while they may be uncomfortable, they're not malicious. Generally speaking, racially insensitive remarks stem from lack of awareness and disconnect, while racism stems from hatred and aggression. Both are important to address, and we should approach both with proper attention to finding the core issues causing them in the first place.

Racism can be broken into three categories: *casual* or *indirect racism*, *direct racism*, and *systemic racism*. Casual or indirect racism can often seem subtle; it may be unintentional or intentional. It is an offensive comment or message that is entirely based on a person's affiliation with a minority group or community. Direct racism is intentional and is premeditated. Systemic racism occurs on an organizational level—in places such as governmental agencies, corporations, and institutions—stemming from oppressive laws and systems that were put into place that have created a shift in power and opportunities.

When you recognize a moment where you feel like you may be acting racially insensitive or racist—even unintentionally—examine the underlying roots (go back to shadow work), then take personal responsibility for your actions and promise to do better. Make a specific commitment or plan to counteract that behavioral or speech pattern the next time you encounter it. You *can* do this. It takes commitment. You are ready.

Inner Work

Use the following incomplete sentences to explore your relationship to the shadow of othering. Be compassionate with yourself with what you find. We all experience and contribute to othering in some way. Knowing how will help you take responsibility, so the poison of othering becomes medicine.

- A specific moment when I have (intentionally or unintentionally) practiced discrimination, prejudice, racial insensitivity, or racism is ________________ ____.

  (Be specific, not hypothetical.)

- Where I think I learned this from was ____________ ____.

- The community/group the person I *othered* was a part of was ______________________.
- The reason I let it be okay to treat this community this way was because ______________________.
- What I didn't know then was ______________________.
- But what I know now is ______________________.
- The way I feel knowing I contributed to this harm is ______________________.
- Where I feel it now in my body is ______________________.
- What I want most for this community/group is ______________________.

There is an additional type of othering we haven't discussed—one that we couldn't teach you until this point and that will pull together everything we've practiced and learned thus far. It's called *inner othering*. Most people only focus on the concept of othering externally, but *you can also other your own self*. The hardest form of othering to recognize is inner othering because it hides in the shadows and then sneakily turns around and *others* others. Justin's personal story will provide you with more context on that. Justin's grandmother Betty—they called Nana—was sick for quite some time. She was on dialysis for over ten years, multiple times per week, and constantly in and out of the hospital. She could barely walk, and this entire time, Justin's mother, whom he loves dearly, was her sole caretaker. He watched her work herself into the ground taking care of Nana, and because of that, her own health started to decline. As a caretaker for someone else, she wasn't taking care of herself. As Justin became increasingly worried about his mother, he would notice that anytime he would get a call that Nana was being sent to the hospital in an ambulance, he would have a thought pop into his head like "It would be better at this point if my Nana dies." He'd immediately push this thought down, as if stuffing something into a closet before anyone could see it. He couldn't even allow himself to think the thought. If the thought lingered for too long, he would shame and blame himself internally, pushing it further into the shadows, thinking he was a "bad" person or that he was going to be "punished" by a wrath of God if he had the thought again. Sometimes he would even think "something evil" was coming into his mind to plant these bad thoughts. He'd tell himself, "I'm not a person who has these types of thoughts." Over and over again, he'd push the thought further into the shadow. This is *inner othering.* We all do it from time to time. For example, when we have a joyous reaction to seeing a person on trial getting punished with a verdict but we push it away, or when we take pleasure in someone else's pain, or when we wish someone harm but then pretend the thought never happened. It also occurs when we're being envious or jealous and then pretend not to be, banishing the envious or jealous parts of ourselves to the shadow. Anytime we consider a part of ourselves to be "unacceptable," it gets pushed into the shadows. This is inner othering—othering inside of our own selves.

Upon closer investigation, the truth about Justin's story with his Nana is that he had two competing thoughts, a paradox of sorts. Holding paradox—the ability to hold multiple truths in duality—is exactly the mindset we need to hold to end racism. On the one hand, he worried deeply for his mother, saw his Nana's poor quality of life, and indeed wished that she would pass away peacefully. On the other hand, he had a deep love for his Nana, possessed an immense gratitude for her presence in his life, and wished she would heal and take better care of herself. The key to moving forward with *both* thoughts/desires is by integrating the two. A good visual representation of this concept is the yin and yang symbol, where light and dark come together in one symbol, are expressed equally, and create something more beautiful than if they were alone.

When we *other* the thought we consider "negative" or "unacceptable," we're denying its natural intelligence and missing out on the

opportunity to learn. But by leaning into what's uncomfortable—by doing the shadow work—we can instead ask deeper questions to discover what life is trying to teach us about ourselves. Justin's unthinkable thought was "It would be better if my Nana dies." When he paused to ask himself, "Where do I feel that thought in my body?," the answer was a tightness in his stomach. When he asked himself what emotion was arising for him when he had this thought, he recognized that it was anger, fear, and resentment. As a child, he was taught to push down feelings of anger, fear, and resentment, and he was told that those were unfeelable and "bad" emotions to have. What he realized by going through this exercise was that by stuffing down his thoughts and the corresponding emotions, he was falling into the same unproductive patterns.

When he sought to understand what that anger and resentment were here to teach him, he discovered that he loved his mom so much that he was frustrated with her for letting her health decline so dramatically in order to take care of his grandmother. He also uncovered that he was afraid of losing *both* his grandmother *and* mom, and that his anger and fear weren't stemming from the desire to fight against something he hated but from the need to protect something he loved. If we can recognize the ways in which we other our own selves and turn toward it with kindness and compassion, we will begin to see changes show up outside of ourselves immediately. Within you there are emotions and feelings that are pushed away; accessing them and acknowledging them with compassion will shift your outside world.

Reflecting back to what we learned in the section about emotions, remember why it's important to acknowledge and allow our feelings to exist, without being judgmental. It is important to fully integrate these "bad" or "unacceptable" thoughts. If those thoughts remain in the shadow, they will seep out somewhere they don't belong. **Suppressed anger and fear always end up affecting other areas of our lives where they don't belong.** They seep out of the cracks in places we don't even notice, and we can find ourselves in a "bad mood" without knowing why; feeling irritated, stressed, and annoyed; or snapping at someone, being aggressive and irritable without a direct reason.

Here's the *big* thing—inner othering always winds up as a projection toward others. These unintegrated emotions and thoughts can open the door to us *othering* other people who are experiencing the exact same unintegrated emotions as we are. Because we can't welcome the experience in ourselves, we shame and blame other people who are having that experience, too. What we push away in ourselves, we push away in others. We see this often in politics, when a conservative politician votes and speaks loudly against LGBTQIA+ rights, only to be discovered with a transgender lover. Or when left-wing folks are fighting on the streets for justice but unwilling to vote or show up for policy change. It shows up as women who've had secret abortions and then fight for the pro-life movement. Or when Black Lives Matter activists discriminate against people of other races. Our inner othering easily becomes our outer othering. This is why inner othering is so toxic.

It is easy to point the finger of blame at people who are feeling the same way you're feeling because you've pushed the feeling away in your own self. But as we've learned, if you could just name and claim the feeling for yourself, you could come to a deeper place of compassion—rather than *othering*—when you witness someone else expressing that which you pushed away in yourself. You recognize that even though you're judging them for what they're experiencing, the same experience has also happened inside of you. You recognize that same experience as a possible point of connection. How does your own inner othering show up in the outside world? Who is exhibiting similar qualities that you've disowned in yourself that you have now deemed as the "other?" When we haven't integrated our shadow, it controls us without us knowing it and wreaks havoc on our lives—and potentially the lives of those around us.

Justin's grandmother did indeed pass away, and he was able to reckon with his emotions. He mourned and felt deep gratitude for her life while finally having a real conversation with his mother about his concerns for her well-being from a place of love, instead of his suppressed anger and resentment. He was able to feel sadness for his grandmother's passing while feeling relief for his mother at the same time. This holding of both emotions in a paradox of duality is where the healing happened.

As we mentioned, we must hold space for paradox to end racism. We must leave the binary thinking and understand that people from all sides, regardless of how despicable you think they may be, are not just a part of you—they *are you*. The next time you catch yourself pushing away a thought, feeling, or emotion, especially as it relates to race, let it arise. Contrary to what you might think, letting it arise is the only way it loses the ability to control you. When it happens, ask yourself, "What's the thought that I'm unwilling to let myself have? If I allow it to arise, what can it teach me? How can I use the energy behind this thought to fuel my mission to create a better world?" This is the pathway to healing and integration—and toward ending racism.

Pillar Six

we practiced forgiveness

13

∞

Offering Forgiveness

Because our shadow is sometimes in control (and will continue to be in ways that we may not realize), the next step of our process is learning how to ***offer*** forgiveness and ***ask for*** forgiveness. Remember, when racism ends, it doesn't mean that the world will be eradicated of all bias, that we will have no more shadow work to do, or that racist thoughts will never occur again. Ending racism means we each *take responsibility* for the racial harm we cause as soon as we become aware of it. From this new reality we operate with an understanding that harm will be caused (because we are human) and that wrong things will be said (because that is normal). This is a part of the process of ending racism. If we expect that when racism is over that people will never make mistakes again, that is not realistic. **Racism cannot end if we cannot make mistakes. This is why forgiveness is key.** When we stand in the future and ask, "What did we do today?," the art of forgiveness is something we became incredibly skilled at. Forgiveness is how a culture processes and releases harm. We must become skilled at it.

Let's begin with ***offering*** forgiveness to another (in the next chapter we will cover ***asking for*** forgiveness). Offering forgiveness is incredibly challenging if you don't first understand *what forgiveness is not.* In our workshops, there tends to be a lot of confusion about this, so let us be incredibly clear. **Forgiveness is not:**

- condoning
- forgetting

- excusing
- encouraging
- being tolerant of disrespect
- minimizing your hurt
- being lenient
- having weak boundaries
- reconciliation
- reestablishing trust
- denying or suppressing anger
- ignoring accountability or justice
- saying what happened is okay

Forgiveness is not contingent on (nor does it automatically result in) any of those things—these things are completely independent of the choice to forgive. Imagine that you are in a parking lot and another person accidentally backs up into your rear bumper, causing damage to your car. You can forgive them, but you would likely still hold them accountable for the cost of repairing your car, right? Well, the inverse can be true as well. Think of all the people who spend energy, time, and money pursuing legal action and get the result they want, yet they still never come out on the other side with any closure. They may have been awarded millions of dollars but they're still holding on to anger and resentment over what happened to them. That is because, as we've been discussing, healing is an inside job. When we realize forgiveness is independent of all of these tangential things we tend to attach to it, it frees us to simply just forgive—without all of the unnecessary strings attached.

One of our favorite definitions of forgiveness is from Oprah Winfrey: "Forgiveness is giving up the hope that the past could have been any different."[1] We love this sentiment because it brings us back into the reality of the present moment. It releases us from what "should have" and "could have" been and allows us to just be with what's in front of us. If we take this a step further, it also asks us to look to the future and ask, "Even though this happened, how do I want the future to unfold from this point forward?" Forgiveness requires radical acceptance of whatever happened in the past, even if we don't like it or condone it, recognizing the present moment for exactly what it is, and realizing the responsibility we play in whatever unfolds next. We can't control what happened in the past, but we can choose how to continue forward. Every time we offer forgiveness, we open a door to new possibilities—a door that remains locked if we choose to hold on to resentment and fear.

Let us be clear—we are not saying that forgiveness equates to a free pass. Remember, forgiveness does not equate to any of the things we usually entangle it with, so be aware of what arises in your mind when you are hesitant to forgive. The true purpose of forgiving someone is to ensure that what was done to you in the past does not affect your life today or, for that matter, how you live your life in the future. We've all assuredly heard this statement before: offering forgiveness is *for you*. However, most of us have a hard time putting it into practice because we allow what happened to us to continue to control us instead of truly moving on, which keeps us in shackles for every moment in our future.

Now that you know this, you should be able to write a simple forgiveness letter, burn it in a fire, release all the difficult emotions, and be done with them for good, right? Wrong. That's because there is a gray area that often gets muddled between the concepts of true forgiveness and *premature forgiveness*.

We've all heard someone say, "I'm over it!" or "I've let it go," all the while knowing they didn't get over it or let it go at all, leaving others in their path to deal with their passive-aggressive behavior. Have you ever agreed to forgive someone so that you could both move on with your lives but still felt stuck or held silent resentment afterward? This is premature forgiveness. While the perpetrator may have done everything right in offering an apology, or even if reparations were made to your specifications, you can still feel activated by what has happened.

What tends to happen in these cases is that the story, the grudge, the victimized you becomes a part of your shadow. We've been down this road together and we already know what happens when we choose to "ignore" what lies in the shadow: it controls your life and actions without you realizing it. What you still harbor comes back to haunt you and is often projected onto different people and in different situations. Premature forgiveness is a shortcut that never works. The creeds of premature forgiveness are "pretend to forget," "ignore," and "suppress" rather than "deal with," "work through," or "confront" what has happened to you. Premature forgiveness means that the one offering forgiveness hasn't taken responsibility for fully processing internally what has happened or how it's still affecting them in the present day. This is why we had to teach you about emotional awareness and shadow work before arriving at this topic.

Know this: *a negative attachment is still an attachment*. When we truly forgive, we release the difficult emotions completely and all the attachments are gone. Releasing attachment doesn't mean that we don't experience negative emotions associated with what occurred ever again but rather that we can think about what occurred without immediately getting reactivated and continue to move on with our life from a healthy place. We stop having to "try not to think about it." We don't hold a grudge, nor do we silently wish for the others' misery and destruction. ***True forgiveness means that you're taking responsibility for what you're choosing to still hold on to.*** With true forgiveness, you realize that you are in charge. In the process toward true forgiveness, you also take heed of Oprah's guidance, releasing the hope that the past could have been any different—and then you can finally understand that what *can* be different is what you do starting now and what unfolds next.

The Three Types of Forgiveness

To get a deeper understanding of forgiveness, we need to know that there are three different types of forgiveness. Each one can be applied differently to each situation depending on the context, and each will produce different results. Expanding our language around the word *forgiveness* will give us the opportunity to practice it more specifically. The three different types of forgiveness are exoneration, forbearance, and release.

Exoneration is the closest term to what we usually think of in Western culture when we say "forgiveness." What it means in practical terms is to wipe the slate clean and restore the full innocence of the relationship before the infraction or harm was done. For example, in the United States, an "exoneree" is a person who has been wrongfully convicted of a crime and has spent time in prison serving a sentence, then released after being proven innocent. They are released without a record and are considered by the government to have their full innocence restored. Exoneration in your personal relationships usually applies in a few distinct ways: First, we can realize that a harmful action was a genuine accident or that no fault can be assigned to that person. Second, the offender may be a child or someone who (for a variety of reasons) cannot understand the hurt they were causing. Third, it can apply when the person who harmed us expresses their remorse, is authentically sorry, takes full responsibility for the harm they inflicted, asks for forgiveness, and we have great confidence that they will not knowingly repeat the harm in the future. Those variables can encompass exoneration.

The second type of forgiveness is *forbearance*. This often applies when the offender offers a partial apology or comingles their remorse with blame that they "had a reason" or that you somehow had culpability in them causing the harm. An apology that warrants forbearance may sound like, "I'm sorry that this happened, but . . ." or "I apologize for the harm that was caused, however . . ." Another way to describe the offering of forbearance is when we decide to "forgive but not forget" or we are determined to "trust but verify." Why even bother offering forbearance? Mainly because it doesn't require us to cut all ties with the individual who caused us harm. Perhaps we work with this individual in some capacity or are related to them and thus have no choice but to continue to engage with them. Sometimes we choose to continue to engage with them because we still care about them or have fun with them, but that doesn't mean we fully trust them.

Finally, there is a type of forgiveness that is warranted when the person who harmed us doesn't acknowledge the pain they have caused, won't (or can't for one reason or another; for example, they may be deceased) offer an apology, and doesn't seek to make amends or offer any form of repair. In this instance, the type of forgiveness we must practice is more like a "release." A *release* offers no exoneration to the individual who caused us harm, nor does it require any forbearance. It offers no demands on the continuity of a relationship. Rather, it requires that you do the work required to not define any part of your life by the trauma or hurt perpetrated so you can redefine your future on a path that isn't comingled with the past. When we release the events of the past without requiring an apology we never got or will never get, we put down the enormous weight that we have been carrying that has managed to define the lens through which we view ourselves and the world. This will likely require you to give yourself permission to experience a period of grieving and allow yourself to deeply feel the pain or emotions of the situation so you can *truly* let it go. The things we don't release eat away at us and cause us harm over time in much the same way a flood can occur in your home by a dripping faucet.

The Five Core Elements of Offering Forgiveness

In our work we have found that there are five core elements to help on the journey of offering forgiveness that allow you to truly move on from the situation that harmed you. To be clear, all five elements don't have to happen for full forgiveness to occur, nor do they need to happen in a particular order. Also, within these elements we will make suggestions about having a conversation with the person who has wronged you, but we know this isn't always safe or possible. In that case, expressing the element to *yourself* is still possible (and the most important action you can take). Think of these five elements like ingredients in a recipe. Each can be incorporated together in a variety of ways or can stand alone as an ingredient on its own. But the more you include, the better the recipe.

1. Express Yourself

The first core element of forgiveness is making sure that you feel like you have been heard. Yes—*you*, as the one who's been harmed, *need to be heard.* In other words, to forgive someone, you must first express the toll of their actions and communicate the hurt or the pain that was caused. Since it isn't always possible or safe to communicate with the person who harmed you, first and foremost, you must admit this to yourself. *Hear yourself.* Bear witness for *yourself.* Let yourself feel the emotions that arise and how the wrongdoing affected you instead of constantly pushing it down or shying away from the difficult feelings. You can do this by writing a letter to yourself about the pain that was caused, how it made you feel, and the deep impact that person's actions had on your life. We often skip this part. Then, if it's safe and you are able, share what arises for you with the person you're forgiving. In all cases, full expression is required for a release to occur, regardless of if you're the only one hearing it.

Often when we're expressing how somebody harmed us, we clam up and withhold the truth about our painful or difficult emotions. We fear that recounting the pain or expressing the emotions may cause us to feel them all over again and so we think it's easier to avoid the truth altogether. Or we want to avoid further conflict and confrontation. Perhaps we don't want to cause further damage, so we resort instead to sugarcoating things and watering down the truth of the harm that was caused. If real forgiveness is to be achieved, this is the one element that cannot be skipped over because even if you manage to get through the other four elements, there will be unresolved wounding, words unspoken, and resentment that lingers and can flare up periodically and fester over time.

We also aren't doing any favors for the person who committed the harm when we don't communicate from a place of candor and authentic truth. We've practiced naming our emotions—this is where it gets real, and we get practice using this skill in real situations. The person listening to our felt and seen experience will have an opportunity to see the truth—the full picture—and thus choose to respond in their own way. If you have the opportunity to be heard by the person who caused you harm, we recommend that you do it. If you're afraid to do it in person, you can always send a letter. As long as you're safe and communicating with the person isn't going to cause you any physical harm, it's one of the most powerful moves you can make for your own freedom. When you get to chapter 16 on *calling forward*, we will teach you more tools that can help you with this process.

2. Release Control of the Outcome

The second core element of forgiveness can be quite challenging: releasing control. Understand that you cannot control the outcome of someone's response after you express yourself and offer up your truth about how you've have been harmed. Similarly, you cannot control how someone apologizes nor fake how you feel emotionally when offered an apology. Pay attention to what you're "already listening for." What this means is that before the person even speaks to offer an apology to you, you're "already listening" for the unspoken stories in your head about what you're hoping they say, what you're expecting they say, what you would say, and making presumed assumptions about how the situation needs to unfold in order for you to accept the apology (assuming that you will even get one in the first place).

When this happens, we end up holding on to *the one sentence* the offending party said wrong instead of paying attention to the totality of the apology. Or we get stuck on someone's bad grammar and harp on it instead of simply asking them to clarify the truth of what they're saying. Or we unfairly hold them accountable for not reading our mind and failing to say that "one thing" we "needed" them to say in order to feel complete. We advise you to drop all of that. If you have expectations about how the situation needs to play out, you'll miss what's *actually happening*. If you don't notice what's actually happening, you'll only be responding to the story in your head instead of the reality of what is unfolding before you. When hearing an apology, do your best to listen generously and mindfully and then respond to what is actually happening instead of the preconceived story you have in your mind about the way it's supposed to go. Mindfully listening to someone means not interrupting when they are talking but taking in all that they are saying. Then, when they are done, you can repeat back to them what you heard them say, without offering your opinion of what they said. Let the person who offered you an apology confirm that what you heard them say is indeed what they said and meant. Then, after this is confirmed to you, you can offer a response.

3. Get Rid of Grudges

We all have grudges that we hold on to, however, some of us have an easier time than others letting them go. Of course, we often hold on to our grudges unwillingly. They interfere with our lives, and while we wish we could drop them and live in the moment, the past winds up occupying so much of our present. A grudge can be painful. Holding on to one means we must keep "picking at a scab" that is trying to heal. Instead of letting nature runs its course, we keep the wound open and active. Because grudges keep us living in past experiences of pain, they prevent us from having healed experiences.

When we hold on to grudges long enough, we begin to identify with them. A person with a grudge is a person who was "wronged." This identity of victimhood can start to define us and subconsciously gives us a sense of purpose—we believe that the pain we are holding on to defines us in some way. Thus, in order to release our grudge, we would then have to be willing to let go of our identity as the person who was "wronged." This can be challenging for people because it also means we have to let go of the narrative and sympathy we sometimes get by rerunning our victim story. But once victimhood goes away, the past no longer defines us—the present moment does.

When it comes to grudges, we need to decide that loving ourselves is more important than possibly not forgiving the person who has wronged us. When we choose ourselves and allow our hearts to heal, we can move our focus off our suffering and into our felt experience, something that we can tend to and nurture back to health. Our hearts are capable of holding two truths in duality—pain and the medicine for our pain; wounds and the salve for our wounds. Our heart can help us understand that, yes, our suffering matters *and* that we are the ones responsible for the healing from our suffering.

4. Take Accountability for Yourself

With forgiveness, what we often desire is a scenario where we can honestly share our pain with the person who has harmed us without any backlash or consequences; where they acknowledge what we are feeling and then take full accountability for what happened. This exact scenario rarely plays out, which is why we need to release control of the outcome, because there is a likelihood that when an authentic truth is delivered—one that may be painful—a wall might automatically go up on either side. The poet Mark Nepo once wrote that "accountability and forgiveness form a paradox."[2] On the one hand, accountability is a yearning for an admission of the pain and hurt caused. On the other hand, forgiveness is the desire to let that pain and hurt go. When you offer forgiveness to someone, you can't force them to take accountability, but you *can* be accountable for what you expect of them and what you continue to hold on to.

5. Let Go

The final core element of forgiveness is letting go or releasing. We want to reiterate that when we say "letting go," we don't mean ignoring what happened. This term has been hijacked somewhat in the past few years, so we are redefining it for you here. **Letting go requires that you trust and have faith that if you've shown up and done your part in the forgiveness process, that all will fall into place as it needs to.** Let the process unfold instead of trying to force it. Once you've shared in an authentic way and listened with an open heart, you have to truly release and let go. Don't keep returning to the situation over and over. Don't keep wishing it could've happened differently. Let go and forgive.

Inner Work

Use the following incomplete sentences to explore your relationship to forgiveness. We know you probably already have a situation arising in your mind, but for the sake of the intention of this book, we'd like you to focus your first answers on topics related to prejudice, discrimination, and racism. If you can't think of a situation where you've *personally* faced prejudice, discrimination, or racism, think of something you've witnessed with a friend, loved one, acquaintance, or coworker, or even a situation from history that you know was unjust. After you've done at least one process around race, you can take a little extra time to go through these prompts again for any other area of your life that's asking for your attention.

- As it relates to race, discrimination, or prejudice, someone or something I may need to forgive is ______________ ______________________________________.
- What happened that upsets me is ______________.
- The emotions that arise as I think about this now are ______________________________________.
- How that's affecting me now is ______________.
- How it might be impacting other situations or relationships in my life is ______________________________.
- How I will show up differently in the world once I let this go is ______________________.
- When I look a little deeper, what *really* held me back from letting this go is ______________.
- Once I really let this go, it will free me from ______ ______________________________________.

Louise, a young woman in her forties in one of our programs, realized that she still held resentment for one of her college professors who constantly made inappropriate jokes about Filipino people. Specifically, Louise was majoring in accounting, but anytime she would offer support to someone in class, her professor would joke about Filipino people being great at caretaking and nursing and that "if things didn't work out with accounting, she should consider a second career" because it was "in her blood." He would then mock a Filipino accent and make sarcastic comments about her naturally loving ways.

Although Louise knew he was just joking and meant no harm, this made her angry and uncomfortable, but she felt afraid to speak up. Louise was the only Filipino (and one of the only women) in the class, and she was shocked her professor would say things like this, especially because he was African American and knew how hard it is to be the first-generation college student in the family, a trailblazer in the field, and "the only one in the room." But her grades weren't great so she didn't want to stand up to him out of fear of retaliation. Instead, Louise stuffed it all inside.

Now that Louise is older, her mother is in need of a caretaker, and Louise is the only one of her siblings that lives close enough to help. But for the last year, she has refused. Every time she goes to help her mom, she gets angry and bitter and can't understand why. She tries to be nice to her mom but often ends up yelling at her, leaving them both annoyed before she eventually leaves. Once we did the inner work exercise with Louise, she realized that although she hadn't thought about it in twenty years, the unprocessed grudge she held toward her professor was actually impacting her ability to help her mom. Before her professor's mocking, Louise was a natural caretaker. But because of his comments, she pushed that loving and caretaking part of herself into the shadow as a protective mechanism to prove her worth as an accountant.

The grudge, although unspoken and out of her awareness for over two decades, prohibited her from doing what she *really* wanted to do, which was to show up for her mom with love in her final years. Forgiveness was the key to unlocking the future that Louise wanted.

We asked Louise to look up some techniques online for processing her anger and rage. She also decided that she needed to go to therapy to work through it with a professional. Once she was able to tend to and honor the emotions that she had pushed down for all those years, she was finally able to let it go and forgive her professor. Louise said, "Forgiveness was like the magic pill I didn't know I needed." Louise now helps her mother three days a week, and she says she is so grateful that she gets to spend these final moments with her and that they are some of the most special, love-filled moments she's ever had.

Holocaust survivor Eva Kor is an inspiring example of how forgiveness can work even in the most drastic examples. Eva and her twin sister, Miriam, were subjects of the horrific medical experiments in Auschwitz administered by Dr. Josef Mengele during World War II. Her sister did not survive. In 2015, Eva was invited to fly to Germany to testify in a trial against a former Auschwitz guard, Oskar Groening. She described the experience of being back in Germany as surreal. The place where she was called "a dirty Jew" so many times in her youth was now the same place she got respect from even the German judges sitting for the trial. After she gave her testimony, Eva wanted to thank Groening for acknowledging his crimes. In subsequent interviews, she stated that if she were the judge, she would prefer to use Groening as a public speaker who could educate young neo-Nazis on what he saw and why the regime should never return to power.

Many misinterpreted her message and gesture as absolving the crimes of not just Groening but his peers, too. But for Eva, forgiveness means something different. "My forgiveness," she said, "has nothing to do with the perpetrator, has nothing to do with any religion, it is my act of self-healing, self-liberation, and self-empowerment. I had no power over my life up to the time that I discovered that I could forgive, and I still do not understand why people think it's wrong." When a victim chooses to forgive, Eva believes that they can take the power back from their oppressors. "They can take a piece of paper and a pen and write a letter to someone who hurt them. Please do not mail it to that person. It's for you to know that you forgive, and you can go on with your life without the burden and pain that the Nazis or anybody else ever imposed on you."[3]

Sometimes forgiving someone requires having a heart-to-heart conversation. Sometimes that isn't possible, necessary, or safe. But you can always take responsibility for tending to the emotions that are still arising in you rather than repeating the pattern of pushing them away. That just keeps you stuck. Remember, "Forgiveness is giving up the hope that the past could have been any different." To end racism, we must accept what has happened in our lives and in our countries. That doesn't mean we don't seek reparations or accountability. It means that we let go of the attachment to those things for our own salvation. From that place, we can release—and realize that although what happened may not fit what we think "should" have happened—it did. And our useful participation in what happens next depends on us to not act from our shadow but instead to stand for the future that we want to create—together.

14

∞

Asking for Forgiveness

Learning to offer forgiveness is not enough. We must also learn how to *ask for forgiveness*. No matter how evolved you are, how much internal work you've done on yourself, or how committed you are to ending racism, *you will make mistakes*. You will say the wrong thing, unintentionally harm someone, and act out of your shadow. In those moments you need to know exactly how to process the experience in a way that opens a door to the opportunity for repair and allows for the poison of harm itself to be alchemized into the medicine needed for transformation. If you know how to practice forgiveness, wrongdoings can become great gifts. Just like offering forgiveness, asking for forgiveness requires you to give up the hope that the past could've been any different, but it also does something more. It frees you from the grip of shame, guilt, and regret. Asking for forgiveness is always your most powerful move, even if another person has a role to play in the harm (which they often do). Asking for forgiveness requires vulnerability, truth, an awareness of your emotions, and understanding your shadow. This is why we couldn't teach it to you until now.

There are five core elements that will help us on the journey of asking for forgiveness. Some of these elements we have control over, others we don't. To be clear, the five don't need to happen in a particular order per se, but enacting all five elements is key to creating space for the possibility of the best possible outcome. As you read these five elements, you may become eager to start the forgiveness process right away, so at the end of this chapter we created a special forgiveness practice for you so that you can apply the five elements directly to your life. *Don't start calling or texting or taking any actions prematurely.* The practice at the end of this chapter will guide you through taking action in a proven way. Let's start with the concepts.

The Five Core Elements of Asking for Forgiveness

1. Speak the Truth

Take everything you learned in chapter 3 about the "truth" versus the "story" and get clear on the facts of the situation at hand. *What happened?* Detach the truth from the stories you've made up about what happened. Keep it simple by first only stating the assertions, not the assessments. This will help you get clear on the situation itself. Remember, the facts are simple, plain, unarguable, and verifiable by any source—for example, "This law was passed," "Jill said this," or "I slammed the door"; not "She didn't like the way I said that," "I know he was thinking this," or "The law that passed is terrible." Start with the verifiable facts.

2. Own Your Emotions

Forgiveness is intrinsically emotional. So, while the facts are important, the process of asking for forgiveness falls flat without a recognition of emotions. To effectively ask for forgiveness, you must create a space of vulnerability. That requires you to use everything we've been practicing about emotions. Remember to *own your emotions.* You can't blame your emotions on another person or situation. While your emotions may have caused you to act in a certain way, they are no one's fault. No one forced you to feel that way. Your emotions are yours. Name them. Own them. Sit with them. Claim them as your responsibility. You're familiar with how to do this now, but if you need a review, go back to the emotions wheel in chapter 4.

3. Be Accountable for Your Side of the Street

Similar to claiming your emotions, asking for forgiveness beckons you to take accountability for cleaning up your side of the street *without pointing to the other person's mess on their side of the street as you do it.* Often people limit their forgiveness by making it conditional on the other person "owning their part." We've all heard people say some version of "I'm sorry I hurt you, but it wouldn't have happened if you didn't mess up first." Asking for forgiveness should never include the word *but.* You don't have control over someone else's choice to take accountability for their actions, so let that go. In fact, the best way to get someone else to clean up their side of the street is to inspire them by taking full accountability for yours.

4. Offer Atonement

The fourth core element of offering forgiveness is atonement. We'll spend a little more time on this one because while forgiveness itself has become somewhat of a lost art, the art of *atonement* is arguably extinct. To begin with, many people don't know what atonement is or that there is a fundamental difference between forgiveness and atonement. The meaning of these terms is often entangled and unclear, but both are essential for us to end racism.

Forgiveness in its simplest form is an exercise of liberation, of setting yourself free. For example, you can forgive me whether or not I offer an apology, and thus you are free. Atonement, on the other hand, requires that we work to restore the relationship to the original state or ideally to a better state. If we spill red wine on a friend's white couch, we can apologize and be forgiven. However, the apology and forgiveness don't remove the stain. Atonement takes the act of seeking forgiveness one step further, into a state of repair. For example, we may hire a cleaning service to remove the stain or buy them a new couch.

Sometimes, though, an actual repair is not possible. But this does not absolve us from the most important part of atonement—the inner work of repairing the relationship with ourselves. The author and teacher Marianne Williamson says that atonement is "the place where you yourself acknowledge where you have been wrong and you ask for that correction of your own perception."[1] It's an "inner reconciliation," where we realize where we went wrong, own it, deeply feel the emotions and understand the toll, and then proceed to first ask for a correction *in our own heart* as a part of offering an apology to someone else.

An example of inner reconciliation can be found in a previous chapter, where Justin shared a story of the cleaning service who used to come to his uncle's home and his family calling all cleaning staff "Lupe." When Justin realized that he used that name in a derogatory and hurtful way (even though his friend did not catch on to it or feel offended), his moment of personal atonement was in the full-stop recognition about what happened, sitting with the emotions he was feeling (shame, disappointment), the promise he made to himself to never repeat that phrase again intentionally, and the understanding that if he did, he would use it as a teaching to help others learn why it was wrong. Justin's atonement process included both the recognition of what he did wrong and an active pursuit to use the wrongdoing in service of doing more good, working toward correcting the perception of how he was conditioned.

Atonement is asking for a correction of our own spirit so that you heal the root of whatever caused the harm in the first place. Sometimes you can include the person who you wronged; sometimes you can't. You never have control over whether someone accepts your offer for atonement, but you can always have control of the correction that happens within yourself.

5. Let Go

This final core element requires that we surrender, trust, and have faith that if we've shown up and made a heartfelt, authentic attempt at forgiveness and atonement, that all will fall into place as it needs to. Once you've shared in an authentic way, *you must release and let go and give the other person permission to respond as they wish*. This can be quite challenging because you do not have control over how someone responds to your apology. Many of us manipulate the truth during an apology to try to elicit a certain response or reaction. Don't waste your time apologizing if you're not going to own it and tell the truth. If you release control and whatever expectations you have of the outcome, you can focus on the only thing that's important—creating an opportunity for healing. **Even if the healing doesn't happen between you and the other person, it can still happen within you,** so show up as fully as you can. Here is a phrase you can latch on to and repeat to yourself, reaffirming your journey forward, when you find yourself in an opportunity of forgiveness: "From this moment on, I release all shame, guilt, anger, and resentment. From this moment on, I completely let go."

Asking for forgiveness does not rely on your being able to actually talk to the other person. Whenever that is possible or safe, we recommend it, but that's not always realistic. Ultimately you are doing this process *for you.* You are of no good to the greater society if you're stuck in the trap of your unforgiven moments. Remember that the best version of the world starts with the best version of you; thus, you are doing this process for the greater good, ensuring that what's left unforgiven doesn't stay in the shadow as unresolved wounding, continuing to control your actions and emotions. Sometimes the biggest act of forgiveness is being able to *forgive yourself.* This process, more than anything, helps you show up as a healed version of yourself. Your work toward ending racism can't be colored by your unhealed wounding. Forgive.

> If we can only name the feet that are situated on our necks,
> but fail to name and recognize the ways our feet are situated
> on someone else's neck, we will never, ever be free.
>
> —DARNELL L. MOORE[2]

In one way or another, each of us has had our feet on someone's neck at some point. Quoting the author and activist Darnell L. Moore, we are referring to the places that we have oppressed or marginalized someone, whether it's somebody of our race or somebody of a different race, background, persuasion, identity, or ability. Our ability to recognize where we have caused harm or where we are still doing it is a skill that can always be sharpened. One of the safest ways that we have found to approach this difficult and sometimes messy topic is through writing a "forgiveness letter." We've compiled a template that has been honed over the years and modified through input and feedback. It builds upon the prerequisite shadow work you've done and encompasses all five core elements of asking forgiveness.

You will feel as you're writing this letter that you are first and foremost processing the experience for yourself. Whether you choose to have a conversation based upon what you find is up to you (we'll give you some tips for that later). For now, focus on writing the letter *for you*. It's important for your first draft that you give yourself space to process your thoughts and anchor into what's true without the intention of anyone else ever reading it. Before you begin writing, ask yourself, "If I wasn't holding back and I could say anything I wanted to say without any consequences, what would I say?" In other words, if you were being less polite, less worried about hurting someone's feelings, and not worrying about any consequences, what would you say?

First, get out the most authentic version of what you need to say to process the experience for yourself. Then if you consider sending the letter to the person you wrote it to and they are able to receive it, you can go back and edit it. Writing the letter is, first and foremost, intended to assist with *your process*—it creates a possibility that a release can happen in your own heart first. If you decide to take this a step further and have a discussion, you have already clarified your own internal experience.

While you can write the letter to anyone about any topic, start by writing a letter that's related to your involvement (regardless of how large or small) in enacting racism, prejudice, discrimination, or othering. The letter can be addressed to someone who is still alive or someone who is deceased, someone you know well or someone you barely know, a person who you've had recent communications with or a person that you haven't spoken to in years. You are writing this letter with the hopes that you can practice asking for forgiveness and atoning for any harm you've caused that would prohibit you from ending racism. If you want to come back again and do a second letter about other topics, you can.

Inner Work

Read the template. Then read the examples. Then write your own letter using the template as a guide.

For a printable version of this exercise, go to HowWeEndedRacism.com/resources.

Forgiveness Letter Template

Dear ________________,

I feel __________________ (emotion) reading/sending this letter to you/telling you this, but I also know it's necessary because ______________________________________.

When I ______________________. *(What did you do?)*

OR

Here's what happened/Here's what I did wrong ______ ____.

(Just state the facts, plain and simple, no sugarcoating.)

What else I need you to know about this moment that I'm most afraid of telling you is ___________________.

What I believed *(about myself/about the world/about life)* then was ____________________________________.

And I did this because _______________________. This is not an excuse for my actions but the ___________ ________________ mindset I was working with at the time, and I think it's important you have that context.

Today I feel _________________ about this moment. *(What do you feel about the moment, about what you did?)*

Knowing that I caused you this harm makes me feel _____ ____.

(What do you feel about the fact that you caused harm to this person in particular?)

I've held on to this for __________________ because I was afraid that __________________. What I really want you to know is that you are ____________________ *(something honoring)* and you did not deserve ____________________ .

I want to apologize from the deepest place in my heart that I ____ .

If we are going to have any sort of meaningful connection moving forward, I want you to be able to make a decision to engage with me or not based upon the truth.

OR

I'm telling you this now to bring us closer, not to tear us apart.

OR

I know we haven't spoken in a very long time, so I know this might seem random.

Since this happened, I've ____________________________ .
(How have you taken greater responsibility for yourself? What work have you done on yourself? Have you changed?)

But I also want to open the space to ask you now: Is there anything I can do to make this better/right?

My wish is ______________________________________ .
However, I know that you may never want to do that after reading this, so I want to wish you ______________________ ______________________________ and I want you to know that ____________________________________ .

If it would feel good to discuss more or if you have any questions, I am very open to that.

I wanted to tell you this in person, but I knew my fear would get in the way of communicating clearly, so I'm writing to you this way.

I am so sorry. I apologize. And I hope that you will forgive me.

With great sincerity and a hope for healing,

__________________________ *(your name)*

To illustrate how the letter works, here are a few examples of forgiveness letters from our students.

(1) The Situation: Mrs. K is an honors teacher who removed a student from her class because she felt he wasn't ready to be an honors student. She later realized she only advocated for him to be removed because of her shadow and unconscious bias and that he should've stayed in her class. This student was in her class seven years ago. Mrs. K says she has thought about this nearly every day since.

Dear Alec,

I feel embarrassed sending this letter to you, and maybe a little apprehension, but I know it is necessary because I did not value your opinion, voice, or needs when I moved you out of my class in the first few weeks of your high school experience. I inaccurately pushed for you to be moved, away from your friends, safety net, and a supportive environment without fully researching and confirming your academic abilities in the way that I should have, and I was wrong. What I need you to know about this moment that I'm most afraid of telling you is that before I came to work at your school, I was at an almost all-white school and still had a lot of learning to do. What I believed then was that my long teaching history allowed me to make instant assessments about students at first glance without having to look deeper or take the full picture into account. All of my assumptions were biased and wrong. This is not an excuse for my actions but indicative of the fixed mindset and the internalization of white supremacy culture in school settings I was working with at the time, and I think it is important you have that context.

Today, I still feel so angry at myself and ashamed of myself. Knowing that I caused you this harm makes me feel extreme guilt. I have held on to this for seven years because I was afraid that addressing it and acknowledging my failure would become your burden. I was also afraid that I would have to acknowledge that the impact of my choices that day deeply hurt you and made you feel disposed and cast off. I failed to acknowledge the impact of my actions. What I really want you to know is you are so brilliant and dynamic. That your emotional safety and well-being in an academic setting should have been prioritized. You deserved a champion, and I failed to be one. I want to apologize from the deepest place in my heart that I made a decision for you that negatively impacted you.

I know we haven't talked in a long time, so this might seem random. Since this happened, I have made sure that I am at the table during student placement meetings to ensure that students who look like you and that share a similar academic profile are not misplaced and moved down in course selection because of biases rather than abilities. I also have earned a whole degree specifically focusing on the barriers for Black and Brown students to access higher education and have begun working in a coalition of teachers to help Black and Brown students thrive in school. In each of these moments I have thought about you and what might have been if I paid closer attention to you when I should have. But I also want to open the space to ask you if there is anything I can do specifically to make this better or right, and I will.

My wish is that this moment did not negatively impact how you saw yourself in an academic setting, nor did it deter you from reaching whatever dream you had for your life. I wish I could validate your feelings in ninth grade and your experience once you left my class. I know that you may never want to do that after reading this, so I want to wish you success and confidence in your absolute inherent brilliance. If it would feel good to discuss more, or if you have any questions, I am very open to that. I wanted to tell you this in person (and thought about it every day I saw you in the hallways for four years), but my fear always got in the way of communicating clearly, so I am writing to you this way.

I am so sorry that I did not show up for you the way I like to believe I show up for students and that I was in such a clouded space when you were in my classroom. I was not the adult you needed. I am so sorry, I apologize, and I hope that you will forgive me.

With great sincerity and a hope for healing,

Mrs. K

(2) The Situation: Sunny is as Chinese American man who was adopted from an orphanage in China. He has not talked to his parents in many years.

Dear Mom and Dad,

I feel ashamed and scared sending you this letter, but I also know it's necessary because for too many years, I have not treated you kindly or appreciated all of the sacrifices you made for me and opportunities you provided me with after my adoption.

When I consistently lashed out at you and blamed you for everything that was wrong in my life, I was mistaken. I was using you both as scapegoats because you were easy targets to lash out at. Therefore, I took all of my anger out on you.

What else I need you to know about this moment that I'm most afraid of telling you is that I never felt like I fit in, regardless of how well you and the rest of our family treated me. Being the only Asian in a family of white Americans, I always felt inferior and out of place. The pain I felt extended beyond just our household and family dynamics and was carried with me into my relationships with friends, into the classroom, and eventually into my adult relationships and professional life.

What I believed then was that I was inferior. I believed that you all also saw me as inferior, even though I know this wasn't true. This pervasive feeling of inferiority always made me feel like an outsider—even in our most intimate and loving family moments. Over time, this feeling of inferiority morphed into feelings of anger. I blamed you both for adopting me into a home where nobody looked like me, nobody provided me with access to my heritage or culture, and where I was always the odd man out. This seething feeling of anger eventually morphed into rage, directed at everyone but mainly directed at you, Mom and Dad.

I did this because I thought that making you feel inferior would make me feel better. However, I realized that causing you pain and suffering didn't ease any of mine. I know this is hard to hear.

This is not an excuse for my actions but the unevolved and disassociated mindset I was working with at the time, and I think it's important you have that context.

Today I feel ashamed and sad about these moments. I feel this way because I know that I squandered many opportunities for joy and connection with the people who loved me most—you two. I know that I can never get those moments back, and that breaks my heart.

Knowing that I caused you this harm makes me feel remorseful. I look at you both now, my aging parents, and I know that you did the best you could for me—for all of us. I know that you adopted me from a pure place of love and the desire to give me opportunities that I would otherwise have never had, had I stayed in that orphanage in China.

I've held on to this for the past few years because I was afraid that you would not forgive me for the harm I have caused you and the rest of the family. I was scared that the damage to our relationship was irreparable.

What I really want you to know is that you are both brave, that you were actually wonderful parents to me and to my sisters, and that you did not deserve to be treated with such disrespect and vitriol.

I want to apologize from the deepest place in my heart that I ever made you feel like you were not good parents to me or that I did not appreciate all that you provided me with. I know we haven't spoken in a very long time, so I know this might seem random. Since my wife got pregnant with our first son, I've taken a deep, hard look at myself. I have known for a long time that I needed to go to therapy and work through my anger and inferiority complex. I connected to my native culture and roots and realized that, even then, among people who "looked like me," I felt inferior. Now that I am going to be a dad myself soon, it is important to me that I never pass this toxic feeling and these patterns of behavior to my own son. With the love and the guidance of my incredible partner, I have been able to make changes in my life that I never thought were possible and I have been able to feel deep connection that—after much therapy—I realized was not a foreign feeling to me after all. Why? Because that connection was available to me in our house growing up and modeled for me by you, my sisters, my grandparents, and so many other people in our community.

I want to open the space to ask you now if there's anything I can do to make this right and to mend our relationship.

My wish is for my son to know his grandparents and for him to experience your love in a way that I never allowed myself to. I want for my wife to finally meet you, and to love and to honor you. And I want to be able to honor you and be there for you as you continue to grow old, to create new memories and to cherish old ones. However, I know that you may never want to do that after reading this, so I want to wish you peace and freedom from suffering. I want you to know that you were incredibly loving parents and that I can see that clearly now, and I love you. If it would feel good to you for us to discuss this more or to meet in person, I will be in the city next month with my wife for the weekend. I would love to see you, to hug you, and to be with you.

I am so sorry. I apologize. And I hope that you will forgive me.

With great sincerity and a hope for healing,

Sunny

You'll notice how these letters—and the process of writing them—integrates *everything* we've learned thus far. Every element is included. We end racism not by never causing harm again but by knowing what to do when it happens, to create a space for greater integration. You are ready.

A Few Notes about Sending Your Letter

If you consider sending (or reading) your letter to the person you wrote it to and they are able to receive it, go back and edit it. The template is a guide to organizing your thoughts, but in most cases should not be the final letter. Remember, there's a way to speak your truth responsibly. Speaking your truth doesn't just mean saying whatever you want with no regard for the other person's feelings. Intensity is okay, but you must anchor the entire experience in love. Don't disconnect yourself from your heart when writing. Before sending or having a conversation with someone, a good approach is to have a trusted friend or colleague read your letter before you send it to look for any hidden shadow creeping in.

Consider having them read this and the previous chapters on forgiveness first, so they understand the process. Otherwise, your proofreader's shadow or tendency to hide from the truth might dissuade you from standing in truth. Consider your letter as *a gift* to the other person. The truth doesn't only set you free; it can set them free, too. Remember, you can only control your part of this exchange; don't attach yourself to a particular outcome. You may have hopes and ideas about how the situation turns out or what response the person might have after receiving your letter, but we recommend you let those expectations and ideas go so you can be accountable to respond to what *actually* occurs. You can intend for the best, but you need to remember that **forgiveness is "for giving."** Don't hold back. You are ready. Write!

15

Making Real Amends

Apologies are not amends. The making of amends is a long-term project where we prove to the ones we have harmed that we have honestly transformed and that we have done so permanently. By behaving differently going forward as a result of our amends, we prove that we have really atoned. Similarly, if we have truly forgiven someone for the harm they have caused us, making amends is our first step on the road to repair. If forgiveness is the internal process, amends is the external manifestation. Of course, making amends takes effort and humility. The choice we have, as we rewrite the future and heal the past, is that we can either remain disconnected or step forward on a new pathway together. **In the introduction, we referenced our experience of living with racism to be like inheriting an old house. When the house is falling apart and caving in, regardless of whether it's our direct actions that have caused the damage, it's our responsibility—and we would even argue that it is our moral obligation—to repair it.** We are the stewards of the metaphorical house. Even if the previous owners are the ones that caused the damage, *we live here now*. And if we don't repair it, the roof will fall down on all of us.

The term *reparation* is defined in the dictionary as "the making of amends for a wrong one has done, by paying money to or otherwise helping those who have been wronged."[1] However, the question of reparations is not primarily about money but rather offering up a form of *healing and action*—acknowledging that harmful, painful, and traumatic acts have long arms that stretch out across time and space, and then doing something to release their grip and prop up whoever was harmed. It is about recognizing that in the wake of these acts, there was (and is) additional pain and suffering that follows/followed in its wake. It is an attempt to marry forgiveness and atonement with the potential to try to make something whole again.

For example, everyone understands that if you've been in a bad relationship or have gone through a divorce, the effects of that relationship last well after the relationship is over. If that weren't the case, there would be no need for therapy, counseling, or divorce lawyers. Getting out of a toxic relationship can have effects on your trust, emotional stability, well-being, finances, and more for years to follow. The same is true for our collective relationship to one another. Yet the idea of reparations gets convoluted with more complexity than need be. We all know that after a traumatic experience, the only way for that experience to stop impacting our future is if we go through a process of repair. We can't undo what was done in the past. We can't make the past any different than what it was. We also can't "pay for" what was done. But we can balance out the effects of the harm that was caused. Most importantly, we can create a better opportunity for the future. **With reparations, we're repairing what was broken so the past harm isn't impacting the possibilities of the future as significantly.**

After World War II and Germany's loss, the country began to pay monetary reparations to survivors of the Holocaust. Jews (and other survivors and victims' family members of the concentration camps) would receive "compensation" from the German government for the harm that was done. Generally speaking, this amount was relatively small; and while many of the recipients certainly counted on that monthly money coming in, the biggest impact that the reparations had was that they were a physical act of repair and public recognition of the harm caused by the German people. It was an admission of fault and culpability and an action to fix it. "Saying" you acknowledge a harm is very different from *doing something about it.* Imagine if in a dramatic fit of anger, your ex-spouse burned down your house on the final day of your divorce. Your ex-spouse apologizing profusely can mean a lot, but buying you a new house means more when attached to that apology, and it communicates a different level of commitment to healing the relationship. The monthly reparation checks served as a symbol that atrocities were committed; it was a public acknowledgment and an action that helped open up the possibility to create a new future based on an agreed-upon truth.

Of course, no amount of money can erase the damage of the experiences in the concentration camps and the loss of life, bring back people's family members, or turn back time. But the "symbolic redress" by individuals who were not even necessarily *directly* responsible for these crimes against humanity helped to create a sense of spiritual closure as described by many of the victims. It provided a tangible testament that the record needed to be set straight. It offered a humane path not only for those who were victims but also for an entire nation shamed by their actions. In giving reparations, we both give to those who once *were* and bestow to those who *are still yet to come.*

Here are some other examples of reparations that have been paid after global harm was caused.

Rosewood, Florida: In 1923, the primarily Black town on the Gulf Coast of Florida was destroyed in a race riot that killed at least six Black residents and two white residents. In 1994, the state of Florida agreed to a reparations package worth around $4.23 million in the equivalent of 2022 dollars, of which $3 million would be set aside to compensate the eleven or so remaining survivors of the incident, $800,000 to compensate those who were forced to flee the town, and $160,000 would go to college scholarships primarily aimed at descendants.

Tuskegee Experiment: Between 1932 and 1972, the United States left 399 Black men with syphilis untreated to study the progression of the disease. In 1974, the federal government reached a $10 million out-of-court settlement with the victims and their families, which included monetary reparations and a promise of lifelong medical treatment for both participants and their immediate families.

Japanese Internment: The forced internment of 120,000 Japanese Americans in camps during World War II resulted in Congress making two attempts at reparations with the Japanese-American Claims Act of 1948 and the Civil Liberties Act of 1988. Between 1948 and 1965, the former authorized payments totaling $38 million (which comes to somewhere between $360 and $471 million in 2022), which didn't come close to matching the economic loss. The latter offered survivors $20,000 each in reparations (which would be the equivalent of $50,000 in 2022). By 1998, eighty thousand survivors had collected their share.

United Kingdom: The UK paid nearly £20 million to five thousand Kenyans who were victims of violence during the Mau Mau uprisings in the 1950s, reports the *Guardian*. The Mau Mau rebellion was a war between Kenyans and their former colonizer, the UK, in a bid for freedom.

Although it's uncertain if we will ever see reparations for slavery in the United States, as well as many of the world's other atrocities, each of us can apply this concept of reparations personally—at a level we can actually accomplish. When we stand in the future and ask, "What did we do today that brought about the end of racism?," we must become people who are skilled at making amends and creating repair. This way, when another atrocity or act of violence occurs in the world, we are the ones in charge, and we know how to turn the poison *into medicine*.

Inner Work

Use the following incomplete sentences to further explore in a deeper way, thinking about how you can take it a step further to make amends. Explore what it might take to actually make a repair.

- Someone who I have forgiven but have not truly made amends with is ______________________________.

- If I imagine an ideal future relationship with this person where things have been repaired to an even greater state than they were before, what I imagine is ______________________.
- A tangible action I can take today to move things in that direction is ______________________.
- Someone I have been forgiven by but have not truly made amends with is ______________________.
- If I imagine an ideal future relationship with this person where things have been repaired to an even greater state than they were before, what I imagine is ______________________.
- A tangible action I can take today to move things in that direction is ______________________.
- A community/group that my ancestors or I have caused harm to that is still in need of repair is ______________________.
- If I imagine an ideal future with this community where things have been repaired to an even greater state than they were before, what I imagine is ______________________.
- What I can do now is ______________________.

Here is a story from one of our workshops that exemplifies how we can make amends and engage in reparations.

To frame the story, here is some historical context: In May 1948, Israel was officially declared an independent state by the United Nations. Starting around the turn of the century and compounded by the Holocaust in World War II, social and political developments convinced Jews and eventually governing bodies/countries that they needed their own country. The ancestral homeland with biblical roots—at the time, the British-controlled colony of Palestine—seemed like the right place to establish a country. In addition to European Jews, many Jews from the Middle East and North Africa also started to arrive in the newly formed country, which caused a displacement of the Arab Muslims and Christians who had been residing there (in addition to other populations). A large segment of this population identifies as Palestinian.

This tends to be a very contentious topic, so without getting into the politics of what occurred or why, we want to share with you a story of one of our participants—who was born in Jerusalem in the 1960s to Jewish parents—who shared this story with us. "Jacob," an Israeli citizen, migrated to Canada with his parents and his sisters when he was five years old. He would visit his extended family throughout Israel every summer and was, in his words, "indoctrinated by my synagogue, Jewish day school education and community to believe that my home country, the country where my father fought two wars and my grandfather lost his life in the war in 1948, was never to be criticized." Growing up, Jacob described, he would stay with his uncle in an old neighborhood in Jerusalem in a home that was called, quite literally, an "Arab house," or *bayit aravi* in Hebrew. He quite honestly never thought of the roots of this terminology and just assumed it was an architectural reference.

As Jacob got older and attended university, he decided to enroll in a history class that taught about the Palestinian-Israeli conflict. In one of the classes, the professor showed a slideshow of houses that were similar to the one that his uncle lived in and told the students that up until the 1948 war, Arab families had been living in those neighborhoods and in those homes for generations. When the Jews/Israelis won the war and were granted that land by the United Nations, almost all of these Arab families were forcibly removed from their homes in a matter of days and sometimes hours. It was such a traumatic experience for the Palestinians that, to this day, the symbol of their movement is a key, or what they call a "right of return" key, with hopes that they will one day be able to return to their homes. Older generations of Palestinians still wear the keys of their old homes around their necks as a symbol of their plight and struggle, but also one of hope.

Jacob began to ask his uncle and his older family members more about the history of the house and what the circumstances were surrounding his family becoming the owners of it. What he learned by speaking to many of his family members, researching archives from the City of Jerusalem, and in speaking to neighbors was that the house was occupied and owned by an Arab family that was Muslim. One elder neighbor recalled that the family was very kind and had seven children and that one day they were "just gone."

Jacob was distraught to learn about his family's role in such an atrocity. Especially because his grandparents survived the Holocaust. He could not fathom that his grandfather and great uncle, once oppressed, could also be oppressors. This piece of his family history gnawed at him for many years. Several of his cousins (all of them still living in Israel) who were around his age or younger agreed with him—that it was reprehensible—but none of them felt that there was anything they could do about it. One of them told him that "the past is in the past," that "this is what happens in wars," and that he needed to just "move on." That wasn't enough for Jacob. He was not deterred and decided that it was important to him to at least try to find the family that was forcibly removed from their home at the hands of his family.

After almost two years of searching archives, public records, and speaking to dozens of individuals from Bethlehem to Jordan to France, Jacob eventually located a descendant of the original owner of the house, who was now living in a refugee camp within Palestinian territories. The family was incredibly apprehensive to engage with Jacob and answer any of his questions, so he decided to write them a forgiveness letter instead, using the same format you learned about in the previous chapter. It read:

Dear Family A:

I feel emotional and apprehensive sending this letter to you, but I also know it's necessary because my ancestors have done a lot of harm to your family and to your future descendants. I also know that it took me over thirty years to wake up to the harm that I was personally doing by not addressing it.

For the first eight years of my adulthood, when I was finally a conscious thinking and supposedly educated adult, I attended rallies in support of candidates that would further contribute to your systemic oppression, I voiced my support of apartheid on our land, and I blamed your family and ancestors for the death of my people. I was the head of a student organization at my university that directly contributed to your suffering and to the perpetuation of the rhetoric of hate and Islamophobia and Palestinian opposition.

What else I need you to know about this moment that I'm most afraid of telling you is that I think that the damage I have done and that my people have done is irreparable. I am afraid of my words being as hollow today as my actions were decades ago.

What I believed back then was what I was taught to believe—that you wanted me dead, that you wanted my people dead and eradicated. And I took all of these actions because I thought I was defending my life and the life of my people. This is not an excuse for my actions but to give you a sense of the fixed mindset I was working with at the time, and I think it's important you have that context.

Today I feel ashamed about this moment. Knowing that my family caused you harm before I was even born by literally stealing your home from you, and knowing that I once felt that they were in the right to do so and that I defended them for years, compounding this harm, makes me feel like a hypocrite.

I've held on to this shame because I was afraid that there is no road back to forgiveness.

What I really want you to know is that you are a victim of my ancestors and of my actions, that you are brave and courageous, that you are so strong and that you deserve more. Your children and grandchildren deserve a home and a future. You do not deserve to be living in this open-air confinement, in this refugee camp.

I want to apologize from the deepest place in my heart that it took me years to wake up, and to open my eyes and my heart, to understand the extent of the damage that has been caused and that is continuing to be caused.

I'm telling you this now to bring us closer, not to tear us apart. I want to support you and your family in meaningful ways that may never make up for the damage that was done or come close but that can help us create a dialogue and create shifts.

I want you to know that I've immersed myself in learning more about the oppression of the Palestinians at the hands of Israelis. I have volunteered in a Palestinian refugee camp for years and have brought dozens of other helpers with me to help open their eyes to your suffering. I have challenged my family on the false history they have shared. I have publicly spoken on behalf of your rights. I have raised funds for you toward the purchase of a new home—a real home—outside of the refugee camp. I know it won't be the home we stole from you, but it is a home you can will to your children and grandchildren.

My wish is to forge a friendship with you. However, I know that you may never want to do that after reading this, so I want to wish you peace; and I want you to know that I will not rest until your people have a homeland, you have a home again, and your children and grandchildren have access to opportunities and privileges that I did.

If it would feel good to discuss more or if you have any questions, I am very open to that.

I wanted to tell you this in person, but I knew my fear would get in the way of communicating clearly and that trust would get in the way of you accepting what I am saying to you, so I'm writing to you this way.

I am so sorry. I apologize. And I hope that you will forgive me.

Sincerely,

Jacob

Two weeks after receiving this letter, Jacob received a phone call from the descendant and began to establish a meaningful relationship. With the help of some of his cousins who rejoiced in this connection, Jacob was able to raise enough funds to help the family purchase property and build a new home. "While it didn't replace the home that my ancestors stole from them or take away the trauma that we inflicted, it created a path for healing and began to repair the holes in all of our hearts." This is amends. This is reparation.

Pillar Seven

we had big conversations

16

Calling People Forward Instead of Out

W[illegible] [illegible] up to this point [illegible] have [illegible] your [illegible] for this [illegible] equipped to [illegible] and listen as you interact with others in the [illegible] pillars will [illegible] to build upon what we've [illegible] the focus to how this work can impact the world around us. This starts with conversation.

In the beginning was the Word. Language is the first pathway through which we [illegible] our vision for the world. Our words [illegible] [illegible] they almost always express our intention [illegible] in conversations [illegible] especially the difficult ones, [illegible] whether a moment becomes an opportunity for growth or [illegible] for more division. Division [illegible] begins with words [illegible] passed, actions are taken, and [illegible] to say something—but we have to [illegible] instead of [illegible]. The first way we call people forward is through [illegible] bigger and more productive conversations. The pillar [illegible] speaking and listening. In the [illegible] pillar, we prepared [illegible] many of the supportive foundations that are helpful [illegible] we step into [illegible] in the moment.

As [illegible] needed is one of the [illegible] [illegible]

16

∞

Calling People *Forward* Instead of Out

We have just crossed a threshold—forgiveness. The pillars leading up to this moment (truth, emotions, shadow, and forgiveness) have prepared you internally to *become* someone who is equipped to end racism as you interact with others in the world. The forthcoming pillars will continue to build upon what we've learned thus far, shifting the focus to how this work can intersect the world around us. This starts with *conversations*.

"In the beginning was the Word."[1] Language is the first pathway through which we bring our vision into the world. Our words start everything. They almost always supersede our actions. Our ability to engage in conversations skillfully, especially the difficult ones, differentiates whether a moment becomes an opportunity for growth or the impetus for more division. Division or connection begins with words. Laws get passed, actions are taken, and situations change *because someone decided to say something—and knew* ***how*** *to say it effectively so their communication inspired action.* The first way to call people forward is through having bigger and more productive conversations. This pillar has two components: speaking and listening. In the forgiveness pillar, we prepared you with many of the supportive foundations that are helpful here, but this is where we step up our game to end racism in the moment.

As we've discussed, language is one of the primary ways we coordinate our experience of reality. But language is not just about *what* we say; it's also about *how* we say what we say. There are certain ways of saying things that will assuredly lead to certain outcomes. This requires us to hold a high level of integrity—remaining centered in truth, faith, and vision—as we approach the teachings on conversations. You are going to affect people's lives as you apply the lessons and techniques you'll learn here. Most people want to begin their journey with conversations—they want to be provided with an instant road map detailing "what to say" and "what to do." Hopefully you see now that starting this book with conversations as the first pillar could have never worked because the shadow energy beneath our words and actions have too great an influence and would regenerate the same patterns.

Before we go any further, we want to take a moment to anchor you in your vision once more. Take a brief moment to review what's important to you as it pertains to ending racism. It may have shifted a bit, given all you've learned. Please take that moment now. Imagine you are in the year 2050 and racism has ended—imagine a future world without racism. What arises for you this time? What do you notice? Slow down, take a few breaths, and see what comes to mind, even if it's changed from before. Whatever comes through is fine, just bring it as clearly into focus as possible. Imagine a future world without racism. Once you're done having an experience with your vision, answer these prompts:

- The main thing I noticed in my vision of a world without racism was ______________________________.
- What excites me most about the vision is ______________.
- For this vision to come true, what I need to cultivate in my life now is ______________________________.
- For this vision to come true, what I need to release from my life now is ______________________________.
- For this vision to come true, who I need to become is ____.

- I am on a journey of ______________________________.
- I am *fighting for* ______________________________.
- I am ______________________________.

Anchoring into your vision has been important throughout this book, but it becomes even more *central* to everything we're going to teach you next. With the tools you've learned, you have arrived at the point of transformation. If you've been doing the work, we want you to know that from this point on, you're ready.

The first conversation skill we want to teach you is the difference between *calling forward* and *calling out*. Standing in the future, we can look back and see that one of things we had to collectively affirm is that *we are done with calling people out*. Calling out leads to cancel culture; cancel culture is ineffective and divides us further. Today we have to commit to graduating beyond that perspective to move in the direction of our vision, so we can stop *fighting against* racism and finally *end racism*. This pillar will help you learn how to have big conversations where you see or experience someone acting from a state that is causing harm.

First, let's make some distinctions. In today's culture, *calling out* means publicly naming a wrong, an infraction, or a mistake; *calling in* means naming it privately. The problem with either approach is that both typically get infused with shame, blame, and guilt. It's well documented in studies in the fields of psychology, anthropology, sociology, and even neuroscience that **shaming, blaming, and guilting someone shuts down the center of their brain responsible for learning and growth**.[2] Thus, regardless of how much a person meditates or prays, or how emotionally or spiritually evolved they believe they are, if you use the tactics of shame, blame, and guilt, it blocks the ability for the person you are speaking with to actively listen, it stunts the capacity for them to learn, and it eliminates any opportunity for growth. We've all experienced this resistance. Think of the last time your partner or a family member said something that triggered you. Regardless of how "right" or "rational" they were, once you were activated by shame, blame, or guilt, all bets were off—you likely ended up *reacting*.

You can usually only come back to the same conversation and see things more clearly after having some time to "cool off," because your brain has had a chance to regulate. After regulation, we hear things differently; we can see the other side of a perspective and think from a logical place that is responsive rather than reactive. In our movement to end racism, we must not use shame, blame, or guilt—*no matter what*. Yes, we really mean *no matter what*. No matter how horrific you think the circumstance is, if you want the situation to transform, shame, blame, and guilt are off the table.

Here are two questions you can ask yourself as a litmus test prior to having a difficult conversation: Do I want to "be heard" or do I want to *be effective*? Do I want to create a bridge or widen the divide? Prior to each interaction, you must be brutally honest with yourself about your true intentions because it will impact the outcome of the conversation dramatically. If you are not ready to show up to the conversation without shame, blame, and guilt, you might want to reconsider speaking at all. To end racism, we must use our language to move us in the direction of our vision.

Another part of "calling out" and "calling in" that is rarely discussed is the fact that both of these acts presuppose that the person who is doing the "calling in" or the "calling out" is right; that the person using these tactics is morally superior and that they have the authority to correct another person. This is precisely the reason that we need to be grounded in truth and commit to understanding pillar 2—the difference between stories and facts. **If you think *your story* is "the truth," then it leaves no room for understanding, discussion, or conversation.** It is binary thinking all over again, requiring the person you are disagreeing with to immediately conform to your thinking and behavior.

Calling forward is a model of communication that we coined several years ago that flips the idea of "calling out" and "calling in" on its head, turning it into something more effective for bringing people together and ending racism. While "calling out" or "calling in" is fighting against what someone did wrong, *calling forward is an invitation to be something greater.* While calling out/in is fighting against what we hate, *calling forward* is building upon what we love. *Calling forward* is inviting people into a greater state of integration and evolution. *Calling forward* opens the door to real transformation, and we've found that the outcome—although not always immediate—is often surprising.

You can call anyone forward, but it doesn't mean they're going to immediately walk toward you. Remember, they may not have the tools yet to do so. When using the model we are about to share, often an opening happens where there once was none.

Use the Ten Essential Steps to Calling Forward the next time you need to have a difficult conversation—specifically when you want to address someone for contributing to the perpetuation of prejudice, discrimination, racism, and othering. Stand in the center of what you believe: that racism can and will end, and that you yourself have the power to end it. When we stand in the future and ask, "What *did* we do today?" *calling forward* became a widely adopted skill that we all had the capacity to learn. It starts with you.

The Ten Essential Steps to Calling Forward

We created the Ten Essential Steps to Calling Forward, as well as the Calling Forward Script, for you to always have handy and to prepare you for your next difficult conversation. Once you learn and practice the skill, it will become natural to you and you will be able to have these conversations without referencing the script or the book. Use these tools anytime you feel someone has done something wrong or immoral, caused a harm, or acted in a way that disintegrates the fabric of Mwe. As with any conversation, you don't have control of what the other person does or says, but *you do have control over yourself—how you choose to respond and how you show up*. These ten steps will prepare you for the best possible outcome. Read the ten steps first, then put it into action using the script.

Calling Forward

Step 1: Center In Your Vision

Step 2: Drop Your Stories

Step 3: Imagine That This Person's Actions Were Coming from a Place of Care, Concern, and Love

Step 4: Prepare the Space

Step 5: Own Your Feelings

Step 6: Create a Space of Connection and Compassion

Step 7: Paint the Picture of the Vision

Step 8: Don't Wait Until It's Too Late

Step 9: Don't Arrive with All the Solutions

Step 10: Don't Attach Yourself to a Specific Outcome

Step 1: Center In Your Vision

Calling forward is, more than anything, *an invitation to something greater.* But you can't invite someone forward if you have no idea where forward is or what you are moving toward. It's important to always know what you are moving toward before you set off on your journey—that is what the collective vision of ending racism is for. That is the finish line. You can ask yourself a few questions while clarifying what you are moving toward: What type of world do I want to live in and how do people in the world treat one another? What *values* are central to this world? What do I see as possible in a world without racism? Now, before you have any conversations, you must remember that the highest possible outcome is that the other person not only sees and acknowledges the mistake they made and harm they caused but also joins you in an elevated state of consciousness. You must approach this conversation from a place of *inviting them forward into something you love*, not just as an opportunity to call out/in what they did wrong.

Stand in the future, orient yourself toward the vision of the world you want to (co)create, and choose your actions based upon what in the future you would do. If you were standing in the future, where your vision had come true and the person you are going to be speaking with is a part of your vision, how would you handle the conversation and speak in way that *took you forward* toward that vision? (That's why it's called *calling forward*). Anchor into this deeply before the conversation even begins. This is key. Otherwise you risk being on the attack from the first sentence.

Step 2: Drop Your Stories

This is hard for many people because we believe so deeply in the assessments and stories we've made up in our heads about people and situations that we don't leave space for anyone to show up differently. We shut the door before they even round the corner. Our stories can block opportunities for connection because they convince us that the preconceived stories we've made up in our heads about a person (or the type of person they are) are true before the conversation even begins. Like fear and faith, *you have to believe in what's possible*. If you don't, the conversation is doomed from the start.

Remember that we tend to default to assessment-making. Thinking things like "I can't trust her," "He isn't the brightest person," "This isn't going to go well," or "People of that gender always do this" is something that we are hardwired to do. Pause before the conversation starts and get clear on the assessments that are going on in your mind. Those assessments may hinder the success of the conversation. Ask yourself, "What are the stories I'm making up, and what are the facts?"

Remaining committed to understanding the origins of our assessments can ground us in a space that staves off reactivity and allows us to be responsible for our biases and beliefs about how things "should" be. ***You may not get rid of all of your biases, but you can be responsible for them so they don't control you.***

Step 3: Imagine That This Person's Actions Were Coming from a Place of Care, Concern, and Love

Even if the person you are speaking with did something you believe is wrong, you cannot approach the conversation from a place of them being a "bad person." Otherwise you'll only speak to and activate the place within them that causes harm (and immediately begin with shame and blame). Every person has within them the capacity for "good" and "bad." You want to prepare yourself to speak to the best part of a person and calling *that best part of them* forward. You do this by trying to imagine yourself in their shoes. This can be incredibly difficult, but here's a trick: Ask yourself, "*If* I forced myself to assume this person's actions were coming from a place of care, concern, and love, then why might they have done what they've done?" Most people are not intentionally trying to cause harm. However, for the purposes of this step, it doesn't really matter. This step of the process is *to prepare you to show up for the conversation* as open, grounded, and clear as possible. This step is an essential part of that process.

Step 4: Prepare the Space

Preparing for difficult conversations is like planning a dinner party. It is not acceptable to invite your guests at the last minute to your fancy dinner party and expect them to show up ready to meet your expectations. You must invite people ahead of time, prepare the menu and food, and set the table. You prepare the space. So, too, must we prepare the space for difficult conversations. Often we've spent hours or even days ruminating and preparing ourselves to have a difficult conversation without giving the other person the opportunity to do the same—often springing the conversation upon the other person unexpectedly without giving them a chance to *prepare to listen*. Getting unexpected feedback is hard for all of us. You may have spent hours mustering up the courage to call someone on the phone, finally ready to spill your heart out, while they may be walking through the grocery store or just getting off a really tough call with their boss, or simply at their wits end and unable to access their heart to listen to you at that time.

A simple way to solve this is by sending the person a message or giving them more than a moment's notice that you want to have a conversation about something important. A message saying, "Hey, I'd love to talk to you about something important. Can you chat after work?" or "Do you have the capacity and space to have a discussion at the moment? It's about something a little sensitive" makes a world of a difference. If the wrongdoing happens in the heat of the moment—for example, in a meeting with other individuals—you might say, "After the meeting is over, I'd love to speak with you about this for a few minutes." More often than not, this is better than letting your emotions take over and flipping out in the middle of the meeting. The primary reason you are doing this is so that when you are ready to speak with that person, they are as ready as they can be to listen. You are inviting them into a conversation.

Step 5: Own Your Feelings

We've covered this at length throughout the book, but we need to take it a step further with the concept of *calling forward.* Every *calling forward* conversation must begin with the words "I feel . . ." If you start the conversation with "You . . ." then you're already down a path to shame, blame, and guilt. As much as we like to blame others, the way we choose to respond is no one else's choice or fault but ours. Regardless of what another person says or does, you own (and are responsible for) your reaction. In these types of conversations, own and name the truth of your emotions first and foremost, and share those emotions with the person you're speaking with. For example, "I felt hurt and insignificant after the conversation that just happened in the boardroom, and I want to share how affected I am by this." Notice the word *you* isn't in that sentence at all. Calling forward starts with *yourself, not the other person.*

Step 6: Create a Space of Connection and Compassion

Creating connection and compassion starts with you being vulnerable. Vulnerability is not weakness—it's your greatest strength, especially in these kinds of conversations. How do you build a space of vulnerability and connection? You begin with sharing your emotions. This is why step 5 (own your feelings) is so important. As soon as you open your heart and allow yourself to be seen emotionally, a space of compassion and vulnerability can be created. For transformation to occur in the most effective way, connection and compassion *must* be cultivated. Remember, it's unlikely that the person you're speaking with will know these steps. Therefore, *you are responsible* for creating and holding the space of compassion yourself and inviting them to meet you there. You already know how to do this. We've practiced it in the previous chapters about emotions and forgiveness. The person you are speaking to may not accept your invitation, but the possibility of them accepting it will never happen if you don't extend the invitation to begin with. As the author and photographer Doe Zantamata once offered, "It's easy to judge. It's more difficult to understand. Understanding requires compassion, patience and a willingness to believe that good hearts sometimes choose poor methods."[3] Judgment leads to separation. Understanding leads to transformation.

Step 7: Paint the Picture of the Vision

Imagine trying to invite someone to a beautiful vacation on a tropical island but only showing them pictures of a volcano erupting or crime, destruction, and violence among the locals. This is what many of us do when we call someone out/in. Don't focus the bulk of the conversation on everything they did "wrong." Instead, describe the world they could be living in *with you* if they chose different actions. Remember, we must remain committed to moving toward solutions rather than continuing to identify and analyze issues. Be specific in your descriptors. Paint a picture of what kind of things we would see in that world. How would people feel? What do you value in your vision? An example would be: "Uncle Dan, it feels so exciting to me to imagine a world where everyone is safe enough to know that they can love who they want without restriction or fear. Where they can walk down the street and go into any restaurant and feel safe and accepted. Think about your grandkids—I know how much you love them. I have witnessed the way you deeply care for and love them. Wouldn't you want everyone to treat them that way, even if they made a choice to love someone different from what's considered status quo? I'm committed to making the world a kinder place, for us now and for our children."

Remember, you're *inviting them in*. A part of (if not most) of your conversation with this person should be painting the picture of the future you're inviting them into.

Step 8: Don't Wait Until It's Too Late

This is big. Most of us wait too long to have these conversations. By the time we do, we're so filled with resentment and fear that we can't find compassion even if we tried. When you notice something has become a problem for you, don't "wait until it happens again" to bring it up. Avoidance and denial only make things more difficult later. Have the conversation early, before the problem gets too big to handle later or before the other person has long passed.

Step 9: Don't Arrive with All the Solutions

We often approach these types of conversations with a premeditated idea of what we'd like the outcome to be, leaving no space for collaborative inquiry. If someone says or does something wrong, and you are hoping they rectify or fix it, the best solutions arise when both parties can explore ideas for solutions together. Otherwise, the person you're speaking with will feel like something is being *forced* upon them or that you are the moral cop—and that never works in the long run. It often reignites the pattern of shame, blame, and guilt all over again. Forcing your solution onto a person or trying to elicit an action that they aren't authentically on board to take leads to empty actions. We're playing a bigger game here. We're going for *transformation*—and that requires remaining open to the possibility that the road to the future you desire has many different doorways into the same room, not just one.

Step 10: Don't Attach Yourself to a Specific Outcome

Sometimes, even after your best efforts, the person you are speaking with is unwilling to or incapable of listening. That should not deter you from standing in your truth, oriented toward our collective vision, and remaining firm in what you believe in. **Think about all the times you've had to learn a lesson multiple times to finally "get it."** Give the person that same measure of grace. We know this can be hard to do when it appears the person is causing harm. Like a flow of water slowly but consistently carving stone, you never know which conversation is going to forge a new pathway forward. If you hold a space of compassion, care, and love, the person *may at least hear you*. It's not up to you how quickly they transform; it is, however, up to you to create a space where transformation is likely to occur based upon the energy you bring to the conversation. Sometimes people will surprise you. Sometimes they will disappoint you. None of that is up to you. Release yourself from having to control it.

You may notice that the Ten Essential Steps to Calling Forward are more about *you* than they are about another person. That's because you cannot take responsibility for what anyone else does, but you can *prepare yourself*. As a beacon of the end of racism, you are responsible for lighting the path for others, regardless of whether someone chooses to walk it with you.

You might be wondering what happens when someone tries to call *you* out, in, or forward for something you've done wrong. All the same steps apply. You get to show up as someone who is practiced and skilled at having these conversations, so that when shame, blame, or guilt arrive in your presence, they get transformed into something greater. Don't fall for the trap of people thinking they have the right or permission to use harmful tactics, even if you are the one who has caused harm. With all of these tools in your possession, you are well equipped to take greater responsibility, make the vision of ending racism a reality, and play a bigger game. Our culture's immune system needs healthy cells that can transform these moments into something greater. Be the one who takes the conversation to a new level.

Inner Work

This is a sample script for *calling forward*. Fill in the blanks to help you prepare for a conversation you might find challenging. Obviously a *conversation* is a two-way street, so you can't plan everything out; having a road map is still useful even if there are detours. This script can be used to help *prepare you and get you in the right mindset* to call someone forward, or it can be used as a letter to send someone. If you choose to send it as a letter, be sure to have a trusted friend proofread it in order to look out for the shadow, which tends to creep in.

For a printable version of this exercise, go to HowWeEndedRacism.com/resources.

Dear ________________________,

I feel ________________________ *(emotion)* sending you this but I want you to know it's from my heart, and I'm sending this to you now because I know ________________________ *(If you assumed the best in them, what would you believe to be true? For example, "I know you believe in love," "I know you believe in equality," or "I know it's important to you that people are treated with dignity and respect.")*

When ________________________ *(What happened; DO NOT start this sentence with "You"! For example, "When we were . . ." or "When I heard . . .")*, I felt incredibly

______________________________ *(emotion),* and I thought it was important that you knew.

The story I've made up about this in my head is ________ ______________________________ *(What is the negative thing you assumed to be true?),* and it's really upsetting because ______________________________.

I know it's possible that we can all live in a world where ____ ______________________________ *(Say a few sentences or more about the vision.).* It's really important to me that ______________. Are these things important to you too?

Although ____________________ really affected me ____________________, I hope that we can use this moment to rise up together to something greater. It would feel so ________________ if ________________. *(What is your request from them? What change are you hoping they make?)*

Optional: It's important to me to have you by my side as we create a world where ______________________________.

I hope you can feel my heart and compassion in this letter.

I'm sending this with a lot of ____________________, and in service of our deeper connection, growth, and healing.

Optional: If you have any more questions about this, or if you'd like to have a deeper discussion, please let me know and I'd be happy to talk.

Sincerely,

____________________ *(your name)*

You may fumble your way through this process at first. It's an entirely new way of being for most of us. No matter what, your main focus should be holding true to the central intention: *that you're inviting people into the possibility of something greater*. Remember, the most important thing about this letter is that it prepares *you* to have the conversation. We want you to strengthen your own *calling forward* muscle. Each repetition makes you stronger. To help you along in your process, we have provided a few *calling forward* preparation letters from our students. These will help you see how it works in context.

Letter 1: John is a gay white man in his thirties who has a mostly white group of best friends. He has a Black boyfriend he's been dating for a few months and needs to *call forward* one of his friends.

Dear Sam,

I feel anxious and afraid sending you this but I want you to know it's from my heart, and I'm sending this to you now because I care deeply about our relationship.

When I hear you making inappropriate jokes about Black people, I feel incredibly sad, hurt, and rejected, and I thought it was important that you knew.

The story I've made up about this in my head is that you're pretending to love and care about my partner but that secretly you might not like him because of the color of his skin, and it's really upsetting because you are one of my best friends. I'm afraid that you might say something racially insensitive in front of my partner and that it could cause irreparable damage or, worse, that you might really believe some of the things you are saying.

I know it's possible that we can all live in a world where no person should be mocked or treated differently because of the color of their skin. It's really important to me that we start to break some of these stereotypes that are simply not true. I want my partner to feel totally safe around and with us, like he is a part of our family. I love him, and I love you, and I don't want to risk or worry about him ever feeling ostracized because of who he is. Are these things important to you, too?

Although the jokes I heard really impacted me and I know I've been silent about them before, I'm learning and growing and I hope we can use this moment to rise up together to something greater. It would feel so valuable to me if we both decided to never put up with any of those kinds of jokes again.

It's important to me to have you by my side as we create a world where we can welcome diversity into our friend group and everyone feels safe always.

I hope you can feel my heart and compassion in this letter.

I'm sending this with a lot of tenderness and a big hug, and in service of our deeper connection, growth, and healing. If you have any more questions about this or if you'd like to have a deeper discussion, please let me know and I'd be happy to talk.

Sincerely,

John

Letter 2: Two family members across political divides.

Dear Stacey,

I feel disheartened sending you this but I want you to know it's from my heart, and I'm sending this to you now because I know that there is love between us. We grew up together, cousin.

When I was at Thanksgiving dinner this year at your house, I felt incredibly uncomfortable and sad, and I thought it was important that you knew.

The story I've made up about this in my head is that you and your family no longer love me, respect me, or want to be in my company, and it's really upsetting because I don't feel this way about any of you.

I know it's possible that we can all live in a world where we coexist and can have different opinions politically. I respect your decision to vote for whom you want and to subscribe to ideals that I do not agree with. For example, I do not agree with abortion and, as you know, I am a (responsible) gun owner. It's really important to me that my freedom to be who I am is respected. I want everyone to feel comfortable expressing themselves in a respectful environment, without feeling like they are less than or that they are not worthy. Is this important to you too?

Although that evening really impacted me for several weeks, I hope that we can use this moment to rise up together to something greater. It would feel so important to me if you and I can figure out a way to coexist together, and even eventually have conversations about these important issues without it escalating to the point where I feel like I am being attacked or diminished as a human. After all, this country was built on the ability to compromise and to have conversations that may be challenging but that ultimately lead to something that can work for everyone.

It's important to me to have you by my side as we create a world where everyone's freedom of expression is protected and where we can model kindness for our families.

I hope you can feel my heart and compassion in this letter.

I'm sending this with a lot of trepidation but hope, and in service of our deeper connection, growth, and healing. If you would like to have a deeper discussion about this, please let me know and I'd be happy to talk. I love you, cousin.

Sincerely,

Anne

Notice the next time someone says or does something that you feel is out of alignment with the vision of ending racism and watch what your tendencies are. Do you get silent? Passively agree? Pretend it didn't happen? Get aggressive? Are you a person who naturally speaks up when the time comes? Are you well versed in these kinds of conversations? In all cases, you now have a new tool. The only way this tool will work is if you use it. When we stand in the future where racism has ended, we know for sure that we are no longer calling people "out" or "in"—we are calling people *forward*. In our collective vision, this skill is cultivated in schools, workplace environments, and everyday life so that each of us becomes a master and contributes to moving the culture toward a vision that's better for us all—one where racism does not exist and where we can all thrive together.

It's time to have big conversations. *You are ready.*

17

Conversations Across Divides

When we stand in the future, where racism has ended, and ask "What did we do today?" one of the most important tools we acquired in our time is the ability to constructively talk across divides with people who have different opinions from us. Just because someone has a different opinion or belief system from you does *not* automatically mean that they need to be invited into something greater. It may simply mean that you see the world differently from one another and that you may have different values, opinions, and beliefs. Just because someone sees things differently from you does not always mean they need to be *called forward*. **In the old way of being, we get stuck surrounding ourselves with people who think and believe all the same things we do,** and we disown and disavow people who think differently. To end racism, our new culture **must learn to talk across divides**, which requires us to welcome people into our lives who think differently than we do. First, this must be done to make discourse possible. Then it must be done to generate solutions to create a better future for *everyone* involved (not just solutions that work for people "like" you).

In our study of *many* processes of communication for talking across divides, we found one of the best and most effective processes was created by Dr. David Gruder, an author and leadership consultant. We have tested his process with people in countries around the world and have seen time and time again that his methodology works. Everything we are teaching you in this section is our interpretation of Dr. Gruder's model as applied to ending racism.

The first thing you must do before trying to have a conversation about a topic that could potentially be divisive is to figure out if the other person is "talkable." Are they open to other perspectives even when they may disagree? Do they have the maturity to engage in a conversation without attacking you? Unfortunately, some people are *not* talkable. These are the people who are stuck in their paradigm and don't have the skill or desire to listen, nor to speak respectfully. They are not yet capable of being emotionally responsible for the energy they bring to the discussion. Untalkable people believe their personal story is the only truth and the *only* reasonable assessment, and they block all other stories under any circumstance. They will usually speak over you, interrupt you, and be degrading, rude, or dismissive in the process. Untalkable people are usually never untalkable because they're right but because they're excessively triggered. Their shadow is in control. When someone is speaking from their shadow, you will not be able to reason with them because their brain is hijacked and the brain centers responsible for learning and connection are shut down.

There are talkable and untalkable people on all sides of every issue. What stops us from having conversations across divides is that we usually take the worst qualities of the untalkable folks on the "other side" of the aisle and apply those as a stereotype to *every* person who shares the same beliefs. We say things like, "You can't talk to liberals. They're all [fill in the blank]," or "Trump supporters always [fill in the blank]." The truth is, however, that there are talkable people on all sides. We (Justin and Shelly) have met with and taught thousands of them, so we know from personal experience. Although there are extremes, we have *always* found *many* talkable people on every side of every issue across all of our work with people representing every kind of divide imaginable. So has Dr. Gruder.

There are a few important traits of talkable people. Although they may have strong and firm opinions, talkables leave room for the idea that the other party has a compassionate reason for their position that is not rooted in hatred or doubt, that there's genuinely a positive intention at the foundation of their point of view. Talkable people are generous listeners, even if their minds aren't going to be changed, and they are open to creating new solutions they haven't considered before. Here's the thing: when we assume *everyone* who thinks differently from us is untalkable, we miss the opportunity to create new solutions that are more diverse in perspective than any one side could come up with on their own.

So, how do you find out if someone is talkable or untalkable? ***You try to have a conversation.* If you see they're untalkable—stop.** Don't waste your energy. Trying to have a healthy conversation with someone who is untalkable is like hitting your head against a brick wall—the only person who comes out harmed is you. If you're harmed, you risk being so damaged and afraid that you decide to close yourself off to having these kinds of conversations in the future, and we need you.

Once you figure out if a person is talkable, you're in for an exciting time, because you get to begin Dr. Gruder's "SUSS It Out" process.

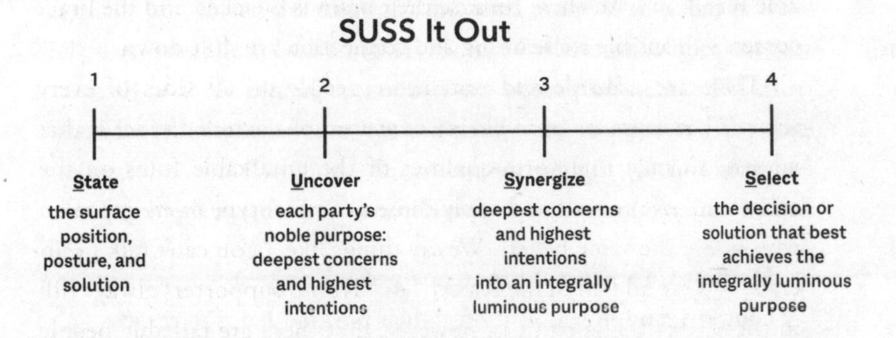
SUSS It Out
1
2
3
4
State
the surface position, posture, and solution
Uncover
each party's noble purpose: deepest concerns and highest intentions
Synergize
deepest concerns and highest intentions into an integrally luminous purpose
Select
the decision or solution that best achieves the integrally luminous purpose

Let's break down each part of the process step by step, with a real example from one of our in-person workshops at the Esalen Institute in Big Sur, California. As with many of our examples, we'll start with something other than race so that we can see the conversation from a vantage point we can all relate to, then we'll apply it to ending racism. These are *actual* responses from our group's conversation in 2021 surrounding one of the most divisive topics of the early twenty-first century: vaccination versus no vaccination (pro-vax vs. anti-vax) as it relates to the COVID-19 pandemic.

The "SUSS It Out" Process

SUSS stands for *State*, *Uncover*, *Synergize*, and *Select*.

Step 1: State Your Surface Position

Start every conversation by stating your surface position.

- In our example, one group's surface position was "I believe people should get the vaccine."
- The other was "I do not believe people should get the vaccine."

The surface position should be plain and simple. It's the foundational content of the situation at hand.

Step 2: Uncover Each Party's Noble Purpose, Deepest Concerts and Highest Intentions

We'll spend a little more time on this since it's usually the hardest step for people, especially when we are convinced that *our* story is the "truth." The main purpose of this portion of the process is to discover each party's *noble purpose*, which has two main elements: (1) deepest concerns and (2) highest intentions. The bulk of your conversation will be centered around these two elements. Let's break them down:

Deepest Concerns: What are the person's deepest worries and concerns, and how do they feel their position helps to resolve those concerns?

Highest Intentions: How does this person believe that their position can help move society forward in a positive, more integrated way?

Together, deepest concerns and highest intentions form the *noble purpose* and always illuminate what people care about most. It is from these elements that their position is born, because in their mind, they are doing something "right" and protecting or advocating for what's important to them. In the case of our example of pro-vaccination and anti-vaccination, our group had an interesting conversation.

- The pro-vax group's deepest concerns were: people with underlying conditions are at risk; our health-care systems are overloaded; more people will die if more people don't get vaccinated; they are afraid of death and illness; they do not want to get their loved ones and others sick.
- The anti-vax group's deepest concerns were: the vaccine's short- and long-term side effects are unknown; there is not enough long-term scientific evidence to prove the vaccine is safe; pharmaceutical companies are historically untrustworthy and are using the pandemic to make money instead of doing what's best for the people; the government (and pharmaceutical companies) has a history of dishonesty for political interest and so they are unwilling to take a risk as it relates to their health or their children's health; healthy people's immune systems will be worse off after getting the vaccine.
- The pro-vax group's highest intentions were: we should trust science; we have trusted science for previous medical issues, global pandemics, and other advancements in our lifetime with positive outcomes; we could protect the most vulnerable people in society by all getting vaccinated even if we are healthy; getting vaccinated is in the best interest of the collective good; the pandemic would end sooner if more people are vaccinated; unnecessary deaths will be avoided and we will have as many people healthy as possible.
- The anti-vax group's highest intentions were: people should have the freedom to choose what to do with their bodies when it comes to their health; we have other options for staying healthy that are not being explored; most people will survive COVID-19 and so people shouldn't be forced to make health decisions for a virus that has such a high survival rate; the government and medical industry should take actions to promote people's health and well-being outside of pharmaceutical drugs and Western medicine.

This is where the gold is. If we argue over surface positions ("People should get the vaccine" vs. "people shouldn't get the vaccine."), we'll never get anywhere. It's a waste of energy and usually causes more division because surface positions are always going to oppose each other, no matter how you slice it. But when we uncover what's underneath our surface positions to identify deepest concerns and highest intentions, the possibility arises for overlap, synergy, and connection. This brings us to step 3.

Step 3: Synergize Each Party's Deepest Concerns and Highest Intentions into an Integrally Luminous Purpose

Essentially this step creates a unified purpose that illuminates the whole picture by taking a holistic view of each party's noble purpose.

- In the case of our example, although each group expressed it differently, you might have noticed that both parties had quite a few things in common. Both groups had a genuine concern for their own and other people's health and well-being, and both wanted safety and health for the people around them, although they each had different stories about whether the vaccine was the right approach to achieve that. Upon further exploration and conversation, additional deepest concerns started to be unearthed. The pro-vax group also decided that they had hesitancy and distrust for the pharmaceutical and medical industry. They pointed to evidence that the American health-care system and the pharmaceutical industry have been known to put profit over well-being. Still, they decided that even if they had some distrust or nervousness, getting the vaccine was ultimately better for them.
- The integrally luminous purpose (which simply means the joint purpose that gets revealed through conversation): *both groups want to be healthy and to protect themselves and their loved ones*. This is one fundamental thing they can agree on that is at the foundation of both positions.

From this point of intersection, the *othering* begins to cease and a connection is made. The opposing groups now have synergy. As soon as this is accomplished, everything changes. Instead of thinking of these two groups as existing in two separate rooms with a wall between them, the groups are now in the same room with different doorways as access points. This is where transformation happens. Think of step 3 as a Venn diagram, where two circles overlap and unite at that intersecting point. That is the integrally luminous purpose. Even if there are areas where they disagree, it is only by finding common ground that we can move forward to find solutions. This leads us to our final step.

Step 4: Select the Decision or Solution That Best Achieves the Integrally Luminous Purpose

In the final step, we move completely away from the surface position to cocreate, craft, and discover a solution that best achieves the integrally luminous purpose described in the third step. This purpose, in most cases, brings about a solution that neither "side" could've come up with alone and solves for most of both parties' overlapping positions.

- In our example, the newly synergized group came up with a solution that everyone loved. The group agreed that their highest intention was keeping as many people healthy as possible, regardless of their vaccine position, especially because in 2021, there were many people (children, immunocompromised, etc.) who wouldn't have the chance to get vaccinated either way. Together, they began to ask an important question: How can we create a solution that works better for and takes care of *everyone possible*? Which led them to wonder why the government and medical industry weren't putting just as much time and resources into creating more instant, *reliable*, and readily available home-testing opportunities as they were spending on creating and distributing vaccines? (For context, at that time, home tests were still not widely available.) Since there were so many people who were unable to get the vaccine, shouldn't they be focused on both?

- The group realized that regardless of how deeply they dug in their feet, no matter what, there were going to be people who were unvaccinated. But since our liberation and health are tied to each other, the best approach was to do everything we could to keep *all people*, regardless of their vaccination status, as healthy as possible. The group's solution was that the government would invest in the creation and distribution of low-cost, instant, safe, quick, and—most importantly—*accurate* testing that could be trusted and used for free at any location. They would fund top labs and universities to create the most accurate testing possible, distribute them globally, and make them free, instant, and easy to access. This way, both vaccinated and unvaccinated people would have better assurance that they were safe and could keep their loved ones safe, regardless of what they believed about the original surface position.
- Our group got excited by this outcome—one of many solutions that began to appear—and began to wonder how and why our government hadn't done this already. Quickly our once divided group was aligned in one integrally luminous purpose and ready to lobby and take bipartisan action toward the creation of a better future together.

Imagine if this kind of conversation was happening in our world, in congressional and parliamentary halls, around every topic—from race to gender, climate change, and beyond. We would be living in a completely different world—one where we could finally rise together instead of wasting energy trying to prove or disprove our surface positions. This will happen when more people learn to converse in this way. We now have the tools and thus we are responsible for holding the torch and leading the way forward. These conversations are part of our collective culture upgrade. These conversations will evolve humanity.

Inner Work

Now it's your turn to practice. Pick an issue that's important to you as it relates to race and use the area below to complete the "SUSS It Out" process for *both sides* of that issue. Being able to understand both sides, especially one that is different from your personal beliefs, will give you the practice of opening your mind and putting yourself in someone else's shoes, which is essential for this work. Better yet, practice it with a talkable friend. If you are having trouble coming up with some examples to practice, here are a few you can choose from that we have tried in our workshops: critical race theory in schools versus no critical race theory in schools; reparations for slavery versus no reparations for slavery; abortions should be legal versus abortions should be illegal.

For a printable version of this exercise, go to HowWeEndedRacism.com/resources.

SUSS It Out Process

The Topic: ____________________

Step 1: State Your Surface Position

Position A: ____________________

Position B: ____________________

Step 2: Uncover Each Party's Noble Purpose—Deepest Concerts and Highest Intentions

Position A Deepest Concern: ____________________

____

Position B Deepest Concern: ____________________

____

Position A Highest Intention: ____________________

____

Position B Highest Intention: ____________________

____

Step 3: Synergize Each Party's Deepest Concerns and Highest Intentions into an Integrally Luminous Purpose

Integrally Luminous Purpose: ____________________

Step 4: Select the Decision or Solution That Best Achieves the Integrally Luminous Purpose

Decision/Solution: ____________________________

While some may complain that this system is "too specific," this model is made for you to practice. To enact this process in real life, you must engage in real conversation. There are two options to do this most effectively:

1. You can sit with a talkable person and ask them if they'd be willing to walk through this process with you step by step. Remember, don't blindside them! Give them an opportunity to accept your extended invitation. You'd be surprised how many people are interested, willing, and would love to learn how to host these kinds of conversations.
2. Guide the conversation in the direction of the SUSS It Out process *without* explaining it. As the conversation unfolds, ask questions like "What are your deepest concerns that cause you to make that choice?" "How do you feel that solution leads to the collective good?" and "Where do you imagine our ideas overlap?"

This process from Dr. Gruder takes practice and intention, but it works. **The sole purpose of this method is not *just* to give you solutions—but also to *bring us closer together*.** We've witnessed its power to bring people together across nearly any divide. Stay talkable and you will be shocked at what can unfold. As we stand in the future and ask, "What *did* we do today that brought about the end of racism?," learning this technique was one of the most important. As hesitation and doubt creeps in and perhaps even failure rears its head as you attempt to have big conversations, we want to remind you to embark on this process knowing that you will make several mistakes along the way and that some people may try to "call you out." Remind yourself often that as long as you are putting one foot in front of the other and that you are anchored in our collective vision, *you are moving humanity forward*. You are making the impossible possible—and you have an entire community here supporting you.

Here are a few reminders for you to embed in your psyche as you embark on this journey: First, take your instincts seriously and listen to your gut. Don't say "I'm fine" when you are feeling hurt or afraid. Don't play things off and say "It's not a big deal" when, in fact, whatever is happening is consuming you. Lean into your truth, follow your instincts about when and how and with whom to have conversations. We don't need you to be a martyr.

Second, create enough space for your continued growth and eventual transformation. Like a plant that has continued to blossom in a small pot, growth requires space—actual physical space and space in your schedule. This process requires self-compassion, patience, and generosity. Give yourself the same grace you would give to others or that you hope others would give to you. As we mentioned in earlier chapters, when you give yourself the things you need, you will begin to pour those same things—compassion, patience, and generosity—back into the world. When your heart is overflowing, the hopeless feeling of impossibility takes care of itself. Don't do this all at once. Allow it to bloom.

Racism isn't "too big" of a challenge for us to handle. The struggle we face doesn't only come from racism itself but rather from the messages that we have heard about what we are capable of. Consider this quote by the Roman Stoic philosopher Seneca: "It's not because things are difficult that we dare not venture. It's because we dare not venture that they are difficult."[1]

Ending racism won't be solved in one big conversation because there are many different systems, structures, and processes that need to be reimagined and radically transformed. But we can't begin to transform them or imagine something new if we don't finally come together. If we all learn to have big conversations about difficult and touchy subjects and take responsibility for bringing these conversations into our corners of the world, imagine the transformation that *could* take place. If we each do our part, however small it may seem to us, there would be dozens, hundreds, maybe even thousands of Venn diagrams overlapping at different points, eventually creating one big intraconnected map of integrally luminous purposes as we each step up to have these conversations with our own unique experiences and expertise—even if it's just with our close friends or family. As it pertains to racism, one set of circles in our diagram could be about mass incarceration, the other about reparations, the next about student loan forgiveness, education, housing, police brutality, medical apartheid, and so on. Each one of these conversations would contain an integrally luminous purpose; sometimes they may even be the same across conversations. This is how new solutions begin to arise. This is how we stop fighting racism and start to work toward ending it.

18

∞

Setting Boundaries

Sometimes instead of *calling forward* or having a conversation across a divide, we need to set boundaries. Boundaries become necessary when the person we are dealing with doesn't accept our invitation (or isn't ready for our invitation!) to work toward something greater and continues to cross a line that is disrespectful or repeatedly harmful, or impairs our well-being. In this chapter we will cover how to set boundaries, the main thing boundaries require to remain effective, the biggest lie we tell ourselves when setting boundaries, and the seven essential steps to setting clear boundaries.

First, we need to understand what boundaries are and why we may need to set them. Many of us focus on boundaries without knowing what they really are. Our favorite definition of boundaries is derived from the writer and somatics teacher Prentis Hemphill: **"Boundaries are the distance at which I can love you and me simultaneously."** Through this definition you will understand that by setting boundaries, you are protecting not only love for yourself but also your ability to hold a space of love for the other person. Simply put, your boundaries are protecting the ability for love to continue to flow between you. Whether the other person is a friend, a family member, or an entire community, boundaries are the distance at which you can love yourself and another at the same time. ***Boundaries are not about fighting against what you hate but rather protecting what you love.***

When most of us set boundaries, we leave love out of the equation completely. We forget that boundaries are about protecting love. Most of us think boundaries require an intense act of pushing away or blocking something. We look at boundaries as trying to "get away" from something that's causing harm. But just as our orientation to ending racism is about liberating love, so are boundaries. Boundaries give love the space needed—first, for yourself, and then for another—in real time. Just like a campfire requires space between the logs for the flames to ignite and thrive, so too do we need space to keep our flame of transformation bright.

If we break down the definition a little further and explore what it means to have enough "distance" to love yourself and another simultaneously, you will notice that boundaries are different from rules. Rules are often rigid and static and allow little to no room for adjustments. In this way, rules can lock people out and block the possibility for forgiveness and the opportunity for connection as circumstances change and when genuine healing occurs. As the author and academic bell hooks once questioned, "How do we hold people accountable for wrongdoing and yet at the same time remain in touch with their humanity enough to believe in their capacity to be transformed?"[1] If you're not careful, boundaries can become walls. Healthy boundaries are flexible and adaptive and thus require honest self-awareness to be effective. You need awareness of your emotional health, mood, capacity for conversation, energy levels, and so on to set healthy boundaries that are appropriate for the situation at hand. In this way, healthy boundaries can change moment to moment. Healthy boundaries are always hoping to *let love in*.

The main thing that boundaries require to remain effective is *tolerance for discomfort and disappointment*. Why? As we've learned time and again, you can't control how another person will react or respond to your boundaries. Thus, you need resilience to hold steady to your boundaries, even if the other person doesn't agree or becomes disappointed by the boundaries you set. In all of our years of working with people, we have found that there is often one big lie that people tell themselves that holds them back from setting necessary boundaries: we call it *the façade of altruism*.

The façade of altruism convinces you that you're not setting boundaries because you "*care so much* about other people's feelings."

That's the lie we tell ourselves. The truth is that we abandon setting boundaries to *avoid having to sit with another person's discomfort and disappointment in response to our truth.* We fool ourselves into thinking that we're protecting the other person's feelings by not setting an appropriate boundary out of "the kindness of our heart." The healer and psychotherapist Kasey Crown says it best: "Many of us are conditioned to be so uncomfortable with disappointment—and with holding another person's disappointment—that we are completely willing to abandon our own knowing and truth in order to ensure that another person is not uncomfortable. Therefore, we don't set boundaries so that we don't have to sit with the disappointment of having *caused* disappointment."[2] You can fool yourself into avoiding setting boundaries under the false guise of "being nice," but that's not usually what's really happening. Instead, you abandon yourself under the false guise of altruism. We can be so committed to keeping the peace that we are willing to abandon what's true in order to avoid having caused disappointment.

The real question becomes this: *What are you committed to?* If we are ending racism, we must be committed to setting clear boundaries to protect our collective vision for the future, with love. Sometimes setting a boundary is the most loving thing you *can* do. By setting a healthy boundary, you give others the opportunity to grow in response to your truth; and in the same instant, you are loving yourself.

Identifying your personal boundaries requires that you first clearly identify whether a person or situation is having a negative impact on something you love. Then you must identify your limits. Ask yourself, "What are my emotional, mental, physical limits?" Reflect on past experiences you have had brushing up against the edges of your boundaries and notice what seems tolerable and acceptable as well as what makes you feel uncomfortable and gives you anxiety. Notice the emotions that arise, leaning on the tools taught earlier. Five common feelings that may come up for you when you think about setting (or engage in setting) boundaries are anger, submissiveness, fear, resentment, and guilt. If a particular situation or person is bringing up these types of emotions, you can take this feedback as a cue that a deeper dive needs to be done. Ask yourself, "Why might I be feeling this way about this situation/person? What do I want to say that I'm afraid of saying? What do I love that I'm needing to protect?"

To avoid backpedaling or failing to create boundaries, you can strengthen your resolve and right by leaning into affirmative statements such as "I deserve to protect my peace," "I am worthy," "I am doing this for love." From this place of strength, begin to shift your view of a boundary as a fence or separation and instead view it as a standard. When you view it as a standard that needs to be upheld in your life, it brings the ownership back to you, empowering you to take responsibility for what *you* can do to improve the situation, rather than looking outward.

The Seven Essentials to Setting Better Boundaries

Step 1: Center In Your Vision

Step 2: Prepare the Space

Step 3: Own Your Own Feelings

Step 4: Don't Wait Until It's Too Late

Step 5: Create a Space of Connection and Compassion

Step 6: Don't Arrive with All the Solutions

Step 7: Don't Attach to Outcomes

Keep reminding yourself that boundaries are protecting what you love. You'll notice that many of the foundational elements for healthy conversations overlap. If you need a deeper dive back into any of the individual concepts, refer back to chapter 16. We will continue to explore them here in relationship to boundaries.

Rita is a young African woman living in America. Her parents were deeply engrained with the social concept that people with lighter skin are better and more beautiful. When Rita was young, her parents constantly encouraged her to use skin-lightening cream. Now Rita is an adult with a high school–aged daughter, Tina, who also has dark skin. After going to therapy and doing deep self-love work, Rita has finally fully embraced and loves her skin tone, but Tina is falling into the same old trap because Rita's parents (Tina's grandparents) keep calling Tina "the dark one," and gifting her with skin-lightening creams. Rita has talked to her parents at length about why this is problematic and the impact it's having on their granddaughter, but they keep doing it. It's gotten to the point where they are making comments about Tina's skin and giving her skin-lightening creams behind Rita's back, even after several requests to stop. Rita realized that this is the moment for a boundary.

With Tina's permission, Rita stopped allowing her parents to see their granddaughter until they offered a sincere apology and a firm promise that they would *never again* mention anything about Tina's skin, nor buy her any creams. Rita also requested that the family read about white supremacy together, so that her parents could get an understanding of where this comes from and how harmful it is to them all. Rita's parents were shocked. At first, they blamed Rita and Tina for "being too sensitive," proclaiming they were "coming from a good place." They scolded Rita for using Tina as a "pawn" in their relationship. When Rita shared this story with us during one of our workshops, we told Rita that we believed that she was doing the right thing and asked her to hold steady.

While working with her, it was clear she wasn't setting the boundary because she hated her parents or because she wanted to distance them from their granddaughter. Instead, she was setting the boundary to reaffirm her love for her daughter and protect her daughter's capacity for self-love. After seven weeks of completely blocking communication, Rita was crushed. She couldn't believe her parents were so stubborn that they actually refused to budge and show up for a healing conversation. We told Rita and her daughter to stay anchored in the vision and continue holding the door open for them to walk through but not to drop their boundaries unless something changed. Finally, after seven weeks, Rita's parents called. They apologized and told Rita that it wasn't until a conversation with an old friend at church that they were able to see the situation differently and how wrong they were.

Rita's experience illustrates something we have pointed out time and again: *you are not in control of how quickly people process their experiences.* You are, however, in control of how you allow people to treat you while they're in that process. You can keep an open heart, drop your expectations, and never disrespect people when you set your boundaries. The healing will happen as it will. In every situation, with all of our clients, healing occurs—even if in some instances that healing means the end of a toxic relationship. There is no prerequisite for healing that necessitates both sides of the party show up. If Rita had not held such a strong boundary, her parents would likely still be engaging in this behavior today and possibly cause irreparable harm to her daughter that could have been, in turn, passed down to her daughter's children one day. Thanks to healthy boundaries, the repeated pattern of trauma is over. The buck stops with boundaries.

Joe's been working at his job for several years. Every time he goes to lunch with his coworkers, they make racist jokes about everyone who isn't white. Even as a waiter leaves the table, they mumble inappropriate stereotypes under their breath and make jokes that would mortify Joe if anyone heard it. Joe is a white man who has been doing his work on understanding bias, as have his coworkers, but every time they leave the office setting, it's like his coworkers just forget everything. They become racially insensitive, offensive, and downright awful, even though they're "just joking." After taking our program, Joe realized he'd had enough, but he was afraid to set a boundary with his coworkers because they were his friends and they had to collaborate closely as a team on projects. We encouraged him to have a *calling forward* conversation. Joe used every step by the book and was even coached by us, but it didn't go well.

In fact, the four friends who were making the racist jokes started calling Joe names and making *him* the butt of the joke. Joe tried one more time to have a serious conversation with them, but it still didn't work. It was time for a boundary.

Joe couldn't protect what he believed in or stay in integrity with his vision or values while hanging out with these friends outside of work, so he stopped having lunch with them. His friends were shocked as they had been having lunch together for years, and they thought Joe was making too big a deal about it. However, Joe held steady and found a new group of coworkers to go to lunch with. Joe was shocked after his first meal with them. He said, "I couldn't believe how deep and amazing of a conversation we had and that these people have been working at my company all along and I never gave them any personal attention."

Joe's old friends never came around. But after meeting his new ones, he didn't care. In a professional context, he is still on some project teams with a few of them, but they keep it cordial; and Joe has made himself a promise that if it ever got to be uncomfortable or unprofessional, he would ask to be transferred to a different team. So far that hasn't happened. Joe letting go of the old hangout crew allowed him to create space for something new, something that was more aligned with who he was becoming. Joe loves his new friend group, and we learned that a year after our course, he became engaged to one of the women in that group.

Inner Work

Now it's time for you to practice setting boundaries. Although you might already have a situation in mind, we ask you to focus your first boundary on something specifically related to discrimination, racism, or othering. Now you have this practice for life, so you can always return to it for anything you need.

- A person who I need to set a boundary with is _______ _______________________________________.
- The way this situation impacts my ability to love myself is ______________________________.
- The way this situation impacts my ability to love others is ______________________________.
- The fear I have about setting this boundary is _______________________________________.
- The story I'm making up about why I *shouldn't* set this boundary is ___________________________.
- If I allow this fear-based story to control my life, the way it will impact my future and my ability to love myself and others is ____________________.
- If I were to set this boundary, the first part of my conversation would be ____________________.
- The next best action I can take, knowing all I know now, is _______________________________.

Setting boundaries allows us to live a life of greater integrity, and it will take a whole lot of integrity for us to *end racism.* Remember, other people are not mind readers. Don't expect them to be. There is no shame in directly asking for your feelings to be acknowledged or your needs to be met. Even our loved ones need ongoing instructions in how to care for us because we are *always* changing—as are our needs and boundaries. As you continue to commit to growth—and as you continue to level up—you may find the need to increase or reduce the number of boundaries you set. Don't forget, you can simultaneously set boundaries and be loving, compassionate, and kind. You can also sit with someone's pain, hold space for their reaction, and reiterate how much they mean to you—all while making clear that *your boundary is nonnegotiable.*

Anytime you set a boundary, you are bringing the outer world into alignment with the inner values that need to be protected to live your personal and our collective vision. Boundaries illuminate and challenge unspoken expectations. They are not "mean." Boundaries draw a line around what we love and protect it as needed so we can keep walking forward without constantly being pushed back.

Setting Boundaries Conversation-Preparation Exercise

This is a sample script for *setting boundaries.* Fill in the blanks to help you prepare for a boundaries conversation. More than anything, this script *prepares you.*

For a printable version of this exercise, go to HowWeEndedRacism.com/resources.

I feel ____________________ *(emotion)* about saying this to you, but the reason it's important we have this conversation now is because ____________________________________ . *(What do you love?)* I've been noticing that ____________ ___________________________ *(What's been happening?)* and it's causing ______________________________ . *(What is the negative impact it's having?)* It's ______________________ for me to do this, but ______________________________ *(What is the boundary you are setting?)* and I hope you will consider _______________ . *(Is there something you want them to consider, do, or learn?)* I'm doing this because ___________________________ . I hope you understand that this is not to ______________ , but to protect ____________________________ .

Example 1: Love's parents keep making racist remarks about his boyfriend, Jo.

I feel afraid about saying this to you, but the reason it's important we have this conversation now is because I'm starting to feel resentment and distance build up between us and I do not want that with you all because I love you so much. I've been noticing that when Jo isn't around, you both keep saying racially insensitive remarks about him and it's causing me a lot of pain, and it's making me afraid to bring him around. It's hard for me to do this, but if I hear one more remark, I will not be bringing Jo around anymore at all. I hope you will consider taking some time to learn to understand how harmful these remarks are. I'm doing this because I love him very much, and I also love the two of you, and I think we all can grow from this. I hope you understand that this is not to spite you but to protect the love I have for Jo and also my deep desire for all of us to be together as a family.

Example 2: Mike needs distance from one of his coworkers.

I feel nervous about saying this to you but the reason it's important we have this conversation now is because I can tell you are feeling my energy shift at work and I want to be transparent and clear about what's going on. I've been noticing that I get extremely uncomfortable when I witness you asserting your politics and beliefs on people in the office. Even when I've asked to change the subject, you refuse to let the topic go and argue until someone submits to your opinions, and it's causing me to be fearful and hesitant to have conversations with you about anything because everything turns into a political argument. It's hard for me to do this, but I'd like to take two weeks away from having lunch together. I hope that you will consider how you might be able to stand for what you believe in without such force or constant anger toward those who believe differently than you. My hope is that after two weeks, we can come together and have a conversation about this, but for now I just need my space and do not want to speak about this until two weeks from now. I'm doing this because I want there to be equanimity in the office. I hope you understand that this is not to blame or shame you but to protect my peace in the short amount of time I have at lunch each day.

Pillar Eight

we took action

19

∞

Tending to Your Garden

At this point in the journey (and at our workshops), people usually have the same questions for us: What happens next? *And what can we tangibly DO to start taking action?* Over the coming chapters, we will present different ways for you to take meaningful action to create a future without racism. As with all of our work, you will stand in the future in the year 2050, where racism no longer exists, and look back at the present asking, "What *did* I do to make this a reality?" If your actions are rooted from this place, anything is possible. Notice how we didn't say that you are asking "What did [anyone else] do to make this a reality?" As we've learned in previous chapters, you cannot control how other people think, react, or what they do. So, let's now turn our focus fully to *your* contribution to the collective vision to end racism.

Wherever we go, we can commit to being a beacon of well-being, love, and care that not only touches but also uplifts those we encounter. The Zen master Thich Nhat Hanh explained it this way: "When crowded refugee boats met with storms and pirates, if everyone panicked, all would be lost. But if even *one person* in the boat remained centered and calm, it was enough to show the way forward for everyone to survive."[1] We want you to imagine yourself as that person on the boat, centering yourself in your vision of a world without racism, understanding that your commitment to being the model of integration and healing affects all those in your boat. Also, by surrounding yourself with other people who are committed to this collective vision, whenever you need to tap out, there will be someone to pick up the workload for you with the same level of integrity and heart while you recharge and the boat continues to sail forward.

As we've stated before, the best version of the world starts with the best version of each of us. Ending racism won't happen overnight. It will happen incrementally, and it requires a steady ship, small but consistent shifts, and commitment from each person to show up as the best possible version of themselves each and every day. When a critical mass of us commit to healing our hearts, racism will end. **No amount of technology or research can stop racism, warfare, environmental destruction, or othering because the source of all these afflictions lies in the human heart.** All of our actions must be deeply sourced from that place.

The seed we are planting with you here is that in order to create the type of transformation needed, we must connect our inner work to the outer world. Every daunting issue in our world needs to first be met with a degree of inner work. Your inner work is not just for you—it is for the world at large. Yet when we say "the world at large," we don't mean that we expect everyone to become the leader of a large movement. You can make a difference exactly where you are, right now.

One of our favorite Buddhist proverbs that illustrates this sentiment beautifully is that you should **"tend to the area of the garden that you can reach."** Your "garden" may seem like a small plot or an insignificant blip on the radar in our grander world. Maybe you harbor doubt that tending to your seemingly tiny area of influence can even make a difference. However, no individual garden is closed off from the greater world. Underground, the roots of trees communicate with one another, and between garden plots there's cross-pollination. Every moment we spend tending to our own garden—intentionally caring for the elements within our reach—contributes to the greater good of the entire world.

If we can each make sure that everyone in our garden is taken care of, then it will have mattered. Because each of those people will go out and tend to their gardens. If you think that this is not practical or your garden is "too small" to make a difference, perhaps the incredible story of how Shelly started Pandemic of Love can illustrate this notion with more clarity.

When the COVID-19 pandemic started in March 2020, Shelly, like most everyone else around the globe, was feeling heightened anxiety, confusion, and fear of the unknown. In those early days, there was so much we did not know about the virus and its potential impact, and we were ill-equipped in terms of the supplies, systems, and infrastructure needed to stay safe, secure, and informed.

Before the stay-at-home orders were official where Shelly was living in Florida, as she was stocking up on supplies, she paused to reflect on her position of privilege. She understood that her own life would be minimally affected by these orders, and while she was scared of the virus itself, she began to turn her attention to her community, both her formalized meditation community (of almost fifteen thousand meditators) and the South Florida community at large. Beyond her personal fear of the virus, she started to think about all the individuals she personally knew who were already struggling to make rent each month, who were reliant on free breakfast and lunch at public schools to feed their kids ten meals per week, who did not have access to reliable Wi-Fi or a computer at home, as well as individuals in the service industry who were reliant on tips to make ends meet. She found herself thinking about every single immunocompromised senior (her own mother included), everyone living alone, the essential workers who would have to put themselves at risk, and everyone without a support structure. She reflected on everyone she knew who did not have enough . . . and the great privilege that her family had. She then began to consider all of the other people she knew in her community (her "garden") who had more than enough and started to make the connection.

Take a moment now and think about who is in your "garden." Who are the people in your circle of influence? Who's in the immediate circle (for example, family, friends, colleagues)? Who's in the extended circle (for example, teachers, children and parents on your kids' sports teams, your friends' and colleagues' parents, and any other communities you may have)?

Shelly sat in meditation for ten to twenty minutes multiple times a day in those early days of the pandemic. She would have a journal and a pen by her side. She would sit with the purpose of listening—to her busy mind, to her heart, to her physical body. Some questions she would ask herself included: "What am I feeling emotionally? Where does it hurt? Where do I feel it in my body?" After each session, she would write down the words that washed over her, without attaching herself to them or judging them. There was typically a flood of emotions, most of them steeped in fear and despair. She would nurture the tender spaces, talk to herself, and remind herself to *accept* that this was the current reality—because only from that place of acceptance could she make a difference. By the third day of this consistent practice, she was ready to shift to a different set of questions. She asked, "What can I tangibly do about what I am feeling right now?" followed by, "And how do I come from a place of love?"

These two questions helped Shelly move from the completely normal, biological response of "fight, flight, freeze, or faint" to a new response, something she calls "empathy-action" mode (also scientifically referred to as "tend and befriend"). So, she started to jot down her ideas. She drew three columns on her journal page. On the left, she wrote down the emotions she was feeling from the emotions wheel—fear and despair. In the center column, she made a detailed list of exactly what she was afraid of and distraught over. Then, understanding the specifics, she could now move to a place of asking herself how she could tangibly *respond* (not react) to one, some, or all of the things on her list. In the final column, she started to list ideas that could directly help with each fear. If the fear was disconnection, she listed people she could call. If the fear was loneliness, she listed ideas for community. If the fear was food insecurity, she listed ideas that could address it. And so on. For each singular idea, she asked herself, "Is this coming from a place of love?" Why is this question especially important? The answer to "What could I tangibly do?" may be something dangerous, could cause trauma, or may be steeped in resentment or vengeance. But if you are coming from a place of love, your response is quality-checked at the heart.

One morning she decided to tackle one of the ideas that came up that day on her list. It was simply to post two hyperlinks on social media titled "Give Help" and "Get Help," with two corresponding Google forms for her community members (her area of the garden) to ask if they needed something tangible or to share if they were able to give something tangible. Her idea was incredibly simple—she would wake up in the morning, look at the spreadsheet of responses from both forms, and match people in need with people willing to fulfill that need. She expected a small handful of people to fill out these forms. By the next morning, she found that more than five hundred people had filled out both forms! Shelly was shocked. But she set about connecting each of the individuals herself. By the hour, hundreds and then thousands more began to fill out the forms, from locations all over the world. The cross-pollination had begun, and she started to get messages from people in different cities asking how they could replicate the forms and help communities start their own versions, in their own gardens. On March 14, 2020, Pandemic of Love was born—a mutual aid organization where people who need help can be supported directly by those who can give help.

Pandemic of Love has proven that coming from a place of love is always the answer and that love is the cure. This may sound like an oversimplification or even a pipe dream to most, but not for the people who have been touched by Pandemic of Love. By August 2022, Pandemic of Love grew to more than 4,800 volunteers around the world, matching individuals and families who *needed help* with those who were able to *give help*, in over three hundred communities globally. More than 2.5 million people have been matched—and counting. Close to $70 million in assistance has been directly transacted between people—and counting. Pandemic of Love has been featured in over 150 media outlets around the globe, including CNN, Forbes, the BBC, Mother Jones, and Upworthy; on every major television network and on talk shows such as *The Kelly Clarkson Show* and *CNN Heroes*. It's been promoted on social media by influential people such as Chelsea Handler, Debra Messing, Busy Philipps, Maria Shriver, Kristen Bell, and other celebrities and influencers. But the most impactful aspect of this movement is that it connects the donor and the recipient directly and lets the best qualities of human nature do the rest—the same qualities that we've been teaching you in this book—the same qualities we need to end racism.

This entire movement started in one fearful person's small garden. She didn't have any big connections or a massive social media following. Fortunately she had a local meditation community, contemplative tools (the same ones that we teach you here!), a heart to help, and the willingness to try. She never even thought about the gardens beyond her own. She just trusted that simply by tending to her own garden, her own community, and by making sure that everything in it could survive and thrive, she could make a difference. It's a poignant reminder that any one of us has the opportunity to show up in this way on a daily basis.

One of the key elements that Shelly's story illustrates is how she neither suppressed nor reacted to her emotions but instead chose to *respond* to them. Reacting is when our subconscious patterns take control; it often comes from our shadow. Responding is a way to *interrupt that pattern*, because you pause, even for just a second, and consciously *choose* how to make a decision. This is something we can all do when we feel outraged by something that is happening in our home, neighborhood, school, community, or our world at large. In this way, the things that make us outraged can serve as fertilizer to help our greatest seeds of action bloom—in our own gardens and beyond. As we learned, Shelly's work was initially only aimed at tending to her area of the garden—her local community. The global movement that happened afterward was not planned; normally with grassroots movements, it isn't. But by people engaging with and being inspired by her garden, pollination happened and the COVID-19 pandemic was met with the force of Pandemic of Love. If we each focus on standing in our vision and tending to our garden, the culmination of this work and its impact will be undeniable. Now it's your turn to practice.

Tending to Your Garden Exercise

This practice builds on a traditional technique that uses the acronym RAIN—*Recognize, Allow, Investigate, Nurture*—originally coined by the meditation teacher Michele McDonald but now taught by meditation teachers and therapists all over the world. The technique is a simple yet effective way of accessing our inner world and creating a pause to respond instead of reacting to what is happening in the world around us.

Sit as comfortably as you can. As you do this practice, you may want to open and close your eyes as you read through the words. Start by closing your eyes or lowering your gaze and taking five deep cleansing breaths. Inhale through your nose and exhale through your mouth. When you feel centered and calm, bring to your mind or your consciousness a problem or issue related to racism, prejudice, discrimination, or othering happening in your life or community that is troubling you. Recall any of the details or nuances that don't sit well with you.

Now we begin, RAIN.

First, **R**ecognize what **emotions** arise when you consider this problem. Name them without attaching yourself to them. Sit with these feelings, just recognizing them. You can use the emotions wheel if you need to.

Next, **A**llow the emotions and physical responses to **arise** without judgment. Say to yourself, "This emotion belongs here right now," "This sensation will pass but for now, I am allowing the experience of it," and "It's okay to feel this way." Spend time allowing the feelings and sensations to exist without judgment or attachment. Let them flood over you so that you don't have to avoid or push them down anymore.

Next, **I**nvestigate. Ask yourself, "What are my beliefs around this?" and "Where does it hurt when I think about this issue or problem in my life/community/world?" Notice during this investigation where you feel this most prominently in your body. Is your chest tight? Does your throat feel like it's closing up? Is your jaw clenched? Place your hand over where you physically feel that emotion most prominently in your body. Invite the feelings to be felt; explore the feelings with curiosity and compassion. How does it feel to live in your body in this moment? As you investigate, continue to also allow.

When you are ready to proceed, move to **N**urture. Imagine that you are listening to a friend you love dearly telling you these same concerns. Ask yourself, "What do I need the most in this moment? What do I need to feel? What do I need to hear?" Tell yourself what you may need to hear. (Perhaps it's "I love you," "I forgive you," or "I accept you.") Imagine that this nurturing presence is pouring in, enveloping you. Let your deepest intention be to be nurtured with whatever you need in this moment.

Finally, once you feel a quality of presence, relax into it. Acknowledge yourself for taking the time to administer self-care. From this place, bring back into your awareness the troubling situation that you originally thought of. Now ask yourself, "How might I *respond*? Ponder, "What can I tangibly do about this situation?" or "How can I tangibly effect change and create impact in even one person's life?" or "Which area of my garden can I reach right now?" Allow any ideas, thoughts, or direction to come up for you, taking note of each idea but not attaching yourself to any one of them or to any associated outcomes. Do not latch on to any one idea; just notice the idea, jot it down if you are afraid of not remembering it, and move on. In this stage, there are no good or bad, better or worse ideas. These are just seeds of ideas.

From a place of possibility, one steeped in response versus reactivity, notice how different you feel in this moment thinking about the troubling issue or situation. You may feel more spacious, open, hopeful. Looking down at your list of ideas, put each one to the litmus test by asking, "Is this idea coming from a place of love?" If the answer is no, cross the idea off your list. If the answer is yes, you can begin to work on expanding upon the idea, figuring out if it is possible for you to act on it, while laying out the tangible steps you can take to make the idea a reality.

Go ahead and do this now.

Looking at your list of ideas, which one resonates the most deeply with you? Which one tends to the area of the garden that you can reach and feels the most "doable" in this moment?

Inner Work

Use the following incomplete sentences to explore your pain point, emotions, and how you might respond with action.

- As it relates to racism, prejudice, discrimination, and othering, the social issues that bother me most are ________________________________.
- The emotions I feel when I think of these things are ________________________________.
- As I dig a little deeper, what's specifically upsetting me or causing me to feel these emotions are ________ ________________________________.
- Reviewing one by one, I might respond to or solve for each of these emotions and situations by ________ ________________________________. (Don't worry about getting it perfect, just see what arises.)
- The ideas that are easy for me to act upon now are ________________________________.
- The ideas that are rooted in love are ____________ ________________________________.
- The ideas I need to release and let go of are ________ ________________________________.
- My tangible action will be ________________.

Greg is a young man living in Oakland, California, who is mortified by police violence, specifically against Black men. When he thinks about it, his heart immediately begins to race and his palms sweat. When he goes to the emotions wheel, he recognizes that police violence makes him feel angry and helpless. What specifically causes him to feel this way is that even though there are countless videos and images and documentation of these issues, no one seems to be doing anything to solve it. He's sick of seeing the images on screen again and again without seeing any tangible action being taken. He's been spinning in this cycle of helplessness for years. But using the exercise you just practiced, Greg became equipped to ask himself, "What could I do to *respond* to this situation instead of constantly pushing down or reacting to the situation with my usual patterns?" He recognized that these patterns never led to anything but more anger and helplessness—an endless loop. Doing this exercise over the course of a few weeks, he had two ideas come to him. One of them was to bomb the local police station. Obviously that answer wasn't rooted in love, so he instantly let that go. His second idea was simple yet one that he had never done before: to do an internet search to see if there were any organizations doing *meaningful* work related to ending police brutality. He was shocked to see a plethora of organizations and specifically one that was founded right where he lived, in Oakland. Greg began to donate funds to this organization, but he realized that in order to properly tend to this garden, he needed to "get his hands dirty." So, he got more engaged by volunteering at events and attending meetings. Now, one year later, he is on the board of directors of the organization. He's even engaged his friends and members of his extended community (also his garden), who previously knew nothing about this cause, to fundraise and support the organization's work. Several of them are now active members of the organization and have invited their communities and networks to be a part. This is cross-pollination—all starting from one person choosing to take action and tend to their garden. Greg knows he is just getting started and is excited to continue deepening his impact.

Mallory (Mal) is a white woman who is completely taken back by the "Karen" complex—she hates the term and thinks it's harmful but also recognizes and gets really upset when other white women respond in disproportionately dramatic ways and keep themselves distant from the reality of the problems People of Color face. She says, "I have lots of friends who act this way. Every time I see them being so dramatic and sensitive, I completely shut down from irritation and annoyance. How can they be so removed from reality?" We asked Mal to do the same exercise you did with your inner work. She discovered that her pent-up anger and irritation were mainly due to the fact that she felt her friends weren't showing up to do the work that was so important to her. They were all retired, empty-nester stay-at-home moms, so they weren't engaged in formal diversity trainings at work, nor were they forced to interact often with people outside of their social group, thus it was easy for them to stay in their little bubbles. However, every time they left their bubbles, in Mal's words, "all hell would break loose." This time, Mal decided that instead of reacting by shutting down and getting annoyed with her friends, she would brainstorm ways to respond. She came up with several ideas through her practice, but two ideas in particular stood out to her that she took action on. Mal and her friends have been part of a book club that has expanded to over one hundred women. As a founding member, Mal decided to introduce into their reading selection books about diversity and from diverse voices. While she faced some resistance initially, a compromise was found in that twice a year, Mal could select a book for everyone to read that fit this description. Next, Mal decided that if she couldn't select books more than twice a year, she would put together a fund and invite others in the group to contribute to it. The fund's purpose was to purchase diverse books that would be donated to other book clubs in their county and neighboring counties, as well as to public and academic libraries that did not have a broad representation of books that could help educate, inspire, and change the narrative of diversity and inclusion. Mal was surprised at how many of the women in her group not only wanted to donate to the fund but also volunteered to help her build a roster of libraries and even start satellite book clubs in other communities around the globe.

Ross is an avid climber and lives in the greater Denver, Colorado, area. His passion is being in the outdoors; communing with nature is when he feels happiest. Every summer, for the past several years, Ross has been working on survival skills with teenagers from the area through a specialized summer camp that involves teaching youth about hiking and climbing, living out in the wilderness for a few days at a time, and helping them to access their own power during their time together outdoors. Ross was in one of our first cohorts of "The Liberation Experience," and during one of the breakouts with three other participants, he reflected on how he never noticed that almost all of the teenagers that he has taught over the past several years were from the suburbs and were white. "It never dawned on me that all of the kids I was working with were exactly like me and that there was little to no diversity," he confessed to the group. He went on to state that it wasn't that there was a lack of diversity in the city where he lived, and he began to contemplate why this was the case. Upon further investigation, Ross's conclusion for a lack of diversity in his program was a lack of diversity among the counselors (representation matters!) and a lack of funding available to help provide scholarships for potential campers to join the program, even beyond the tuition costs—things such as hiking boots, appropriate socks, a backpack, and other gear required really began to add up. Ross resolved that during the fall and winter months, he would try to raise the funds and hold a collection drive for gear. The owners of the local coffee shop where he works as a barista were very supportive of the idea and allowed him to set up a collection box for gear in the shop. They also committed to donating a portion of each hot chocolate sold in the winter to help fund the camp. Ross also called a few of the local gear manufacturers and other local shop owners in the area to see if they wanted to assist in some way and he managed to get two additional shops to run a campaign during the winter months. During the spring months, Ross worked on recruiting his first ten campers for the summer program; he had raised enough money to support them. At first it was challenging for him to find the right partners who could recommend and promote the program to local teenagers. But after connecting with program directors at after-school programs and mentorship organizations locally, he was able to recruit his first two participants and then, through word of mouth, the teenagers began to recruit their friends. Ross's first summer program was wildly successful as he saw a transformation in the kids that were a part of the experience. To test the waters, that first summer he ran the program separately for these children. In subsequent summers he began to integrate the teens into the wider program, helping them build connections with the other teens from around the county. Today the program underwrites the cost for close to one hundred diverse teens to attend this program each summer, and four of the program's former participants have become counselors themselves, helping to address the lack of representation of mentors. Ross identified a problem in his garden and brought in the seeds and the nurturing required to close a gap that he identified.

None of us are going to end racism alone. We are going to end it by committing to being the best version of ourselves, tending to our own gardens, and taking every opportunity we have to cross-pollinate other gardens. But good ideas and intentions aren't the only ones that get pollinated—harmful and bad ideas do, too. We must make sure our seeds are sewn with love and the intention of bringing us together and calling us toward a greater collective vision, not tearing us apart or creating more division. You have the power to tend to your garden now. Begin with whatever came to you in the inner-work exercise in this chapter. If nothing came up yet, don't worry. Something will. It may take days or weeks. Go back and try again. Stay present. Don't worry about your idea being "the next big thing"; the idea or organization may already be in motion in your community. You just have to commit to showing up, seeking it, or building it.

20

∞

Creating a Personal Passion Project

Taking action by responding to your emotions and pain points, like we taught you in the previous chapter, is ideal for some people, but there's another way to get inspired toward meaningful action using a more systemized approach. When we stand in the future where racism has ended and ask, "What did we do today?" we know that *everyone* used their greatest passions, talents, interests, and skills to help the world get there. This not only makes ending racism possible but it also makes the journey *enjoyable.* When you can bring your greatest gifts to the world in service of something greater than yourself, you will receive a boost of joy and purpose unlike anything you've ever experienced in your life. In our workshops, we use a worksheet called "The Seed of Action"—continuing with the metaphor we used in the last chapter—to help participants get started on figuring out how to best take action toward ending racism in a way that aligns with their passions.

Inner Work

This exercise will be a little different than our previous inner-work practices. Begin by completing the sentences, then proceed to the following table and instructions.

For a printable version of this exercise, go to HowWeEndedRacism.com/resources.

- Of the social issues that intersect racism, prejudice, discrimination, and othering, the three specific issues that pull on my heart strings *most* are ________ ____ .
- When I stand in the future where these problems have been resolved, what I imagine is _______________ __________________________ . (Give some details.)

Now, use the following Personal Passions and Assets table and circle every item that you have expertise with, have passion for, or that brings you joy. Then continue with the final incomplete sentences.

Personal Passions and Assets

Music Playing an instrument, singing, writing songs	**Art** Painting, drawing, sculpture, graphic art	**Writing** Writing poetry, stories, and plays; blogging	**Movement** Dancing, martial arts
Building Wood working, construction, welding	**Volunteering** Being of service to the community, giving back through nonprofits	**Entrepreneurship** Business, marketing, inventing things, investing	**Sports** Group activities, active
Teaching Mentoring, tutoring, teaching, reading to kids	**Nature** Exploring nature, wildlife, gardening	**Speech** Debate or public speaking, broadcasting	**Computers** Software development, social media, web design
Spirituality Prayer, meditation, communal healing	**Drama/Theater** Acting, directing, theater	**Photography and Film** Taking pictures, making films, animation	**Reading** Reading fiction, nonfiction, poetry
Advocacy Politics and government, commitment to a cause	**Journalism** Newscasting, writing, radio and TV production	**Outdoor Recreation** Fishing, hiking, bicycling	**Creative Arts** Cooking, sewing, fashion, knitting

- Of the items I circled, the ones I enjoy most are ______________________________.
- A way I might use some of the things I circled to help achieve the vision I see is ____________________.
- Another idea is ____________________________.
- A final idea is ____________________________.
- Of these three ideas, the one I feel most excited to start is ____________________________.
- My first tangible step will be __________________.
- And I will do this by __________. *(Pick an actual date!)*

You naturally possess certain passions and interests; you are gifted with certain talents and skills. You will find that you also lean toward caring about certain subcategories related to ending racism more than others—that's okay. If we all bring our passions, skills, hobbies, and interests to the wide variety of subcategories related to ending racism—areas that we are drawn to—then every issue can and will be solved. There are enough of us working in every arena of the world—politics, art, business, education, finances, family, entertainment, activism (the list goes on!)—that if we each showed up in our gardens and did the work that was ours to do, and if it were the work we are passionate about, racism would definitely end in one generation. Of course, there will be hard moments and challenges to overcome to end racism—we don't fool ourselves into thinking that it's all going to be easy. But when you balance those challenges by bringing *what you love* to the mission, you avoid burnout and continue to feel inspired even when you encounter obstacles, because you're doing something you are passionate about for a cause that's greater than you.

We hope you already have ideas running through your head. To help inspire you more, we want to share some examples of the personal passion projects from people in our community.

Kate is a seventy-three-year-old British woman living in the UK. Her partner, John, was diagnosed with Alzheimer's in 2009. She joined our program because she wanted to understand what she may be missing in her life and work as it relates to connecting across divides. Kate had cared for John for twelve years as his health declined, and over these years they had created and shared a real love for finding and supporting caregivers and people living with dementia. Through being involved with providing sustaining care for John, she became acutely aware of just how many people were impacted by dementia and how large and global a community it is.[1]

Because of the work she did learning to care for John, she has now become a leading expert, through lived experience, in the field of dementia care. Kate now volunteers in her community, writes articles, has coedited a book,[2] presents at conferences, gives talks, and sits on panels for people with dementia and their caregivers. Needless to say, this is one of her passions. Through the same assignment that you have just explored in this chapter, Kate realized her work to promote equality of access could include an activism approach. She said, "There needs to be a revolution to reimagine a creative way of helping *everyone* to participate in life, even if they have disabilities from living with dementia." Soon after doing this assignment, she joined a local group of dementia activists. Next, she began using her voice, experience, and privilege to speak boldly about the need for more equity and care for minority groups living with dementia. A year later, Kate is now on the steering group of an international coalition, Reimagining Dementia: A Creative Coalition for Change,[3] which has created a global campaign called "Let's Reimagine."

Since its launch in September 2020, the coalition has emerged as a beacon for those interested in using creativity to build diverse communities of belonging. One of Kate's biggest realizations through this experience and her mindfulness practice was that "you just have to start somewhere." She says, "What I learned is that *there's an unfolding*. You can't plan it all out. One small action leads to a phone call, which a few weeks later leads to an email that then leads to a conversation, and soon you find yourself making a difference you never imagined you could make. What I want everyone to know is that *the key is showing up*." Soon after completing our program, Kate's dear partner, John, died peacefully, having lived "proud with Alzheimer's" for twelve years. His legacy lives on through Kate, and with this incredible work she continues to bring greater inclusion, equity, and diversity to a very specific area of the world that she is uniquely placed to reach.

Tammy is a young Black woman who for years worked as a leader in nonprofit spaces, but her biggest passion is entrepreneurship and connecting people. When she joined our program, she wasn't clear on how she could help or, honestly, if she even *needed* to help more with ending racism because she was already in the nonprofit space working to support People of Color. After doing this inner-work exercise, Tammy lit up. She had an idea that made her jump out of her seat. She always complained that so many Black-owned businesses failed because they never had enough support. She said, "Every time I support a Black-owned business, within a few years, they're closed." Doing this practice was the first time she ever considered that *she* could be the solution.

Within months, Tammy and her husband founded a company that supports local Black-owned businesses to network and connect with one another, serving as a guide for consumers to learn about and support Black-owned businesses in her community. She discovered that one of the biggest issues in the community was that Black business owners were working so hard at their own businesses that they didn't know of each other. They would end up getting their needs met by other businesses instead of circulating wealth within the community. Tammy's work helped to address and solve for that problem, and several businesses have said they would not be open today if it were not for her work.

The stories from our workshop participants are endless: Barbara started an online racial justice training for elders in her community; Chris made a film and made sure all of the main characters were diverse; Alonzo recorded a music project supporting mental health for Black men; Elissa started free yoga and healing sessions for Native American women; Jen started a "common ground" group that brings together Muslim, Jewish, and Christian members in her community to discuss the issues that affect them and develop friendships and conversations across seeming divides; and Jerome started a mentoring program for young Black men at the high school football team he coaches in Texas, helping to provide them with positive role models and support in practical ways during their years with the team.

The things you love and enjoy can be a part of the mission to end racism. The work doesn't *only* have to be what's considered standard activism. That work is important, too, *and* each of us has a passion, an interest, or a hobby that can be a gateway to us starting to contribute now. This is your chance to create a passion project that has the power to change the trajectory of humanity forever. All you have to do is show up. Start right here, where you are right now. Use the resources you already have in your garden, where they will create the most immediate impact. What's your personal passion project going to be? Take the first step. Use the guide to support you. The time is now.

21

∞

The End Is the Beginning

In 2020, we, Justin and Shelly, stood in the future and asked, "What *did* we do to end racism?" First, we decided to launch a virtual workshop and bring together hundreds of participants from all over the world with the purpose of providing them the fundamental tools needed to end racism. Based on the success and response to our workshops, we eventually decided to codify the pillars and write this book. We understood that our workshop and this book alone won't end racism, but we know—from experience—that we could inspire more people to dream as big as we do, to help them take steps toward the vision in powerful ways that moved far beyond anything we could ever dream of. Now that you've made it this far, and we know you're on the journey, we're ready to invite you to sign the pledge that we created to end racism. This is just a small and simple way for those of us who believe in this possibility to say *yes* and stand *together* as we walk into this dream. It would mean the world if you add your virtual signature with ours and the signatures of thousands of others who are on this path, here at this special link (or use the QR code below): HowWeEndedRacism.com/pledge. The world will change as we stand together.

In his book *Tattoos on the Heart*, Father Gregory Boyle, a Jesuit priest in Los Angeles, writes about all the human tragedies that play out in neighborhoods riddled with gang violence in Los Angeles, where he serves. One story that stood out to us was about Soledad, a mother of four who was so proud when her oldest son got a high school diploma and was deployed to the Marines. One day he came back to his hometown for a visit and went out to pick up some fast food. Moments after he left the house, Soledad heard shots in the distance on the streets near their home. Her son, Ronnie, died in her arms, right outside their front door.

Soon after that, her oldest son, Angel, also managed to graduate from high school, and he helped pull Soledad through the internal and external hell that she was living in. Six months after Ronnie's death, he pled with his mother to put on some clothes, put on some makeup, do her hair, get up, and be a mom to her three remaining children. That afternoon while sitting and eating a sandwich on their front porch, Angel was shot by the kids from a rival gang, and Father Boyle writes, "the few of us there found our arms too short to wrap around this kind of pain." At one meeting, Father Boyle asked Soledad how she was doing, and she responds, "I love the two kids I have, I hurt for the two kids that are gone," and then crying and sobbing to him, she admitted, "the hurt wins, the hurt wins."[1]

Several months later, she was in the emergency room after experiencing some chest pains when suddenly a kid with multiple gunshot wounds was rushed in on a gurney and placed in the spot right next to her. It was such an emergency, the nurses didn't have time to draw the curtain between them. She was able to actually witness him fighting for his life. When she was able to see his face, she recognized this kid from the rival gang that killed her boys. She knew that her friends might say to her in that moment, "Pray that he dies." But that's not what happened.

She heard the doctors yelling, "We're losing him! We're losing him!" Something in that moment caused her heart to just crack open. She told Father Boyle, "I began to cry as I had never cried before."

She actually laid there in the gurney next to this boy who killed her sons, and she started to pray the hardest that she had ever prayed before. She said, "God, please, please don't let him die. I don't want his mom to go through what I have been through." That boy survived—as did she—and so did her capacity for loving. Her heart was cracked open and expanded by what seemed like insurmountable grief, and in time it actually became unimaginably vast.

What we wish for you is the knowing that **whatever is happening to *us collectively* as it relates to racism right now, whatever is happening to *you* as it relates to racism right now, and whatever *has happened to you in the past* as it relates to racism can be transformed into what wakes you up.** That what we've taught you in this book helps you transform the poison into medicine, the pain into purpose, a vision into action, and the *impossible into the possible*. The future we reach depends on what we believe is possible now. The future is nothing but a possibility in the present. *We can't be certain the future you believe in will arise, but we can be certain that it won't arise if you don't believe in it.* It doesn't mean that everything you want will happen. But you can trust that if you can be in relationship with your emotions and shadow, practice forgiveness, stay skilled in having conversations that matter and are sometimes difficult, and take action, then you will be a healthy cell in the collective immune system. With each person who reads this book and commits to taking action, that immune system is growing stronger—strong enough to end racism on arrival.

In these final few moments together, we'd like to end with the practice we started with—*creating from the future*. Give yourself permission to pause as you read this and have an experience with this vision.

Place both of your hands over the center of your chest, one on top of the other. Take a moment now to pause and take five deep breaths. After your fifth breath, begin to imagine that you are projecting yourself into the future—a future where racism has ended globally.

Now, imagine your personal contribution to the end of racism succeeding beyond measure. It doesn't matter if the vision comes through clearly or if it's fuzzy or incomplete. Just trust what arises in this moment. You may choose to bring yourself to a specific moment in the future or imagine a cascade of many moments. Whatever comes through is fine; just bring it as clearly into focus as possible.

As you imagine a future without racism, what do you notice in the vision? What images are in front of you? What colors do you see? What emotions arise for you? Where do you feel them in your body? What's different about this future world? Who is there with you? Most importantly, what's happening in the vision that indicates to you that racism has indeed ended?

Finally, expand that vision to include all of us who are standing here ready to take action with you. We invite you to take a few moments right now to close your eyes and let this vision unfold in front of you. Once you're done having an experience with your vision, continue reading.

Inner Work

As the final step in our guidance, we want you to create a clear vision, knowing that you have the tools you need to equip you on your journey to get there. The purpose of your vision is to guide you inward, using this vision as a reference point that drives the decisions you make and actions you take. As you've done throughout every chapter, complete the following sentences:

- The vision I have for a world without racism is _____ ____ ______________. (Give us much detail as you can.)
- What's changed about the world in this vision is ____.
- What excites me most about the vision is ________ ____.

- What inspires me most about the vision is ________ ________________________________.
- What's changed about my vision from the time I started reading this book is ____________________.
- The emotions this vision brings up in me are ________________________________ __________. (You can still use the emotions wheel.)
- What I need to release to be more in alignment with this vision is ____________________.
- Some more specifics about this vision are ________ ________________________________.
- An action I will take to bring this vision to life is ________________________________.
- I am committed to ____________________.

Shelly's Vision

I envision a future where every single person in this country has enough, where every single person's basic needs are met so that they do not have to focus on surviving anymore but can instead shift their attention to thriving. We've paid reparations to those we have harmed, and we have offered atonement, making sure to teach our children the harsh truth about atrocities of the past. We've created a reality where every person has access to a defined and acceptable standard of health care, education, social services, and safety. No child or adult is without a home or experiencing food scarcity. Mental health is not stigmatized, and there is free help in many different forms for all who need it. In America, our leaders are limited in their power and are no longer influenced by corporations who are ruled by the mighty dollar. Services that affect the lives of our community and each person living in it are not monetized; services such as hospitals, prisons, and schools are no longer for-profit. Rather, they are here to serve the stronger cornerstone from which we can build from. Every office and position of power in our nation reflects the diversity that makes up our country. In this vision we all live in community with one another and understand our intraconnectedness and how what one of us does affects the others. I am "safe," "at ease," "peaceful," and "hopeful."

Justin's Vision

I envision a new political party that is in full power in America. It even has a name: the United Party, a party that isn't just an amalgamation or center point of Republican or Democrat but a completely new party that represents the truth of what I believe most people in America really are: good people who want the best for themselves, their families, and one another, along with economic prosperity and no limits on their dreams. This new political party changes the context from "right" and "left" and instead does exactly what its name suggests—*unites us* to create a better world. America has become a beacon of peace, well-being, and hope throughout the world that sets an example so successful that it shifts leadership on the planet. America itself has set the model for how to end racism, and other countries around the world have followed suit because they saw the measured economic, societal, governmental, personal, and political positive impact of an America that finally came together to embody its promise.

Every school is a safe haven of learning, education, and well-being; where each child is nourished and fulfilled physically, mentally, and emotionally. All students across the world are given the highest standard of education, offering them the opportunity to be contributors to society in ways that light up their passions, beyond basic survival. Well-being is truly accessible to everyone. There is healthy food in every neighborhood and people can easily make healthy choices about what to put in their bodies. Whenever a challenge arises around race in this new society, it is embraced with compassion, love, and care—because everyone in the society, from the children to the adults, is equipped to handle conflict around race in a way that easily transforms breakdowns into breakthroughs that guide us even further forward.

We've all learned how to celebrate our and one another's cultures in a way that doesn't detract from the Mwe, including white people also being able to embrace a new culture of whiteness that isn't centered around harm or old tropes but instead re-indigenizes folks and allows them to celebrate what they've contributed to the collective good. In this vision, we all have sheer reverence for one another. We respect each individual's way of being and what each of our groups offers to the collective by way of the sheer diversity. We are more together. We are stronger together. We rise together.

Together, we envision a world where everyone is able to believe in a possibility of a world without racism. We realize that racism can never exist on its own and that it only exists in us and through us. It is *with us* that it must end. We all realize that the tools we need to end racism are here and that all we need to do is learn them, implement them fervently, and say yes to a bigger dream. We envision that we all realize we are much more alike than we are different, and that race itself becomes a concept of the past. That we can stand together, not in division but in love, with our differences. That our children learn the truth so it never gets repeated again. And that *every* person is given the chance to thrive.

This is our collective vision, but the most important vision in this moment is yours. Our hope is that as you work toward bringing that vision to the world, you are not just creating the vision as some external experience outside of yourself but remember that you *are* the vision. You are not creating the end of racism, *you are the end of racism*. You are only able to end racism as much as you are willing to reveal the end of racism as it exists inside of you. When racism arrives in your presence, it ends—not just because of what you do or say but because of *who you are*. You are, yourself, *the end of racism*.

The end of this book is only the beginning. We hope that the tools we offered you serve as springboards toward the belief in a new vision. That you know how to stand in a future that may seem impossible. That you believe in something bigger than you believed in before. We hope that you have awakened from the trance that racism is a given and know that you're now part of a community that believes that racism can and will end, and you have a role to play in ending it.

Now you have the tools to be more confident of your expanded role in this vision. If you're already in politics, continue on that path. If you're a parent, continue on that path. If you're an artist, continue on that path. If you're an activist, continue on that path. Whatever path you are already walking, keep moving forward knowing that with each step forward, you can also make a choice to end racism right where you are. You can keep returning to the vision of a future where racism has ended, and ask yourself, "What *did* I do now that made this vision a reality?" The more of us there are that are willing to work toward that future, the more likely we will be able to realize a new possibility in one generation.

Keep walking toward that impossible future. Every step makes it possible. **Racism will end. We'll meet you there.**

Acknowledgments

We recognize that this work was built on the backs of so many heroes of the past, and many who are contributing in the present—from teachers to community organizers and spiritual leaders, to writers and academics, activists, and politicians, without whom we would not have the tools, history, language, or perhaps even the rights to offer this book to the world. We would be remiss to not also mention all the human beings who have suffered, continue to suffer, and lost their lives at the hands of racism. To that end, it is with a great bow of gratitude that we thank everyone who came before us—some whose names are widely recognized and those whose contributions to the world may largely have gone uncelebrated but are equally important nonetheless.

Specifically, we would like to thank Martin Luther King III and Arndrea Waters King, whose tireless work continuing the legacy of Dr. Martin Luther King Jr.'s work has inspired us to contribute to realizing The Dream. Your encouraging support has fueled us to dream big.

We also want to thank Jim Selman for the tireless support in bringing this book to life and igniting the spark that gave us the courage to start writing.

We want to acknowledge the immense contributions that our time as Garrison Institute Fellows and with the MWe Council had on bringing this big idea to light. In a safe container with our peers and mentors, we had the space to create, test, experiment, and make mistakes as this body of work was put together.

We are grateful for all the brave and beautiful souls who researched, studied, and signed up for our first cohorts of The Liberation Experience and our in-person retreats. The content, your feedback, our conversations, and your inspired actions in your communities let us know that we were on the right track and that we had something worthy of sharing here. Without your participation, and without you showing up for humanity, we never would have written this book.

Many people read and contributed to this book in all of its drafts and forms before it ever made it to the publisher. We are so grateful for every person's input, perspective, and counseling. This book is a reflection of OUR collective work, together—we thank you.

Finally, we want to acknowledge the reason why we are here: *our families*. The complex, winding, and seemingly impossible histories, events, and decisions that led us to this very moment, and that contributed to who we are today and who we are becoming. We are sustained by the affection and support of our grandparents, parents, siblings, partner and child, nieces and nephews, aunts, uncles, and cousins. Thank you for surrounding us with your love and encouragement and showing us what courage looks like in action.

Justin & Shelly

Notes

Introduction: Who WE Are

1. Amishi Jha, "Experiencing Wellbeing: Developing Resilience & Supporting Recovery," Wellbeing Project (webinar, June 8, 2021).

Chapter 1: Creating from the Future

1. Walter Mischel, *The Marshmallow Test: Understanding Self-Control and How to Master It* (New York: Little, Brown, 2014).
2. "Learning from the Future," *Harvard Business Review* 98, no. 4 (July/August 2020), hbr.org/2020/07/learning-from-the-future.

Chapter 2: The Skeptic in All of Us

1. George Jean Nathan, *Materia Critica* (New York: A. A. Knopf, 1924).
2. Jason Marsh, Rodolfo Mendoza-Denton, and Jeremy Adam Smith, eds., *Are We Born Racist?: New Insights from Neuroscience and Positive Psychology* (Boston: Beacon Press, 2010).
3. Tessa E. S. Charlesworth and Mahzarin R. Banaji, "Patterns of Implicit and Explicit Attitudes: I. Long-Term Change and Stability from 2007 to 2016," *Psychological Science* 30, no. 2 (2019): 174–92, doi.org/10.1177/0956797618813087; Nilanjana Dasgupta, "Implicit Attitudes and Beliefs Adapt to Situations: A Decade of Research on the Malleability of Implicit Prejudice,

Stereotypes, and the Self-Concept," in *Advances in Experimental Social Psychology*, vol. 47, ed. Patricia Devine and Ashby Plant (San Diego, CA: Academic Press, 2013), 233–79.

4. Marilyn A. Brewer, "The Psychology of Prejudice: Ingroup Love and Outgroup Hate?" *Journal of Social Issues* 55, no. 3 (Fall 1999): 429–44, spssi.onlinelibrary.wiley.com/doi/abs/10.1111/0022-4537.00126.
5. Toni Morrison, interview with Stephen Colbert, on *The Colbert Report*, Comedy Central, November 19, 2014.
6. "Why You Must Do This One Thing to Achieve Your Goals," Dr. Phil (website), December 14, 2017, drphil.com/videos/why-you-must-do-this-one-thing-to-achieve-your-goals/?fbclid=IwAR1Aq_f7KvkahsnPL1TuQsEzE3OYuPaMEtaqXzPH03P4Hq4L2PEsma2Fhmc.

Chapter 3: The Truth about the Truth

1. Fernando Flores, *Management and Communication in the Office of the Future* (self-pub., 1982).
2. Matthew Clarke, "U.S. DOJ Statistics on Race and Ethnicity of Violent Crime Perpetrators," Prison Legal News, June 1, 2021, prisonlegalnews.org/news/2021/jun/1/us-doj-statistics-race-and-ethnicity-violent-crime-perpetrators/.
3. See Qasim Rashid, *Extremist: A Response to Geert Wilders and Terrorists Everywhere* (AyHa Publishing, 2014).
4. Daniel Frank, ed., *The Jews of Medieval Islam: Community, Society, and Identity* (New York: Brill Academic, 1995).

Chapter 4: Describing How You Feel

1. Brené Brown, *Atlas of the Heart: Mapping Meaningful Connection and the Language of Human Experience* (New York: Random House, 2021).
2. Ludwig Wittgenstein, *Tractatus Logico-Philosophicus* (New York: Harcourt, Brace, 1933).
3. Brown, *Atlas of the Heart.*

Chapter 5: The Emotions of Race

1. Isabel Wilkerson, *Caste: The Origins of Our Discontents* (New York: Random House, 2020), 152–53.
2. Henry Louis Gates Jr., "The Truth Behind '40 Acres and a Mule,'" *African Americans: Many Rivers to Cross,* PBS, pbs.org/wnet/african-americans-many-rivers-to-cross/history/the-truth-behind-40-acres-and-a-mule/.
3. History.com editors, "Black Codes," History, last updated January 26, 2022, history.com/topics/black-history/black-codes.
4. Wilkerson, *Caste,* 133. See also South Carolina Black Code 72, *Acts of the General Assembly of the State of South Carolina* (Columbia, SC: Julian A. Selby, 1866).
5. Wilkerson, *Caste,* 80–82.
6. Marianne Williamson, "We are the only advanced industrialized nation that bases our education funding on property taxes," stated on July 28, 2019, on *Face the Nation,* CBS, Politifact, politifact.com/factchecks/2019/jul/31/marianne-williamson/fact-checking-marianne-williamson-school-funding-u/.

Chapter 6: Becoming Mwe

1. Daniel J. Siegel, *IntraConnected: MWe (Me + We) as the Integration of Self, Identity, and Belonging* (New York: W. W. Norton, 2022).
2. Siegel, *IntraConnected.*
3. Daniel J. Siegel, interviewed by Justin Michael Williams, "The Power of Connection," *The Kingdom with Justin Michael Williams*, November 16, 2020, youtu.be /HRSLn81LbKQ.
4. Ram Dass and Mirabai Bush, *Walking Each Other Home: Conversations on Loving and Dying* (Boulder, CO: Sounds True, 2018).

Chapter 7: What's in Your Shadow?

1. Abstruse Goose, September 10, 2009, abstrusegoose .com/183.
2. Rachel Yehuda, "Trauma in the Family Tree," *Scientific American* 327, no. 1 (July 2022): 50–55, doi:10.1038 /scientificamerican0722-50.

Chapter 8: Intergenerational Change

1. "Epigenetics and Child Development: How Children's Experiences Affect Their Genes," Center on the Developing Child, Harvard University, developingchild .harvard.edu/resources/what-is-epigenetics-and-how-does -it-relate-to-child-development/.
2. Rachel Yehuda, "How Parents' Trauma Leaves Biological Traces in Children," *Scientific American*, July 1, 2022, scientificamerican.com/article/how-parents-rsquo-trauma -leaves-biological-traces-in-children/.

3. Alice M. Graham, Jerod M. Rasmussen, Sonja Entringer, Elizabeth Ben Ward, Marc D. Rudolph, John H. Gilmore, Martin Styner, Pathik D. Wadhwa, Damien A. Fair, and Claudia Buss, "Maternal Cortisol Concentrations During Pregnancy and Sex Specific Association with Neonatal Amygdala and Emerging Internalizing Behaviors," *Biological Psychiatry* 85, no. 2 (January 15, 2019): 172–81, ncbi.nlm.nih.gov/pmc/articles/PMC6632079/.

4. Erika Beras, "Traces of Genetic Trauma Can Be Tweaked," *Scientific American*, April 15, 2017, scientificamerican.com/podcast/episode/traces-of-genetic-trauma-can-be-tweaked/.

5. Michael Price, "Protests Over Killings of Black People Could Erode Racism, Researcher Says," *Science*, June 4, 2020, science.org/content/article/protests-over-killings-black-people-could-erode-racism-researcher-says.

Chapter 9: The Big P

1. Janaya Future Khan, "Janaya Future Khan's Guide to Understanding White Privilege," *British Vogue*, June 3, 2020, vogue.co.uk/arts-and-lifestyle/article/janaya-future-khan-privilege.

2. Adam Grant (@AdamMGrant), "Too many people spend their lives being dutiful descendants instead of good ancestors," Twitter, February 18, 2022, 11:22 am, twitter.com/AdamMGrant/status/1494708914922954759?s=20&t=bqvcewF6AGCyr4OicSeaOA.

Chapter 11: Doubt and Faith

1. Dictionary.com, s.v. "faith," accessed July 22, 2021, dictionary.com/browse/faith.

Chapter 12: The Other in Me

1. Yuval Noah Harari, *Sapiens: A Brief History of Humankind* (New York: Harper, 2015).

2. Marie Beecham (@marieibeech), "Why and how I've learned to be very particular with deeming something racist," Instagram, March 9, 2022, instagram.com/p/Ca5Pfk4uoS4/?igshid=YmMyMTA2M2Y.

Chapter 13: Offering Forgiveness

1. Oprah Winfrey, "Oprah Explains How Forgiveness Can Change the Way You Move Through the World," Oprah Daily, July 25, 2021, oprahdaily.com/life/a37117486/oprah-forgiveness/.

2. Oprah Winfrey, *The Wisdom of Sundays: Life-Changing Insights from Super Soul Conversations* (New York: Flatiron Books, 2017), 115.

3. "'It's for You to Know That You Forgive,' Says Holocaust Survivor," *All Things Considered*, NPR, May 24, 2015, npr.org/2015/05/24/409286734/its-for-you-to-know-that-you-forgive-says-holocaust-survivor.

Chapter 14: Asking for Forgiveness

1. "Marianne Williamson: Atonement and Forgiveness," interview by Elliot Mintz, May 18, 2015, YouTube video, 5:14, youtu.be/T8n7wa_aeho.

2. Justin Michael Williams, "Darnell L. Moore: Break the System Through Inner Transformation," *The Kingdom with Justin Michael Williams*, podcast interview, February 3, 2008, podcasts.apple.com/us/podcast/darnell-moore-break-system-through-inner-transformation/id1341565149?i=1000401407255.

Chapter 15: Making Real Amends

1. Dictionary.com, s.v. "reparation," accessed July 27, 2021, dictionary.com/browse/reparation.

Chapter 16: Calling People *Forward* Instead of Out

1. John 1:1.
2. Coralie Bastin, Ben J. Harrison, Christopher G. Davey, Jorge Moll, and Sarah Whittle, "Feelings of Shame, Embarrassment and Guilt and Their Neural Correlates: A Systematic Review," *Neuroscience & Biobehavioral Reviews* 71 (December 2016): 455–71, doi:10.1016/j.neubiorev.2016.09.019; Petra Michl, Thomas Meindl, Franziska Meister, Christine Born, Rolf R. Engel, Maximilian Reiser, and Kristina Hennig-Fast, "Neurobiological Underpinnings of Shame and Guilt: A Pilot fMRI Study," *Social Cognitive and Affective Neuroscience* 9, no. 2 (February 2014): 150–57, doi:10.1093/scan/nss114; Theresa Robertson, Daniel Sznycer, Andrew W. Delton, John Tooby, and Leda Cosmides, "The True Trigger of Shame: Social Devaluation Is Sufficient, Wrongdoing Is Unnecessary," *Evolution and Human Behavior* 39, no. 5 (September 2018): 566–73, doi:10.1016/j.evolhumbehav.2018.05.010; Daniel Sznycer, John Tooby, Leda Cosmides, Roni Porat, Shaul Shalvi, and Eran Halperin, "Shame Closely Tracks the Threat of Devaluation by Others, Even Across Cultures," *Proceedings of the National Academy of Sciences* 113, no. 10 (February 22, 2016): 2625–30, doi: 10.1073/pnas.1514699113; Daniel Sznycer, "Forms and Functions of the Self-Conscious Emotions," *Trends in Cognitive Sciences* 23, no. 2 (February 2019): 143–57, doi: 10.1016/j.tics.2018.11.007.

3. N. Raman, *221 Ways to Success: Timeless Quotes of Great Masters for a Fulfilled Life* (Chennai, India: Notion Press, 2021).

Chapter 17: Conversations Across Divides

1. Seneca, *Letters from a Stoic: Epistulae Morales ad Lucilium*, trans. Robin Campbell (New York: Penguin Books, 1969).

Chapter 18: Setting Boundaries

1. Interview with bell hooks and Maya Angelou, interview by Melvin McLeod, *Shambhala Sun*, January 1998, hartford-hwp.com/archives/45a/249.html.
2. Justin Michael Williams, "Kasey Crown: Power of Boundaries," *The Kingdom with Justin Michael Williams*, podcast interview, March 10, 2021, podcasts.apple.com/us/podcast/the-kingdom-with-justin-michael-williams/id1341565149?i=1000512384124.

Chapter 19: Tending to Your Garden

1. "Quotes," Thich Nhat Hanh Foundation, thichnhathanhfoundation.org/covid-resources-quotes.

Chapter 20: Creating a Personal Passion Project

1. Across the world, currently fifty-five million people have been diagnosed with dementia. "Dementia," World Health Organization, who.int/news-room/fact-sheets/detail/dementia.
2. Kate White, Angela Cotter, and Hazel Leventhal, eds., *Dementia: An Attachment Approach* (London: Routledge, 2019).
3. Reimagining Dementia: A Creative Coalition for Change is an international campaign with a vision of care and support that promotes inclusion, relationship, creativity, joy, and the possibility of growth for everyone impacted

by dementia leading to the end of stigma and the predominant tragedy narrative. Take a look at the "Let's Reimagine" video and share with others in your life: reimaginingdementia.com.

Chapter 21: The End Is the Beginning

1. Gregory Boyle, *Tattoos on the Heart: The Power of Boundless Compassion* (New York: Simon and Schuster, 2011).

About the Authors

Shelly Tygielski

Shelly Tygielski is a humanitarian and community organizer who has been hailed by individuals ranging from President Joe Biden to Arianna Huffington and Dr. Jon Kabat-Zinn to Maria Shriver. She is the founder of the global grassroots mutual aid organization Pandemic of Love and the cofounder of Partners in Kind, a company that brings purpose to production, development, and investment in film and entertainment projects aimed at inspiring acts of kindness and compassion while building community and momentum around social change. She is an executive producer and a cohost of the non-scripted television show *All Hands on Deck*.

Shelly's work has been featured in over one hundred media outlets including on *CNN Heroes*, *The Kelly Clarkson Show*, *CBS This Morning*, the *New York Times*, and *Washington Post*. She is a trauma-informed mindfulness teacher and a Garrison Institute Fellow who has been named one of the "12 Powerful Women of the Mindfulness Movement" by *Mindful Magazine*. Shelly has taught formalized self-care, resilience, and belonging at organizations around the world and is widely considered to be a thought expert on building community.

She is happily married to her husband, Jason, and is the mother of a son, Liam, she adores. She is currently pursuing a doctorate in philanthropic leadership at Indiana University's Lilly Family School of Philanthropy.

Justin Michael Williams

Justin Michael Williams brings people together across divides with his multigenerational message of hope, empowerment, and unity. He is an award-winning author, Grammy-nominated recording artist, and keynote speaker who has captivated audiences at some of the world's most prestigious organizations such as Google, Apple, Bloomberg, and SXSW®. He has shared the stage with luminaries such as Marianne Williamson and Deepak Chopra.

Whether he's speaking, penning books, recording music, or hosting conversations with thought leaders on his podcast, Justin is hailed for harnessing the power of media as a vehicle for personal growth and social transformation. He has been celebrated in publications like Grammy.com, *The Wall Street Journal*, *Mindful Magazine*, *The Root*, and *Billboard*.

Justin's groundbreaking first book *Stay Woke: A Meditation Guide For The Rest Of Us* (Sounds True, 2020) made history for bringing mindfulness to young people across America, earning him the Next Generation Award from the New Thought Walden Awards, alongside contemporaries like Jay Shetty. The book was endorsed by Jon Kabat-Zinn, Yung Pueblo, Shaun King, Patrisse Cullors, and other influential figures in both diversity and mindfulness.

Despite the adversity of growing up in a home harmed by gunshot holes and violence, Justin has dedicated his life to helping people transform pain into power. With nearly two decades of teaching experience and a global digital reach spanning more than forty countries, Justin's work has touched countless lives. He is proud to be a champion for *all* people and is committed to making sure everyone, regardless of their age, ethnicity, background, or circumstance, has the tools to transform their lives and transform society.

To learn more, visit www.justinmichaelwilliams.com.

About Sounds True

Sounds True was founded in 1985 by Tami Simon with a clear mission: to disseminate spiritual wisdom. Since starting out as a project with one woman and her tape recorder, we have grown into a multimedia publishing company with a catalog of more than 3,000 titles by some of the leading teachers and visionaries of our time, and an ever-expanding family of beloved customers from across the world.

In more than three decades of evolution, Sounds True has maintained our focus on our overriding purpose and mission: to wake up the world. We offer books, audio programs, online learning experiences, and in-person events to support your personal growth and awakening, and to unlock our greatest human capacities to love and serve.

At SoundsTrue.com you'll find a wealth of resources to enrich your journey, including our weekly *Insights at the Edge* podcast, free downloads, and information about our nonprofit Sounds True Foundation, where we strive to remove financial barriers to the materials we publish through scholarships and donations worldwide.

To learn more, please visit SoundsTrue.com/freegifts or call us toll-free at 800.333.9185.

Together, we can wake up the world.